CHINA, HONG KONG, TAIWAN AND THE WORLD TRADING SYSTEM

Also by Penelope Hartland-Thunberg

BOTSWANA: AN AFRICAN GROWTH ECONOMY
THE POLITICAL AND STRATEGIC IMPORTANCE OF EXPORTS
WORLD TRADING BLOCS, U.S. EXPORTS AND WORLD TRADE
GOVERNMENT SUPPORT FOR EXPORTS: A SECOND-BEST
    ALTERNATIVE *(co-author)*
BANKS, PETRO-DOLLARS AND SOVEREIGN DEBTORS: BLOOD
    FROM A STONE? *(co-editor)*

China, Hong Kong, Taiwan and the World Trading System

Penelope Hartland-Thunberg

in association with
CENTER FOR STRATEGIC AND
INTERNATIONAL STUDIES

MACMILLAN

© Center for Strategic and International Studies 1990

All rights reserved. No reproduction, copy or transmission
of this publication may be made without written permission.

No paragraph of this publication may be reproduced, copied or
transmitted save with written permission or in accordance with
the provisions of the Copyright, Designs and Patents Act 1988
or under the terms of any licence permitting limited copying
issued by the Copyright Licensing Agency, 33–4 Alfred Place,
London WC1E 7DP.

Any person who does any unauthorised act in relation to
this publication may be liable to criminal prosecution and
civil claims for damages.

First published 1990

Published by
MACMILLAN PROFESSIONAL AND ACADEMIC LTD
Houndmills, Basingstoke, Hampshire RG21 2XS
and London
Companies and representatives
throughout the world

Typeset by LBJ Enterprises Ltd
Chilcompton, Somerset

Printed in the United States of America

British Library Cataloguing in Publication Data
Hartland-Thunberg, Penelope
China, Hong Kong, Taiwan and the world trading system
1. China. Economic policies. International economic
aspects
I. Title
382.10951
ISBN 0–333–54376–9

Contents

List of Tables and Figures	vii
Preface	x
Foreword by Leo Cherne	viii
Map of Chinese Provinces	xi

1 Introduction	1
2 China's Economic Reforms	13
Introduction	13
Origins	14
Crises of Increasing Intensity	17
Inheritance of the Reform Effort	26
The Course of the Transition	28
Autonomy of Enterprise Management	28
Dual Price System	31
Inflation, Corruption, and Future of Price Reform	43
Foreign Trade and Investment	53
Conclusion	70
3 China and the World Trading System	73
Introduction	73
China's Interest in the World Trading Organization	78
Problem Areas for China in the GATT	82
Non-Discrimination, Transparency, and Reciprocity	82
Safeguards, Subsidies and Dumping	84
Concerns About China's Import Regime	89
Concerns About China's Export Regime	91

v

vi *Contents*

4 "Greater China": The Special Problems of
  Hong Kong and Taiwan 97
  Introduction 97
  Hong Kong 99
    Relations with China 99
    Relations with GATT 101
    Growth in Late 1980s 102
    Joint Declaration and the Basic Law 103
    Citizenship and Emigration 105
    The Future of Hong Kong 106
  Taiwan 112
    The Economic Miracle 113
    The Role of Trade 115
    The Financial Sector 117
    Political Change 118
    Foreign Policy 122
    Taiwan and the GATT 123
    Reactions to Tiananmen Square 128

5 The Outlook and Implications for U.S. and
  Western Policy 133
  Outlook for China 133
  Implications for Western Policy: China 144
    The Status Quo 144
    Progressive Economic Reform 148
  Implications for Western Policy: Hong Kong 152
    Potential Benefits of GATT Membership 153
  Implications for Western Policy: Taiwan 158
    A Window of Opportunity 158
    Conditions for GATT Membership 159

Notes 166
Bibliography 179

Index 187

List of Tables and Figures

Tables

2.1	Total Factor Productivity: Organization for Economic Cooperation and Development, United States and Japan, 1973–1985	14
2.2	Chinese Foreign Trade and Investment	55
2.3	Chinese Utilization of Foreign Capital	62

Figures

2.1	Chinese Industrial Production (year-to-year change)	19
2.2	Chinese Trade Deficit: Balance of Imports and Exports	20
2.3	Chinese Budget Deficit	21
2.4	Chinese Currency Circulation	22
2.5	Chinese Cost of Living Price Index: Year-to-Year Change	23

Foreword

We live in a revolutionary era. The forces that are sweeping across the Soviet bloc, the West, and the developing world deprive us of many longstanding reference points to interpret events. Ideological conflict is fading while economic competition among allies sharpens. Military might no longer seems the controlling factor in the global equation. The limits of national sovereignty are being tested as never before.

The contemporary revolution is being driven less by men or ideas than by breathtaking gains in technology. When the television and the xerox machine ushered in an information age decades ago, few realized that they marked just a starting point. Today, the microchip, the computer, and the fiber optic cable have begun to restructure economics and politics on a worldwide scale. The capacity to process and transmit data almost anywhere within split seconds has transformed manufacturing, finance, and global markets for goods as well as services. New economic realities, in turn, are shaping new political realities.

Although the dynamic of global change is at best dimly understood, a few patterns are already discernable. First, receptivity to the new technologies holds the key to building economic strength. The success of the Pacific Rim illustrates this vividly. Secondly, go-it-alone economic strategies look increasingly unrealistic. The penalties for being isolated from the network of global innovation have become prohibitive. Third, the new information-based technologies foster pluralism. The diffusion of knowledge, far from reinforcing central authority, increases demands for participation in decision making.

The dilemmas of structural change have been especially acute for China. Beginning in the 1970s, China's leaders made an extraordinary break with the past by opening to the West and launching a program of domestic economic reform. They promoted decentralization and introduced market incentives to speed modernization. But these adjustments generated political pressures for freedom of expression that the ruling Communist Party found intolerable. Just as China seemed to be moving irrevocably toward liberalization, the clampdown in Tiananmen Square called into question the nation's future course.

Foreword

Dr Thunberg illuminates China's dilemmas with clarity, insight, and nuance. She has combined a firm grasp of international economics, a feel for China, and painstaking research to produce a remarkable, forward-looking assessment of the Chinese role in the world economy. She looks beyond the interplay of personalities that so often dominate Western analysis and applies hard data to the fundamentals of China's position. This approach yields a truly strategic perspective.

Dr Thunberg's analysis of China's economic reforms corrects a number of widely shared misperceptions. We realize that the reform process did not run smoothly but lurched in fits and starts. Despite stunning achievements in some sectors, Chinese modernization proved vulnerable to bottlenecks and inflationary pressures as well as corruption. The logic of economic reform did not create an imperative for political reform. Rather, it ran headlong into the determination of the Communist Party to retain control.

The same cautionary note applies to China's trade and financial relations with the external world. Although a persuasive political case can be made to include China in the multilateral trading system, and China continues to seek admission to the GATT, Dr Thunberg argues that politics alone cannot be the controlling factor. Both China and the West must take account of very real differences between market-based and planned economies.

Dr Thunberg's treatment of Hong Kong and Taiwan is particularly helpful. Their successful efforts to manage structural change strike a vivid counterpoint to China's more problematic adjustment. Although Chinese retrenchment has had a most adverse impact on Hong Kong, the author points out that it has created a strategic opportunity for a democratizing Taiwan.

Looking ahead, Dr Thunberg argues that China has a fundamental stake in establishing itself as a great economic power. This objective, she hopes, will renew the process of political as well as economic reform and will speed China's integration into the world economy. One cannot help but share this hope.

Leo Cherne
Executive Director
The Research Institute of America, Inc.

Preface

This book attempts to set forth the facts and their consequences necessary to an understanding of the implications of China's "open door" policy for China, for the world trading system, for Hong Kong and Taiwan. Comprehension of those interdependencies is essential to the fashioning of a sound U.S.-China policy. The book makes no pretense at being a complete discussion of the enormous changes wrought in the Chinese economy during the first decade of reform. Nor does it pretend to be a complete treatment of the problems confronting the world trading system or the complex web of political, economic and strategic relationships between China on the one hand and Hong Kong and Taiwan on the other. Only the problems and relationships relevant to U.S. policy formulation are discussed.

The book is written for intelligent, interested laymen and policymakers; in consequence, it avoids jargon and discussions of complex analytic techniques. Nonetheless because it views economic problems in their political context, it is hoped it will interest professional economists, international relations experts, and area experts as well as laymen and policymakers.

I have benefited from discussions with many individuals concerned with some aspects of this subject–businessmen actively engaged in trade with China, government officials, academic sinologists and trade experts. Many have asked for anonymity. Among the others, I am especially indebted to Mary Wadsworth Darby, Kerry Dumbaugh, Clark Ellis, Gerrit Gong, Isaiah Frank, James Frierson, Harry Harding, Amos Jordan, Albert Keidel, Cecelia Klein, Douglas Newkirk, Ernest Preeg, Michael Samuels, and Kaarn Weaver. The encouragement and support of my colleague John Yochelson was essential to my initial undertaking of this effort, as well as its completion. No one of these, of course, bears any responsibility for any errors the book may contain.

Among the many interns who have helped me with the research, special recognition is due to Charles Matt whose fluency in the Chinese language was invaluable.

Research was supported by a grant from the Kearny Foundation as well as by the Dr. Scholl Foundation.

Penelope Hartland-Thunberg
January, 1990

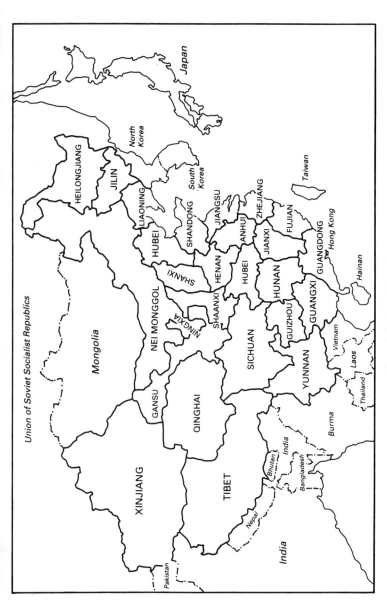

Map of Chinese Provinces

1 Introduction

Perhaps it is their respect for orderliness that explains the proclivity of the Chinese people for numerical slogans. Whatever the cause, such formulations as "the four modernizations," the "three noes," or "one country, two systems" are uniquely Chinese in their whimsy.

Paramount leader Deng Xiaoping first used the slogan "one country, two systems" in 1984 during Sino-British discussions about the future of Hong Kong. It was a tidy summary of Deng's promise that the British colony could retain the status quo – its existing free enterprise, free-trading system – during the first half-century of its reunification with the mainland, to begin in 1997. The PRC would have a "socialist commodity" system (i.e., a mixed socialist and market economy) while Hong Kong continued with capitalism and undiluted free enterprise under the sovereignty of the People's Republic.

The slogan applied equally well to Taiwan whose reunification with the mainland had been a prime goal of both governments on either side of the Straits of Taiwan since the Nationalists (the Kuomintang) had established themselves on Taiwan in 1949 claiming to represent all of China. After Deng's advent to power in Beijing in the late 1970s, the PRC had ceased its three decades of beligerence toward the island and commenced a series of friendly overtures. The Government of Taiwan continued to claim that as the Republic of China it represented all of China and that the Communists were a group of bandits. China promised that Taiwan could retain its capitalist, market-based economic system, its integration into the world trading system, and even its armed forces and its Nationalist party after reunification: clearly "one country, two systems." Taiwan wanted none of it.

Although it was not done, the slogan could also have been applied to the economic reform program initated in the PRC in the late 1970s. That program aimed at rapid economic development through much enlarged participation in world trade (the "open door" policy) and a shift to a socialist market economy. China would modernize and stimulate its economy by adopting the mechanisms of capitalism while retaining government ownership over most

2 *China, Hong Kong, Taiwan and World Trade*

means of production and government control over priority sectors of the economy. The two systems would be directly or indirectly controlled by the Chinese Communist Party. Thus the two systems, capitalism and socialism, would be combined in the PRC on the mainland itself as well as through the reunification of capitalist Hong Kong and Taiwan with the still socialist mainland.

From the beginning the dominating question was "would – could – 'one country, two systems' work?" The Chinese on the mainland, in Hong Kong and in Taiwan all asked themselves the question, but with little urgency. So did the rest of the world. The question was not compelling while the emphasis was on economic growth, and all three parts of China grew apace. In significant measure their rapid development was due to rising commerce among the three. Between 1980 and 1987 the average growth rate of the People's Republic at over 10 percent a year was the second highest among the countries of the world. More modestly but still impressive for a period that encompassed the most serious recession in the post-war era, growth in the colony of Hong Kong (7.6 percent) and on the island of Taiwan (7.8 percent) also boomed. Exports in the three parts of China played a key role in their rapid development, both exports to the rest of the world and exports to each other.

The shift to a conservative regime in Beijing and its accompanying repression in mid-1989 raised to a level of immediate concern the basic question of the feasibility of "one country, two systems" and changed its emphasis. Whether elements of capitalism could be successfully combined with elements of socialism became less important. More important was the question of whether the Communist Party in a single party system was capable of adjusting to a lessened degree of control over the country. A much-diminished degree of control was implied by a shift to a market mechanism, with the loss of party privilege and status that necessarily accompanied such a shift. The reformulated question had been answered on the mainland where the tanks and guns in Beijing had responded with a resounding "no." But that was only the first reaction and could change.

The question took on a new urgency in Hong Kong and Taiwan. During the past five years many Hong Kong businessmen have been concerned over whether Communist Party stalwarts after 1997 would be able to resist meddling with Hong Kong. Even with the best of intentions in Beijing, could local party officials in the former colony be restrained from attempts to "improve" Hong Kong's

Introduction 3

system? After the shift in Beijing the answer appeared unequivocal. In Taiwan, where the Chinese Communist Party had long been reviled, the reformulated question appeared finally to get at what Taiwan considered to be the heart of the matter.

The dramatic conclusion to the first decade of economic reform in the People's Republic of China in mid-1989 was a many-faceted tragedy. For China it was an ironic tragedy because the Deng Xiaoping regime itself had recognized the danger to social and political stability in China contained in the combination of high inflation and corruption that had emerged in 1988. Deng and his colleagues had lived through – and benefited politically from – the rampant inflation and corruption that marked the last days of the Nationalist government of Chiang Kai-shek in the 1940s. That potent combination has been widely credited in China and abroad with bringing the Communist regime to power. With memories of Chiang's downfall still sharp, the Deng leadership itself was calling for an end to corruption some months before the students demonstrated in Tiananmen Square demanding the same thing. The Deng regime had also taken steps to slow the frenetic rate of growth that was the source of China's inflation.

The tragedy was compounded by the fact that the chosen path of Chinese economic reform, especially in regard to price reform, had placed increasingly monumental temptations before minor as well as major Chinese Party officials – temptations that became irresistible to more and more Party members. Because the rule of law was only partially established in China, corruption was the inevitable outcome of the dual price system; the dual price system, however, was by no means an essential part of the process of shifting from central-control to a market-oriented economy. Economic reform need not have exploded in the face of its designers; political tensions which are the inevitable handmaiden of a society experiencing rapid change would not have been so great if a different path of reform had been chosen.

The shift to a conservative regime in Beijing in the spring of 1989 may also have been a tragedy for the world and for Hong Kong and Taiwan, whose economic and political futures are so intimately connected with developments on the mainland. The final page of China's economic reform effort, however, has yet to be written. The Deng regime will, at least at first, attempt to retain it. Other regimes will follow. The future could still be bright.

The opening of China to the West in the late 1970s was widely viewed throughout the West as an event of considerable geo-

4 *China, Hong Kong, Taiwan and World Trade*

political moment. It was that, but it was – and remains – much more. When nearly one quarter of the world's population, with a national history encompassing 22 centuries and about to embark on a policy of rapid growth, decides to join the world economy, it is an event whose economic proportions are potentially seismic.

A decade later the economic significance of China's turn toward the West was still little appreciated. Some multinational business had been enthusiastic about the opportunities in China – perhaps too much so. In the United States, China experts and some trade experts were alert to the importance of the event, but these specialists constituted a small, and highly select, group. For the most part the business, government, and economic communities in the United States viewed the emergence of China as yet another less-developed-country seeking rapid economic growth through international trade.

It is not size alone that gives immense significance to China's emergence into the world economy. Its timing is crucial. China hopes to model its development in part on the course that has proven successful in its neighbors – especially Japan, Korea, and Taiwan. It plans to use exports as the source of the foreign exchange required to finance imports of technology, materials, and supplies necessary for catching up with the industrial West. In the meantime, it plans to protect its domestic market while its infant industries, made increasingly efficient by the necessity for earning profits, become acquainted with the new technologies. China enters the world economy, however, at a time when the industrial countries, especially the United States and Europe, are showing increasing impatience with the operation of the international trading system and specifically with the way that system has encouraged developing countries to use the system for exports but not for imports.

The rules of proper international trading procedures prevailing today were established in the late 1940s by the General Agreement on Tariffs and Trade. The GATT, created at about the same time as the World Bank and the International Monetary Fund, is less well known than its two financial counterparts. Its influence on world growth and development, nevertheless, over the 40 years of its existence has probably been of much greater importance than that of the Bank and the Fund, even in combination. The three international economic organizations together, however, established the rules that determined the nature of the post-World War Two international economic order and continue to do so today.

Introduction

The successes of the GATT in stimulating world trade and world economic growth through successive rounds of tariff reductions are history. World trade has grown faster than (and has led) world output. Tariffs of industrial countries are now so low that the stimulus to trade achievable through further tariff reductions has declined sharply. Meanwhile, for the past decade or two the industrial countries have resorted increasingly to non-tariff barriers against imports in order to counter more intense competition from the developing countries and Japan as well as among themselves.

By the late 1980s, the GATT had become a sickly organization, with a larger volume of world trade taking place outside of GATT rules than within them.[1] Ambiguous in many areas, having no enforcement mechanism and in fact possessed of only an informal ad hoc system of governance, the GATT was unwieldy, lethargic and toothless. Even the most successful of the developing countries, the Newly Industrializing Countries (NICs), according to the rules and practices of the GATT, were relieved from fulfilling GATT obligations – that is, from trading according to GATT rules. Impatience with GATT operations induced members to seek solutions to trade problems increasingly outside of the GATT in the form of bilateral agreements, regional agreements, or by flouting GATT recommendations.

The GATT was widely perceived in Europe and North America as being out of date, badly in need of revision, and essentially irrelevant. For the GATT to survive as an effective administrator of international trade rules multilaterally agreed, the trend toward bilateral, extra-GATT solutions to trade problems clearly had to be reversed. It was imperative that more trade disputes be settled within the GATT, that GATT procedures be accelerated, and GATT ambiguities clarified.

Widespread dissatisfaction with the weaknesses in the General Agreement led to the initiation in 1986 of the Uruguay Round, the eighth in the series of multilateral trade negotiations sponsored by the GATT. The Uruguay Round was an international undertaking to modernize the GATT. If its agenda were to be successfully completed, the GATT would be strengthened, world trade would be more orderly, trade disputes among trading partners less rancorous and divisive.

China was aware of the fragility of the existing rules of international trade. It had benefited from them and hoped to benefit even more in the future as its capacity to export increased. It

6 *China, Hong Kong, Taiwan and World Trade*

applied for membership in (technically, "accession to") the GATT to ensure GATT benefits for itself and to be able to participate in the determination of such changes in GATT rules as might come about. A rapidly growing China with a potential for accounting for an increasingly significant fraction of world trade could make the difference between a healthy or moribund multilateral trade mechanism. How China might behave as a member of the GATT could be crucial.

China was in fact a founding member of the GATT. It participated actively in the multilateral discussions of 1946–47 which hammered out the original General Agreement, vigorously supporting the interests of the less developed countries in those debates. China was represented by its then-ruling Nationalist government under the leadership of Chiang Kai-shek. When the Nationalists retreated to the island of Taiwan in 1949, they took with them the GATT China seat, only to withdraw from the GATT less than a year later in mid-1950. Since then China has not been a member of the GATT, although it has participated in GATT meetings as an observer, first represented by the Republic of China on Taiwan from 1965 to 1971 and since late 1984 by the People's Republic of China on the mainland. Whether the PRC was returning to the GATT or joining the GATT anew was a contentious and complex legal issue in China's application for membership.

China's eventual membership in the GATT was never in doubt. When it would assume membership and under what conditions were being laboriously negotiated within the GATT and bilaterally between the PRC and the United States in the late spring of 1989. After the traumatic events of June 1989, further negotiations were postponed and remained moribund through the winter of 1990. Meanwhile the GATT itself was in the process of change as the Uruguay Round attempted to extend and adjust the terms of the General Agreement. GATT officials were aware that China as a member would make a notable additional difference, but they were unsure whether that difference would help or hinder the modernization of the General Agreement.

The impact of China on the GATT – and of the GATT on China – has been further complicated by the relationships between the GATT and Hong Kong and Taiwan. Hong Kong, scheduled to be incorporated into China in 1997, became a full member of the General Agreement in 1986. The People's Republic has repeated many times that Hong Kong can continue to be an independent

Introduction 7

GATT member after China itself assumes full membership and after 1997 on the basis of its policy of "one country, two systems." China has promised that after 1997 Hong Kong can continue as a capitalist economy for fifty years while being politically a part of a country with a socialist economic system.

The PRC has also promised that the policy of "one country, two systems" will apply to Taiwan when it is once again reunified with the mainland. The authorities on Taiwan in the meantime began actively exploring independent GATT membership in the late 1980s and startled GATT members by filing a formal application of accession on January 1, 1990. The People's Republic has informally let it be known that China would not oppose Taiwan's membership after the PRC has been admitted, provided Taiwan enters under an acceptable name.

What Taiwan calls itself is an issue of enormous sensitivity and emotional involvement on both sides of the Straits of Formosa. It is difficult for outsiders to appreciate its importance. The name issue is likely to be resolved only by a decision at the highest level in each country – if ever. The Chinese are a very proud people; pride reinforced by ideology seems to be the prime emotional source of the dispute. But the economic gains that, in the perception of each side, might flow from a resolution of the name issue will be the basis of agreement on an acceptable name if and when it is reached, and the economic gains to each could be substantial.

The experience of Hong Kong in the years before and after 1997 will play a large role in fashioning the attitude of China's trading partners toward the PRC and thus in determining both the commercial and political environment that the Chinese will confront at the turn of the century. If China proves itself both willing and able to take control of Hong Kong without deleterious effects on the freewheeling economy there, widespread doubts about both its intentions and its abilities will be assuaged. Hong Kong will be immensely relieved, the rest of the world will be reassured, and Taiwan's resistence to open, direct economic intercourse with the mainland will disintegrate. Even eventual reunification could become feasible.

The bloody repression of the students' demonstration in Beijing in June 1989 diluted (at the least) the widespread good will and support for the PRC's new efforts that the Chinese met around the world during the first decade of their economic reform. It has severely jolted confidence in Hong Kong. If China continues to

8 *China, Hong Kong, Taiwan and World Trade*

mismanage the absorption of Hong Kong, Chinese membership in the GATT could be threatened, Hong Kong could be expelled, and the peaceful reunification of Taiwan and the PRC would be impossible. China's stake in the future of the Hong Kong economy is large and complex.

In addition to China's size and the timing of its shift toward the West, the significance of China's emergence into the world trading system is heightened by the enormity of the task that China has set for itself. The shift from its system based on total government control over the economy to one based primarily on market control and direction implies in effect a shift from stability to dynamic change.

For nearly a quarter of a century after the mid-1950s, some of the basic determinants of Chinese economic activity were fixed at the levels prevailing then. Many prices did not change by a fen (100 fen equal one yuan, the basic unit of the Chinese currency) over those years; the technologies in place or introduced by the Russians in the 1950s remained largely unchanged until the 1980s; an industrial structure emphasizing heavy industry at the expense of light, consumer-oriented industry persisted; incentives continued to be based on ideology and importuning entreaties, while the "iron rice-bowl" continued to deny the relevance of material incentives and ensure that everyone was equally well off. Meanwhile, consumers and producers were insulated from the effects of changes in the rest of the world by a pervasive system of controls over information, communications, and mobility.

Such pervasive and enduring stability has profound implications for the human beings experiencing it. Stability becomes comfortable; it requires no effort on the part of individuals to adjust. Change is disruptive; it creates apprehensions and the necessity for an expenditure of effort either to adjust or to resist. The turmoil of the Cultural Revolution was of course greatly disruptive for China and the Chinese people, in part because it was in contrast to the stability that had preceded it. Although the Cultural Revolution introduced change primarily in the socio-political realm, it did have economic ramifications. Its insistence on self-sufficiency for individuals, villages, and localities forced many into new pursuits, some into new locations. Prices, technologies, industrial priorities, and economic incentives, however, remained largely unaffected.

China's turn to the West and the market mechanism is an embrace of change. It is welcomed by many Chinese as stimulating

Introduction 9

and rewarding, resisted by others as discomforting or demoting. The abandonment of stability in China, moreover, is a greater challenge than it would be elsewhere because of the importance in traditional Chinese culture of order and avoidance of turmoil. If change in China should fringe on turmoil, it would lose its acceptability. How long it will take the majority of the Chinese people to accept change and the necessity for adaptation as ongoing facts of life is a basic question hanging over China's new economic policy. No one knows. Perhaps the majority already has accepted change.

It is infinitely more difficult to remove controls – especially after a quarter of a century has passed – than to impose them. It is especially difficult in an economy that is at once backward and complex, as is China's. Although, in terms of numbers employed, China is still primarily an agricultural country, industry has grown in importance steadily since the 1950s, and accounted for an estimated 48 percent of GNP by 1980. Before the 1980s, emphasis on self-sufficiency and growth necessitated building a varied and complex industrial structure, but one based on obsolete or obsolescent technologies. Further, even if the Chinese price structure had made sense in the 1950s – as reflecting world prices or relative scarcities – it would have made no sense at all in the 1980s. When prices were rigidly fixed in the 1950s, however, producer goods prices were set at artificially high levels and raw material and consumer good prices at artificially low ones to promote industrialization and control inflation.[2]

The industrial mix inherited by the new regime almost certainly falls short of maximizing the productivity of China's labor and capital, but how far short and in which industries cannot be known until prices – including wages and interest rates – are permitted to reflect market forces. Without a scarcity value for basic inputs, prices and profits are not indicative of absolute or relative efficiency and thus are not a meaningful guide to resource allocation decisions, either among industries or at the micro level, within enterprises.

For political reasons China has determined that it cannot remove all price controls at once. Further complicating the decontrol process, China has determined, also for political reasons, that the prices of certain important inputs like petroleum, coal, cotton, steel and transportation will remain under central government control even when the shift to a market mechanism is completed. Then, if controlled prices differ from market prices, they will impose a constraint on the operation of market forces and thus throw doubt

10 *China, Hong Kong, Taiwan and World Trade*

on how successful China eventually can be in raising productivity in the industrial sector. If controlled prices are to be the same as market prices, there is no reason for controls.

The success of China's effort at modernization and rapid growth and the imposition of limits on the extent of market forces in operation in China also raise questions about the success of China's incorporation into the GATT-based world trading mechanism. The General Agreement is founded on the assumption of market-directed economies – that trade responds to prices and that prices reflect demand and supply in world markets. In a non-market economy, prices and trade volumes are determined by the central government and trade is unresponsive to prices. China's shift from a centrally controlled to a market-directed economy made great strides in the first decade of the new economic orientation, but much remains to be done. The shift of control from Beijing to farms and enterprises around the country has frequently resulted in a shift of government control from the state to the provinces and localities, with the market and local governments sharing in the basic determinants of price formation. Because local governments have been given – or have assumed – different degrees of authority over enterprises, the effect on prices and trade often appears chaotic. This appearance of chaos is only in part the ordered chaos of a market mechanism in operation; it is also in significant part the consequence of multilayered controls and shifting degrees of authority among governments at different levels and in different locations. The consequence has been not only widely different prices for the same good in different parts of China, but at least two prices for the same product in the same place. In addition differences in tariffs, trade and investment regulations, wages, taxes, and interest rates have led some observers to comment that China's provinces should be admitted to the GATT one by one as each more closely approaches a market-determined economy.

Further, for a variety of reasons, it is likely that China will for many years find it impossible to eliminate subsidies to enterprises. Continued widespread subsidization runs the very real risk of stirring up a blizzard of unfair trade charges and accompanying litigation against China in China's trading partners. Substantial numbers of such trade actions have already been brought in the United States and won an affirmative finding; the more rapidly China's exports grow, the more such charges will multiply, encouraged as they have been by changes in the 1988 U.S. trade act and

Introduction 11

recent innovative interpretations of unfair trade practices in the European Community.

Mushrooming trade disputes embitter international relations. In the case of China, where political support for the new economic course is not yet fully rooted, multiplying barriers to its exports in major world markets could promote a reevaluation of its economic policy and a retreat from the kind or degree of participation in the world economy that it had previously envisaged.

Such a retreat would represent a serious loss to the United States and the world. A rapidly growing, increasingly prosperous China, extending its economic relations with the rest of the world on the basis of an evolving comparative advantage, can mean an increase in the size of the world economy large enough to make a difference. China has the potential for serving as a growth-locomotive, helping to propel the rest of the world as well as itself on to higher incomes.

China will be able to play this role only if its productivity experiences a sustained rise over many years and only if it is willing to extend its economic relations with the rest of the world *pari passu* with its internal growth. There are two potential sources of rising productivity for China: a shift of resources into enterprises and industries where they are most efficient – where they produce goods of higher value on a world scale in relation to cost; and a shift of technology employed from the obsolete to the more modern – not necessarily to the most modern. Tapping both sources of productivity-enhancement requires China's participation in the world economy. Competition in world markets is necessary to determine which firms and industries are most efficient and which exports can most efficiently pay for imports of more modern Western technology. Thus for some years the success of China's growth program will be dependent on its participation in world trade.

The opportunities for both China and the world entailed in China's new economic program are immense. The loss to both China and the world would be equally immense if China were to retreat from this program.

The challenges to U.S. and Western policy in this complex of relationships are intricate and difficult. It is in the U.S. national interest to support China's new economic program and to encourage China's continued participation in world trade and membership in international economic organizations. It is also, however, in the U.S. national interest to support political pluralism and human rights around the world. The United States must move cautiously between the hazards of supporting a repressive regime that may not be representative of its people and that of pushing the Chinese people back into isolation and poverty. The United States also has an interest in the future of the people in Hong Kong and Taiwan and must be alert to the repercussions of its policies fashioned in regards to the mainland on those other parts of China.

2 China's Economic Reforms

INTRODUCTION

During a long taxi ride in Beijing in September 1988, a 22-year-old Chinese college student mused: "My country is an old country. Years ago it was the world leader; people came from all over to learn from China. We invented gunpowder. We invented porcelain. But today we are so backward! How did it happen?" Fortunately the poignant question was rhetorical, for it would have taken one with the courage of an Oswald Spengler or an Arnold Toynbee to respond.

The Chinese are a proud people who believe with deep conviction that their country should be a world leader. "China must resume its rightful place in the world" is a comment one hears from all sectors; the implication is clear that China must once again make itself powerful and rich on a world scale. In the late 1970s, the Deng Xiaoping regime determined that to do so China must catch up with the West technologically and that this would require extensive reform of the Chinese economy.

"Catching up with the West" is a code phrase of deceptive simplicity, appearing to offer in a word – technology – an answer to the Chinese student's rhetorical question. The emphasis on technology seems to suggest that China's backwardness can be eliminated by imports of Western machinery and equipment. One manifestation of China's backwardness, however, is its very low level of productivity – output per unit of combined labor, capital, and material inputs. Total factor productivity is a function of production practices including, but not confined to, technology.

Western production practices involve much more than modern machinery and equipment. They involve a system of incentives based on fluctuating incomes and prices and mobile labor and capital that leads to maximum output from minimum inputs. It is in this sense that catching up with the West technologically entails extensive economic reform in China. It is to their credit that Deng and his supporters recognized these verities soon after their assump-

14 *China, Hong Kong, Taiwan and World Trade*

tion of control – in contrast to their counterparts in Eastern Europe, some of whom still cling to the notion that imports of advanced machinery and equipment by themselves will reverse their long-standing declines in productivity.

ORIGINS

Sustained increases in the productivity of China's labor and capital inputs are essential if China is to overcome its backwardness.[1] Total output can always be raised by increasing inputs, but if it takes ever-more inputs to raise output by the same amount, productivity growth is negative and real costs will rise sharply.

The hallmark of Western economies in the post-World War Two period has been rising total factor productivity; the most rapidly growing economies are those experiencing sharply rising productivity. From Table 2.1, it is clear that Japan's ability to catch up with Western Europe and the United States is based on the extraordinary growth in the productivity of its inputs sustained for long periods of time.

TABLE 2.1 *Total Factor Productivity: Organization for Economic Cooperation and Development, United States and Japan, 1973–85 (Business Sector, Average Percentage Changes at Annual Rates)*

	OECD Average	United States	Japan
Pre–1973	2.9	1.5	6.3
1973–79	0.7	– 0.1	1.8
1979–85	0.6	0.0	2.0

SOURCE: Organization for Economic Cooperation and Development, *Economic Outlook*, no. 42 (Paris: OECD, December 1987), p. 41.

Chinese statistical data are not adequate for computing similar estimates for the Chinese economy. Nonetheless, it is generally agreed that from the mid-1950s to the late 1970s Chinese productivity, at best, remained stagnant.[2]

China's industrial output during these years increased primarily because of increased inputs of capital, supported by high levels of Chinese savings. Although output per worker increased, output per

China's Economic Reforms

100 yuan of fixed capital declined.[3] The increase in Chinese national income resulting from successive additions of 100 yuan of fixed capital investment declined, probably not smoothly, from 52 yuan in the first Five-Year Plan to 34 yuan in the late 1970s (1976–79).[4]

Industrial output, and probably productivity, varied greatly during the three decades before 1979, with output growth ranging from an estimated 16 percent per year during the first Five-Year Plan (1953–57) to 2.8 percent during the second Five-Year Plan (1958–62), reflecting the collapse after the Great Leap Forward.[5] Growth was especially rapid in the favored sectors of industry, those producing heavy industrial goods, and slower in the neglected sector of light industry. Industrial growth rates were higher in the central and western parts of the country than in the already more highly industrialized coastal areas, again reflecting plans that favored the geographic dispersal of industry for security reasons and the inland provinces of Mao Zedong's origin.

In agriculture, which has always been accorded high priority because of the crucial importance of food availability to political and social stability, output per acre had typically been uncommonly high for a developing country using traditional agricultural techniques. In the 1930s, yields per acre for most major crops were higher in China than in the United States.[6] Even in agriculture, however, labor productivity declined in the 1960s and 1970s and, by 1977, was below its 1952 level.[7] Lagging agricultural growth in the face of an inexorable population increase and in spite of a steady increase in inputs is generally credited by China specialists as a major factor motivating economic reform.[8] Similar developments in industry led to an emphasis on improved efficiency in the Chinese economy and to increased labor productivity as a top priority of economic reform.

The ability of the Deng Xiaoping leadership to identify the major sources of China's economic problems was a remarkable achievement. The leadership's willingness to talk openly about China's backwardness (and the underlying reasons for it) was stunning at the time. China's previous isolation from the world was intensified during the decade of Mao's cultural revolution when, from 1966 to 1976, self-reliance was its theme. To purge the populace of mistaken leanings, intellectuals were scorned and, together with "capitalist roaders," banished to the countryside to do hard physical labor. Universities were either closed or their curricula converted to teaching party precepts. No new scientists, economists, engineers, or managers were trained, and those appointed to high positions

16 *China, Hong Kong, Taiwan and World Trade*

were chosen for their political reliability, not for their expertise. How well the new leadership understood the implications of its modernization program is debatable; at least its intuition was sound: It recognized the need for more efficient use of China's labor and capital resources.

Further, despite declining productivity, China's economy had grown at very respectable rates during the Mao years, and this growth had been widely bruited in China as a series of accomplishments. In fact, between 1952 and 1975, the annual growth of total output averaged 8.2 percent, with 11.5 percent in industry and 3.1 percent in agriculture.[9] Per capita income nearly doubled, rising from roughly $117 to $230. From the mid-1960s on, however, China's output growth dropped to a little more than 7 percent annually and this at a time when China's neighbors – Japan, Taiwan, South Korea, and Singapore – were enjoying growth rates of 10 percent or more. In the face of China's declining rates of productivity advance, China could realistically only expect to slip further and further behind.

In early 1978, little more than a year after Mao's death, the new leadership announced a detailed and highly ambitious new 10-year progam of economic development for the then-current Five-Year Plan (1976–80) and the Five-Year Plan to follow 1981–85), as well as broad guidelines for the remainder of the century.[10]. The program was endorsed at the 3rd Plenum of the 11th Party Central Committee in December 1978. Specifically, the plan called for agricultural output growth of 4–5 percent annually for 1978–85, industrial growth of more than 10 percent annually, and a quadrupling of net national product by the year 2000. China was to be transformed into a major industrial economy by the turn of the century.

The plan placed a high priority on agricultural development and the expansion of China's basic industries and transportation structure. Major emphasis was placed on industries that had accounted for existing bottlenecks in the economy – fuel, electric power, raw and semifinished materials, and metallurgy, as well as transportation, harbors, and ports. To alleviate these shortages, 120 large-scale projects were included. The program also called for "vigorous" development of light industry and an extraordinary reduction of China's population growth. The goal was to lower the rate of population increase in three years to less than 1 percent annually. (Estimates of the rate of China's population increase at that time varied from 1.2 to 1.7 percent annually.)[11] Finally, the program also included a large increase in foreign trade, incorporating new facilities for supplying industrial, mineral, and agricultural products for export to pay for imports of advanced technology and equipment.

In the 30 years of China's history as a centrally planned economy, only one Five-Year Plan had been completed satisfactorily by 1978 – the first. The second Five-Year Plan had been overruled by the Great Leap Forward, the third by the Cultural Revolution, the fourth by the Gang of Four, and the fifth by the economic reform and modernization program.[12] In light of such consistent political interference in the economic planning process, Chinese and foreigners alike had reason to be skeptical about the newly announced economic program. In fact, however, skepticism was little in evidence: The Chinese were euphoric, and foreigners were wildly optimistic. Hope and optimism in China had been rising during the previous year or two with the decline of the Gang of Four, as the idea of a Chinese renaissance took hold. Foreigners were being welcomed to China; Chinese leaders scheduled visits to Western Europe and the United States.

By early 1978, the Chinese were energized by optimism.[13] Industrial production and foreign trade, in particular, spurted forward in 1978, and, following after four years of stagnation, agricultural production also finally increased, although modestly.[14] With enthusiasmn for implementing the new program at a high pitch, China entered negotiations with almost all the interested Western companies (of which there was a multitude) to contract for large-scale projects included in the program, as well as smaller undertakings. Toward the end of that year, however, the constraints imposed on the economy – the many bottlenecks in infrastructure, materials supply, available foreign exchange, and lack of trained or experienced personnel – were becoming increasingly evident.

CRISES OF INCREASING INTENSITY

In 1979, a period of restraint and consolidation was announced together with a review of how best to implement the new program. This was the first of a series of stop-and-go policy changes that was to characterize the decade of the 1980s. The first period of retrenchment extended through 1981, the second covered 1985 and 1986. Then, by the autumn of 1988, yet another interval of restraint was necessary. In each of these efforts, growth was slowed by slashing

18 *China, Hong Kong, Taiwan and World Trade*

investment, curtailing budget expenditures, and limiting the trade deficit. In each succeeding period of advance, however, the excesses of the economy became more acute – rates of growth increasingly exceeded plan goals, as did investment, wages, imports, consumption, money supply, and prices. Corruption became increasingly troublesome.

Industrial output, having grown by nearly 9 percent in 1979 and 1980, fell to 4 percent in 1981. It recovered in each of the succeeding four years, reaching a growth rate of 18 percent in 1985 before collapsing to 9 percent in 1986. In 1988, it was nearly 21 percent.[15] (See Figure 2.1)

Similarly, after negative trade balances of $1–$2 billion in 1979 and 1980, trade was balanced in 1981, in surplus in 1982 and 1983, and negative again in 1984. In 1985, the excess of imports amounted to an awesome $15 billion, which by 1987 had dwindled to about $4 billion.[16] By the first half of 1989, it had risen again to nearly $12 billion at an annual rate[17] (see Figure 2.2).

Official data for investment and the budget deficit are misleading especially after the mid-decade. Substantial investment occurred that was not included in the central government's investment categories; investment financed from non-budgetary sources jumped in 1985 and after. Some central government spending financed investment activities by local governments.[18]

Figure 2.3 corrects official budget data for the fact that China treats drawings on foreign credits and loans as a revenue item. These credits and loans (converted into yuan from dollars) are added to official budget deficit figures.

The broad measure of China's money supply (currency and demand deposits) grew by 33 percent in 1980, dropped to 15 percent in 1982, recovered to 41 percent in 1984, then subsided to 18 percent in 1985.[19] By 1987, the growth was nearly 30 percent; in the second half of 1988, money in circulation jumped by more than 45 percent.[20] Figure 2.4 shows official data for the predominant part of the money supply, currency in circulation. Thus, in each succeeding period of advance, rates of growth were generally higher than those achieved previously, although the lows reached during periods of retrenchment never fell to previous levels.

Inflation became more intense as the decade progressed. Aggregate demand in the People's Republic of China (PRC) had always exceeded aggregate supply, although in the pre-reform period rigid controls kept prices stable. With decontrol, excess demand was

China's Economic Reforms

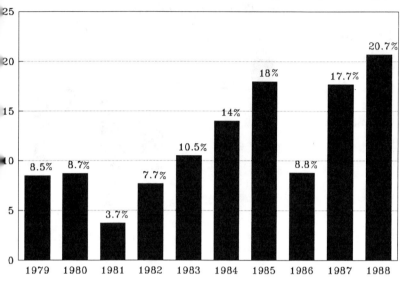

FIGURE 2.1 *Chinese Industrial Production (year-to-year change)*

Year	In Billions of Yuan	Year-to-Year Change (in percent)
1978	423.1	—
1979	459.1	8.5
1980	499.2	8.7
1981	519.9	3.7
1982	557.7	7.7
1983	616.4	10.5
1984	703.0	14.0
1985	829.5	18.0
1986	902.8	18.8
1987	1062.6	17.7
1988	1282.6	20.7

SOURCES: State Statistical Bureau (PRC), *Statistical Yearbook of China: 1987* [English edition], p. 220; *Statistical Yearbook of China: 1988,* p. 19; *Beijing Review* (March 6–12, 1989): p. II (documents).

evident in price rises. Price increases were moderate in the early years of reform, averaging about 2 percent until 1985. In that year, the consumer price index rose by nearly 12 percent. Inflation then moderated to 7 percent in 1986, but rose to 9 percent in 1987 and, in

FIGURE 2.2   *Chinese Trade Deficit: Balance of Imports and Exports (in billions of U.S. dollars)*

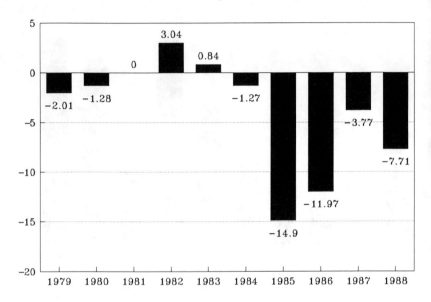

Year	Exports	Imports	Balance
1979	13.66	15.67	− 2.01
1980	18.27	19.55	− 1.28
1981	22.01	22.01	0.00
1982	22.32	19.28	3.04
1983	22.23	21.39	0.84
1984	26.14	27.41	− 1.27
1985	27.35	42.25	−14.90
1986	30.94	42.91	−11.97
1987	39.44	43.21	− 3.77
1988	47.54	55.25	− 7.71

SOURCES: State Statistical Bureau (PRC), *Statistical Yearbook of China: 1988* (English edition]; *Beijing Review* (March 6–12, 1989): 26.

1988, took off.[21] By the end of 1988, the government officially recognized that inflation had reached 27 percent countrywide and was higher still in the cities (see Figure 2.5). Unofficial estimates indicated that in some cities it was as high as 50 percent.[22] Earlier in

China's Economic Reforms   21

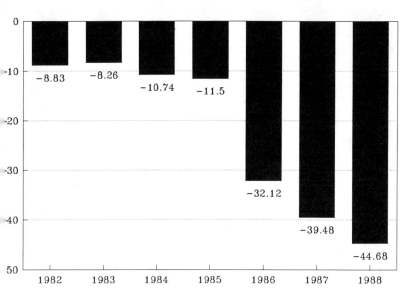

FIGURE 2.3 *Budget Deficit (in billions of yuan)*

Year	In Billions of Yuan	Year-to-Year Change (in percent)
1982	8.83	—
1983	8.26	– 6.5
1984	10.74	30.0
1985	11.50	7.1
1986	32.12	179.3
1987	39.48	22.9
1988	44.68	13.2

SOURCES: State Statistical Bureau (PRC), *Statistical Yearbook of China: 1988* [English edition], pp. 655, 665; *Beijing Review* (March 6–12, 1989): 26. Official budget deficit data were adjusted by adding utilization of foreign capital converted from dollars at average annual exchange rates.

1988, rising prices had caused panic buying and hoarding in urban areas and withdrawals of savings deposits from banks on a scale that clearly sobered the authorities; the culmination was retrenchment at the end of the decade.[23]

FIGURE 2.4 *Chinese Currency Circulation (in billions of Yuan)*

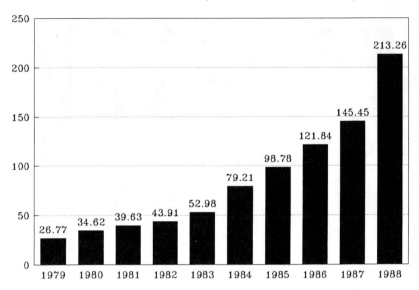

Year	In Billions of yuan	Year-to-Year Change (in percent)
1979	26.77	—
1980	34.62	29.3
1981	39.63	14.5
1982	43.91	10.8
1983	52.98	20.7
1984	79.21	49.5
1985	98.78	24.7
1986	121.84	23.3
1987	145.45	19.4
1988	213.26	46.6

SOURCES: International Monetary Fund, *International Financial Statistics: 1989* (Washington, D.C.: IMF, 1989), 289; for 1988, *International Financial Statistics, December 1989*, p. 167.

The reasons for the stop-and-go policies and for the increasing intensity of the cyclical swings were several. From the late 1970s, China had known where it wanted its economy to go, but it had been – and still is – unsure about how to get there. The Chinese

FIGURE 2.5 *Chinese Cost of Living Price Index: Year-to-Year Change (in percentages)*

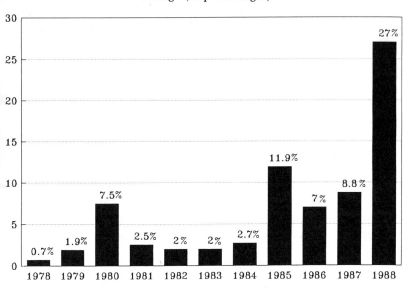

SOURCES: State Statistical Bureau (PRC), *Statistical Yearbook of China, 1988* [English edition], p. 691; *Asian Wall Street Journal Weekly,* August 7, 1989, p. 1.

were agreed that rapid growth and modernization were essential if China was to take its rightful place in the world. How best to achieve these goals, however, has been the subject of ongoing dispute.

The fact that China has been successful in achieving its prime goal of accelerated growth during the first decade of economic reform is illustrated by the clear rising trend underlying the cyclical swings in the major aggregates discussed above. Between 1978 and 1987, according to official sources, China's real gross national product (GNP), measured in 1980 yuan, grew at an average rate of nearly 10 percent a year.[24] It was supported by investment, which rose nearly 20 percent annually, and exports, which grew at nearly 17 percent.[25] Although statistical comparisons – especially among developing countries – are hazardous, it seems safe to conclude that China was among the most rapidly growing countries in the world during its first ten years of reform.

24 *China, Hong Kong, Taiwan and World Trade*

Controversy about how best to achieve rapid growth and modernization was prolonged, if not intensified, by the highly eclectic and pragmatic trial and error approach adopted by the Deng regime. Experimentation with economic reform commenced in a small group, an individual enterprise, or a single city; then, if successful, it progressed to a province or two or to the entire country. Starting with the micro and proceeding to the macro, however, frequently entailed side effects either not anticipated or ignored. What worked for one farm, commune, or enterprise in a few months frequently worked less well on a national level during an extended period in which social costs or externalities could overwhelm any progress.

Then, too, although some of China's professional economists rank with the top of their profession on a world scale, their advice frequently was ignored or adjusted because of political considerations. China's economists, moreover, like their brethren worldwide, did not speak with one voice; they too argued among themselves. Whether or not conflicting advice was responsible for the stop-and-go policies, such conflicts did not facilitate the reform process.[26]

Further, the Deng regime never aimed for capitalism. Rather, it attempted to substitute market mechanisms and government regulationjs for centralized administrative controls as the instruments for directing a socialist economy. (A "commodity economy" is the quaint term used by the Chinese). Specifically, China's economic reform tried to separate ownership of the means of production from control of production processes by giving farmers and enterprise managers the authority to make decisions about production, marketing, and prices. Decision-making acumen and hard work would be rewarded by higher, differential incomes; poor performance would suffer lower incomes, although the issue of how much income inequality would be tolerated was left ambiguous. The state would direct the overall course of the economy by adjusting such indirect levers of market control as the money supply, interest rates, taxes, and government expenditures in the same fashion as Western economies.

In addition, the goal of economic reform was not the eventual complete replacement of administrative controls by market controls. Rather, from the beginning, the Chinese agreed that certain sectors would remain administratively directed. The question therefore arises: Does market socialism itself lead to periodic crises of increasing intensity? This leads to two questions: First, can market socialism work as efficiently as capitalism? Second, if it can, can

China's Economic Reforms

limited market socialism also be as efficient as capitalism? There is a long history of discussion of the first question in the literature of theoretical economics, dating back to the seminal work of the Polish economist, Oskar Lange, in the 1930s. Lange's work, *On the Economic Theory of Socialism*, stimulated a lively debate that continues to this day.[27] The chief points of dispute concern the efficiency of management and especially of resource allocation decisions under market socialism. The main question is whether professional managers under socialism, receiving a salary plus a small percentage of profits, would be as efficient as their counterparts under capitalism for whom risks and rewards both would be much greater. No consensus seems to have developed.

Most of the theoretical discussion assumes that pragmatic market socialism would insist on a more equal distribution of incomes, and especially of property returns, than would be the case under capitalism. The state as the owner of the means of production would collect rents and most profits, and would distribute them to households in proportion to labor income. Thus, all the people – the true owners of the means of production – would benefit from their ownership. The manager, however, not being able to sell a full ownership share, would not be able to benefit from the long-term effects of his decisions; thus, his incentive to exert extraordinary effort, especially in regard to long-term planning for the enterprise, would be limited.

Whether in fact pragmatic market socialism, if it existed in any country, would find its managerial capacities *significantly* limited in practice, is unlikely to be truly tested by empirical evidence. This is so because political necessities would be as compelling under socialism as under capitalism, would cause at least as many deviations from the theoretical ideal in the former as the latter, and therefore would distort the system away from its best possible performance.

Thus, both questions can only be answered with a "perhaps." The second question, can limited market socialism be as efficient as (limited) capitalism, is the only relevant one. China hoped to be able to demonstrate a positive response. In the context of the present discussion, there is nothing inherent in ideal market socialism itself that would lead to crises of increasing intensity.

China's periodic crises were primarily related to the nature of the economy the Deng regime inherited – especially the geographic structure of production and the structure of relative prices – and to

26   *China, Hong Kong, Taiwan and World Trade*

the fact that it was in transition from a centrally controlled, planned socialist economy to a market-controlled, growth-oriented socialist economy. The inheritance of the reform, at least in part, constrained the nature of the specific transition course that China could realistically choose.

THE INHERITANCE OF THE REFORM EFFORT

Despite having been modeled on the USSR, the economy of the PRC was never as monolithic, concentrated, or planned as that of its Soviet neighbor. During the Mao period, industrial development and especially heavy industry was dispersed away from existing centers of industry and commerce along the coast to the inland provinces. This dispersal was motivated by security concerns that led to increasing emphasis on regional self-sufficiency and to industrial relocation to inland areas because of Mao's personal interests; there was little economic justification for this industrial move. The consequence was greater geographic dispersal of industry than in the USSR or Eastern Europe.

Furthermore, Chinese economic development under Mao was unique in the socialist world in its reliance on small-scale industry, a consequence both of the dispersal of industry and Mao's emphasis on self-sufficiency, which peaked during the Cultural Revolution. In fact, in the pre-reform period, China was comprised of a collection of largely segmented, autonomous local economies, self-sufficient to a sizable degree and cut off from each other by lack of transport and communications. China was never a national market to the degree found in Eastern Europe or the USSR. Large numbers of small enterprises across the country together with primitive communication facilities made it unfeasible for central output planning to be concentrated in Beijing. Thus, from the 1950s onward, an active and increasingly important role in output planning was assigned to the provinces and localities.

The process of rapid industrialization throughout the country and decentralization of the planning process to the provinces, municipalities, counties, prefects, and villages combined to make the non-central government planning sector almost as important as the central government in the planning process by the late 1970s.[28] By 1977–78, for example, the central plan included only an estimated 50 percent or so of the gross value of industrial output; the rest was planned at the local level or was not subject to official planning. Although the central plan included nearly all the output in centrally administered enterprises, it accounted for less than 20 percent of output in rural collective enterprises, for one-fourth to one-third of output in county and prefectural enterprises, and for an estimated one-half to two-thirds of output in provincial and municipal enterprises.[29]

The central plan included almost the entire output of state enterprise, but little of the output of collectives. "Collective" enterprises in fact covered a variety of ownership patterns. Owners of collectives included groups of individuals, local governments, state enterprises, and semiofficial organizations. Even the Chinese had acute problems in identifying enterprise ownership, especially in distinguishing among different kinds of state ownership (e.g., ministerial, municipal, or enterprise). The main difference between collective and state enterprises was that most collectives were not included in the state plan.[30]

The largest enterprises were all state-controlled, under the domain of the central plan and under the supervision of the central industrial ministries in Beijing and their branches throughout the country. Medium-sized enterprises were largely owned and administered by provinces and municipalities. Small-scale enterprises were owned and administered by localities (county, prefect, or village) or collectives; small businesses were primarily outside of plan control. Thus, under Mao, although China had a primarily government-controlled economy, it was only partially a centrally controlled or centrally planned economy.

The relationship between local authorities and enterprises within their boundaries (whether locally or centrally administered) that developed under Mao was by no means adversarial in nature; rather, it was largely symbiotic. Local authorities and enterprise managers worked with considerable harmony to achieve mutually agreed goals. This relationship, based on family connections and long established ties of confidence and congeniality, continued in the reform period.

In the sphere of prices, under Mao, the relative price structure established to encourage industrialization made raw material and food prices cheap in relation to industrial products' prices and in comparison with world market prices and with internal Chinese scarcities. Such price relationships set the stage for a shortage of raw materials and overinvestment in industry as market forces were given more scope. Market forces indeed operated in a more limited

28   *China, Hong Kong, Taiwan and World Trade*

fashion in the pre-reform period of incomplete output planning, thereby aggravating raw material shortages. In a similar fashion, the overvalued foreign exchange rate for the renminbi (RMB) (1.52 RMB = \$1 in 1978) provided the basis for depressed exports and buoyant imports in the reform period. Even the official depreciation to 3.72 RMB to the dollar by 1988 still left the Chinese currency considerably overvalued.

Finally, the economy under Mao was one of hidden shortages. Prices and wages were fixed at low levels and remained almost unchanged through the 1970s. Investment absorbed a high proportion of output, averaging 28 percent from 1952–80, financed by savings that were forced on consumers by the scarcity of consumer goods for which they might spend their incomes.[31] Costs were largely ignored in the state-determined prices, with differences between revenue and outlay by enterprises being made up by the state budget. Because employment was guaranteed, and social services like health, education and housing were provided by the employer, and because wages bore no relation to output, incentives to better performance were nonexistent. Low prices for raw materials, fuel, power, and transport encouraged wastefulness in their use. Rigid controls plus long waiting periods kept demand down to the level of supply.

THE COURSE OF THE TRANSITION

Autonomy of Enterprise Management

Despite its rocky course of stop-and-go policies, the first decade of reform was marked by the continuous introduction of new reform measures. Even during intervals of retrenchment and reimposition of central controls, China extended existing reform measures over larger areas and continued to experiment with new reform measures. During the clampdown of 1988–89, for example, a system of unemployment compensation was tested in Shenyang, and China reportedly started to offer special insurance against political risks for foreign investors in Hainan, designed to stimulate foreign investment by allaying foreign fears of changes in Chinese policy.[32] Similarly, during the slowdown of 1985–86, Beijing eliminated mandatory quota deliveries by farmers, instead signing production contracts for grain and cotton. The contracted amounts were less than the previous quotas, and the state withdrew its commitment to buy all above-quota output at premium prices. Also, controls on prices of nonstaple farm products were removed.[33]

The process of extending reforms incrementally expanded the operation of market mechanisms more or less continuously after the late 1970s, thus creating new opportunities for the entrepreneurial Chinese to make money in production or commerce or by wheeling-dealing. During the past decade, the mainland Chinese have proven that they have not lost their interest in or skill at making money.

Even if the division of the economy into a market sector and an administratively planned sector had remained fixed, it is likely that growth of output in the market sector would have been more rapid than that of the state-controlled sector. Because the potential financial rewards would be greater, incentives for investment in the market sector would be greater than those in the controlled sector. Thus, a tendency would exist for the market share of production to expand over time at the expense of controlled production or for the economy "to grow out of the plan."[34] There is considerable evidence that such tendencies were operating in China.

Economic reform was intended further to decentralize control and to expand enterprise decision-maiing autonomy in an effort to raise output from the same amount of inputs. In its first decade, it was notably more successful in decentralization than in expanding enterprise autonomy. Although the withdrawal of government at all levels from direct involvement in the day-to-day economic decisions of enterprises *and* the decentralization of decision making to enterprise managers were the combined intent of the reform process, in fact, decentralization proceeded in large part from the central government in Beijing to local governments at all levels, where it remained stalled. Decisions by enterprise managers concerning production, purchasing, marketing, investment, and finance remained subject to the approval of local authorities in most cases.[35]

Compulsory and guidance plans declined in importance during the economic reform, but were replaced to a large degree by informal mechanisms of government control. The power of local governments to continue to influence the operation of enterprises located within their boundaries was broad and deep, based on their control of local resources (e.g., workers, managers, raw materials, finance, fuel, and power) and, thus, of costs and their control of prices and taxes and, thus, of profits. Governmental administrative organs retained their power to appoint enterprise managers and to provide

30   *China, Hong Kong, Taiwan and World Trade*

investment capital to the enterprises they administered. They often determined the access to raw materials and supplies of the enterprises within their boundaries; in consequence, all levels of government were able to continue to exert significant control over enterprises.[36] In addition, local governments were motivated by strong pressures for growth. The combination fueled much of the overheated growth in China's economy in the late 1980s.

Pressures for rapid growth were both political and economic. The reform program itself, of course, provided the setting by giving official blessing to a goal of rapid growth. Also, Beijing, in pointing to and lauding specific cases of success around the country, constantly urged other cities, provinces, or localities to go and do likewise. Whether economically rational or not, emulation drives were successful.

Further, governments had the responsibility for providing employment for all their citizens. Because arable land was fully cultivated and declining in availability as farmers chose to use more of it for housing or rural industry, governments were under pressure to provide more and more nonagricultural employment because of increasing population growth. To do this, they needed more investment funds and, therefore, more revenue. What better way to accomplish these ends than to encourage the processing of the raw materials within their own regions, which had previously been shipped to other provinces. The new industries would provide both employment and a source of tax revenue for the local government.

In addition, the relative price system inherited from the Mao era made processing more profitable than the production of raw materials. Thus, establishing new processing industries not only provided employment within the producing provinces, but was especially lucrative in tax revenues and perquisites for local officials. The new capacity locally installed, however, raised demand for already scarce materials, fuel, and power and thereby aggravated existing shortages.

The China Enterprise Management Association at a meeting in 1988 cited "three pests" harassing enterprise managers. Each stemmed from interference with enterprise operations on the part of local governments. The greatest pest was judged to be the resale by local officials at high prices of goods in short supply. Managers asserted this pest to be most threatening because punishment was elusive: Higher officials typically pleaded the case for the "speculators," thereby enabling speculators to escape punishment. The

China's Economic Reforms

second pest took the form of indiscriminate and arbitrary charges levied by local governments on enterprises. As enterprises accumulated funds from successful operations, they faced repeated requests by local authorities for "aid" of some sort. If such requests were denied, the enterprise would be charged with an unlawful act, such as pollution, and would be subject to a fine. Third, as enterprises were accorded more rights to autonomous actions, local authorities were extremely inventive in finding new means for retaining power. Local bank branches were pressured to make or withhold loans from enterprises; land for housing or schools was denied; personnel for health clinics were withheld from recalcitrant enterprises; administrative bureaus even set up "companies" to perform the control functions of the bureaus.[37]

Each of the three pests represented a form of corruption that Beijing attempted to eliminate, but halfheartedly and with little success. The reform had multiplied political and economic opportunities for personal gain. As rapid growth made shortages more acute, temptations to profit personally from one's official position became more irresistible. In part, this corruption was transitional and would disappear when the transition to market socialism was completed; in part, it was inherent in the price system.

Dual-Price System

The bulk of China's economic and corruption problems during the reform period was traceable to its dual-price (two tier) system, designed as a technique to alleviate the shock to the economy that would result from an abrupt shift from controlled to market-based prices. With controlled prices clearly too low, the inflationary implications of an all-at-once shift to market prices were deemed so severe as to be socially destabilizing. A transitional dual-price system was perceived as necessary for the interval during which supplies were expanding toward the level of demand.

Rural Reform

The dual-price system was broadly established in the early 1980s during a period in which rural reforms preceded reform in urban areas, although the practice of two prices for the same commodity had originated with the appearance of small farmers' markets in rural areas in the 1950s. By 1983, most of the collective forms of agricultural activity had been replaced by household farming. Farm

32 *China, Hong Kong, Taiwan and World Trade*

families were allocated sections of former collective land that they could use as they chose in exchange for certain obligatory deliveries to the state. Production quotas were fixed and sold to the state at established low prices. Production above the quota could be sold on the free market at prices the market would bear.

Long-standing concern about an adequate food supply led China to experiment with incentive prices for grain deliveries (and for other food items) to the state, while continuing to sell grain in urban areas at the low prices fixed in the 1950s. The incentives were hugely successful in increasing output, but the impact on state subsidy expenditures was explosive.

A series of bumper crops caused prices in the free market to decline in 1984. By 1985, China felt that its food supply was secure enough to slash compulsory state quotas and to talk in terms of their eventual, complete abolition. Quotas were replaced by targets for procuring a limited number of products – especially grain, cotton, and other important industrial crops. The government offered to sign purchase contracts for these amounts and guaranteed to buy at a minimum price agricultural produce for which no other market could be found.[38]

By the mid-1980s, China (and many China-watchers) considered its agricultural reforms a resounding success. Growth rates for agricultural output had been boosted from an annual average of about 4 percent during 1971–78 to 13 percent during 1982–86. Although this dramatic overall result represented to a large degree the exceptionally rapid growth of rural industry (processing of output, manufacturing of inputs and consumer goods in the rural areas), total factor productivity in agriculture appeared to have increased substantially as well.[39] The reform, however, was by no means complete. The dual-price system continued in both producer and consumer markets, and controlled prices in both markets were too low; relative price distortions still existed; huge subsidies still added to budget deficits and festering problems – for example, irrigation system maintenance, rural health, education, and rural roads – were ignored.[40] Nonetheless, the PRC officials were sufficiently heartened by the success of agricultural reforms that they felt confident in stepping up the pace of industry reform in urban areas.

Urban Reform
Urban industrial reform was vastly more complex an undertaking than was agricultural reform. Some free markets in agricultural

China's Economic Reforms

produce had existed under Mao, but none existed for industrial goods. Enterprises had no experience in autonomous decision making. The complexity of modern industrial processes entailing many inputs, a varied output, and a structure of interdependencies among enterprises, both wide and deep, complicated urban reform. Awareness of the complexities induced the Chinese to approach urban reform with special caution.[41]

Experimentation in industrial reform began in 1978 when existing plan quotas for some enterprises were adjusted to permit above-quota output to be marketed independently at prices that could vary by 20 percent from the fixed state price. (The 20 percent limit was canceled in 1985.)[42] Some state prices were adjusted in an attempt to make them better reflect costs and scarcity. As the 1980s progressed, the major thrust of the reform effort was directed toward enhancing the scope for market forces to determine prices. The number of industrial and consumer goods sold at state-fixed prices was reduced periodically. Brookings Institution Scholar Harry Harding notes that in 1982 enterprises were given authority to set their own prices for 160 commodities; in 1983, another 350 were added to the free list, and, in 1985, when mandatory agricultural quotas were eliminated, prices of meat, fish, poultry, and vegetables were made subject to market determination.[43]

Free enterprise (collective and private) was the most rapidly growing sector of the Chinese economy during the 1980s. Comprising private and collective business, its share of employment, output, and retail sales expanded rapidly. By the same token, the share of state enterprise dropped. In contrast with 1978 when 90 percent of retail sales was conducted in state stores, by 1987 only 40 percent of retail sales was so sold. The decline of the state sector was far less dramatic in employment and output, however. The share of state enterprise in urban employment dropped from 78 percent in 1978 to 70 percent in 1986 where it remained; the state share of industrial output fell from 81 percent to 60 percent at the end of the 1980s.[44] Thus, the economy showed signs of "growing out of the plan."

At the end of the 1980s, all large-scale enterprise remained in state control; private and collective enterprises were confined to small businesses primarily in rural areas. Although rates of private-sector growth were far in excess of those in the state sector (the average rate of output growth of individual enterprise from 1980 to 1985 was 80 percent and of collective enterprise, 17 percent, as compared with 8 percent in the state sector) and despite the rapid

34   *China, Hong Kong, Taiwan and World Trade*

growth of employment in the private sector (35 percent for 1980–86), the state sector still remained dominant and the economy still remained primarily state-controlled and regulated.

In the important area of state enterprise, reforms were directed toward giving managers more authority – making them more autonomous in production and marketing decisions, in part by introducing a new tax structure and permitting state factories to retain more of their profits. By the end of the decade, state enterprise was directed by both the plan and the market and was subject to many inherent contradictions as a result. Pursuit of efficiency and higher profits were frustrated because state enterprise was forced to provide additional employment although already overstaffed, because state enterprise frequently was required by the plan to produce priority goods at a loss, and because chronic shortages created a need to hoard raw materials. Such state-imposed constraints on efficiency, moreover, contributed to the perception by plant managers that plant modernization and long-term investment were the responsibility of the state, not the factory.[45] Enterprise subsidies rose during the decade to an amount equal in 1989 to two-thirds of China's total investment.[46]

Only one-third of the state enterprises operated at a profit; the remainder either suffered losses and had to be subsidized (up to 20 percent) or broke even.[47] Most of the important industrial inputs – raw and semiprocessed materials, fuels and power, transport and machinery – as well as many industrial and consumer goods and food were state-controlled, with prices fixed in whole or in part by the state and distribution subject to state allocation.[48]

Contract System

The contract system for factories, a key feature of urban reform, obligated an enterprise manager to give to the state a predetermined amount of profit each year in exchange for freedom to run the enterprise as the manager saw fit and to retain profits above the contracted amount. Through this system, the state maintained a posture of factory ownership while encouraging market-directed operations. The system was more successful in the private and collective sector than in state enterprise. In the latter, where, by 1989, 80 percent of state-owned enterprise had instituted the contract system, for each 100 yuan spent on capital investment, enterprises earned 20 yuan in 1987, compared with 25 in 1979,

China's Economic Reforms

according to official estimates.[49] Because collectives had to seek out their own inputs and markets, their competitive skills were sharpened. Further, because the contract system had no provision for penalizing those who did not meet their profit targets and only the small private and collective plants were allowed to go out of business while larger state enterprises were subsidized, collectives had a strong incentive for efficiency. The contract system provided the carrot for state enterprises, but wielded no stick in their direction.[50]

Beijing realized through most of the reform period that recorded profits of state enterprises did not reflect enterprise efficiency, but rather the historical accident of the relation between state-fixed prices for key state enterprise inputs and its finished product, as well as the quality of the plant and equipment the enterprise happened to have inherited. Nevertheless, it was the only even approximate measure of efficiency available for administrative purposes, and Beijing attempted to improve it by adjusting actual profits better to measure efficiency according to the specific conditions of each factory. Because only local officials were in a position to know the conditions prevailing in each locality, they were authorized to make the necessary adjustments to profits for purposes of taxation. As a consequence, profits were determined primarily as a result of bargaining between enterprise managers and the local bureaucracy for lower tax rates or higher allocations of low state-priced raw materials.[51]

What Beijing appeared to have had in mind was a step-by-step iterative approach to realistic profits using plant history and actual prices as a guide to managerial efficiency. To be even partially successful, such an approach required a corps of skilled, experienced, objective accountants with extensive knowledge of actual commodity and product markets. Such talent was – and remains – sadly lacking in China. In fact, the great preponderance of enterprises checked their own books for accuracy.[52] Further, the established pattern of congenial relations between managers and local authorities and the motivations of each to further the success of their region (to say nothing of themselves) militated against success. Clearly, the opportunities for corruption latent in such an approach were enormous.

Despite the high degree of state control, most goods sold at two different prices – a low state-set price for supplies subject to allocation and a higher free market, fluctuating price for production

36 *China, Hong Kong, Taiwan and World Trade*

in excess of state quotas. Those enterprises whose output and, therefore, revenues were primarily determined by state allocations at low state-set prices were clearly at a disadvantage. Those individuals and enterprises that had access to low-priced allocated supplies clearly were in a favored position. Their costs were lower; hence, their profits were higher than the costs and profits of those who had to purchase in the free market. Temptations for diversion were immense. Temptations were enlarged with growth, moreover, as demand for further inputs outran supply, and the difference between the two prices expanded.

Bottlenecks
The differential between regulated and market prices for basic industrial inputs widened during the reform period as demand for raw materials, fuels, and infrastructure services – electric power, transportation, communications of all kinds, warehouses, and such – grew more rapidly than supply. Although production in all of these areas increased during the reform, it still did not keep pace with demand. According to official sources, from 1978 to 1987 industrial production increased at an average annual rate of 12 percent, while energy output grew at less than 5 percent, steel at about 6 percent, coal at a little more than 4 percent, cotton at about 7 percent, and electricity at nearly 7 percent.[53] According to a 1984 survey, the importance of planning and allocation in the production and distribution of raw and semifinished materials was far greater than for other goods.[54] In fact, planned supply (both mandatory and guidance plans) exceeded actual output, requiring costly adjustments in the production plans of their consuming enterprises.

A more rapid growth of industrial output than of the main industrial inputs could have been the consequence of greater efficiency in the use of inputs. This may have happened to some degree in enterprises that were forced to buy at free-market prices because their allocations of low-priced inputs from the government never arrived. The reduction in demand that would flow from such increased efficiency, however, seems to have been counterbalanced by greater hoarding and spreading physical shortages of materials, power, and such that were not available at any price.

Shortages of coal became especially acute during the late 1980s. Power cuts, blackouts, and brownouts were chronic in late 1988 and 1989, forcing factories and hospitals to close or operate for only a few hours a day, and even Tiananmen Square, the symbol of China, was periodically darkened by power cuts. Because coal provided the great bulk of China's energy requirements (more than 70 percent), shortages brought complaints from all quarters. They resulted primarily from three interdependent causes. Industrialization, and therefore the demand for energy, outpaced the expanding output of coal, and low official prices discouraged efficient use. The consequent increase in the price of free-market coal widened the differential between the market price and the fixed price for state allocations, causing more coal to be diverted from the state market to the free market and "profiteering" of all sorts to become rife. Also, because coal was produced largely in the west (especially Shanxi Province), but used all over China, and because China's rail network of 50 000 kilometers was growing only 500 kilometers a year (1 percent), railway traffic became jammed.[55] Coal frequently piled up at the mines because of a shortage of rail cars.[56]

All coal-consuming industries (most of manufacturing activity) were affected in a similar fashion. Steel output was limited by the coal shortage, for example, and costs of production were raised because of the necessity to use more high-priced free market coal. Thus, the differential between official and market prices for steel widened. Those with access to official allocations – primarily party members – could buy a ton of steel at 200 yuan and resell it at 700 yuan, becoming instant millionaires in the process. The effects on steel consumers were similar to those on coal consumers; cost and price increases rippled through the economy.

Coal and other raw material producers were typically large-scale industries, requiring sizable amounts of capital investment and long construction periods before production could commence. Inadequate credit markets kept private and collective enterprises from entering these industries except on a very small scale. Individual and collective enterprises were consequently poorly represented, and most raw material production was carried on by government enterprise. Thus, the stimulating effect of free markets on the supply of raw and semifinished materials was negligible; supply remained inelastic.

As local governments, under pressure for rapid growth and more revenue, built new capacity for themselves to process raw materials produced within their borders, raw material scarcities were aggravated. Rising market prices created wider incentives for the diversion of supplies from state allocations into the market sector and

38 *China, Hong Kong, Taiwan and World Trade*

contributed to the rising costs of finished products. Intensified shortages also created competition among the provinces for the scarce but essential materials that was so intense that it was termed by one observer "economic warlordism."[57]

The consequences of the dual-price system and decentralization were totally predictable. Enterprises receiving a quota allocation were sometimes able to make more money by selling the allocated quota in the free market than by using it in manufacturing. Others with a low quota could profit by offering to reward enterprises or officials who might direct low costs supplied to them. Although such trading was illegal and, therefore, definable as "corruption," it was also evidence that the market mechanism was alive and well in China. Such corruption was the direct consequence of the dual-price system. In late 1988, an economist at the Guangdong Academy of Social Sciences estimated that three-fourths of the goods produced under the state plan were being sold illegally in the free market.[58] It created Chinese millionaires overnight, at all levels of the civil service.

The distortions resulting from the dual-price system were exaggerated by the fact that the process of reform gave more autonomy to some localities than to others. The coastal provinces were especially favored in this regard – Guangdong and Fujian in particular and, toward the end of the decade, the island of Hainan also. The philosophy of Deng's "open door" policy was grounded in the notion that China's coast with 14 "open cities" and 5 Special Economic Zones (SEZs) would grow and prosper through foreign investment and trade. (Three of the five SEZs were located in Guangdong, one in Fujian, and the fifth was the island of Hainan.)[59] The government believed this prosperity would spread from the coast to the interior. The favored localities were authorized to keep a larger share of tax revenues, to approve foreign investments of larger amounts, to give tax holidays to foreigners, and to retain a larger share of foreign exchange generated within their boundaries.

The "open door" policy was most notably successful in Guangdong, the province bordering Hong Kong. There, foreign businessmen – especially those from Hong Kong, but also Japanese, Americans, and others – established joint ventures to provide labor-intentive finished products or labor-intensive processing for imports to be reexported and finished abroad. Many workers in Guangdong factories came from neighbouring provinces, many illegally.

China's Economic Reforms

Chinese policy during the 1980s continued to discourage labor mobility among localities and also between enterprises because of laws restricting the movement of workers to cities larger than that of their original employment, and because of the Mao-era practice of tying housing, education, and health services to the place of employment. A worker shifting his job might be forced to give up his apartment, change his child's school, and seek alternative sources of medical treatment. Continued shortages of housing, schools, and medical facilities meant that only those with a low level of risk-aversion were willing to take the chance. Employers, moreover, under pressure to improve productivity, were reluctant to release the most productive workers who stood the best chance of finding another job, and social pressures made it impossible to fire the inefficient.[60] In addition, the state itself was hesitant to enforce measures (like bankruptcy) that would release workers and reduce the budget deficit (through reductions of subsidy payments). Lacking any operational system of unemployment benefits, the state was concerned about the potential for social unrest of sizable unemployment.[61]

Some progress toward more flexibility in the labor market was made during the 1980s. In 1985, new workers entering the labor force were no longer assigned to a job for life, but rather received from the state a contract for a fixed term of employment with specified duties.[62] Workers dismissed from a job for any reason also became eligible for unemployment compensation for as long as two years. Except for an experimental project in the city of Shenyang, however, no implementation of unemployment compensation was evident.[63]

Despite such restrictions, much illegal migration did take place, motivated by declining employment opportunities in agriculture and, in the late 1980s, in construction and by the rapid growth and relatively high incomes available in the coastal areas. Guangdong especially was attractive to the migrants. It was the recipient of much foreign investment because of its available labor, low wages, and easy access to the trade and commercial facilities of Hong Kong. Its attraction was magnified by the depreciation of the dollar after 1985 against many of the currencies of the region. The province boomed. Between 1978 and 1987, the province absorbed one-half of the foreign investment used in the entire country.[64] Beyond workers, it devoured coal, steel, and aluminium from the

40 *China, Hong Kong, Taiwan and World Trade*

interior as well as grain and pork by paying high market prices. "Trickle down" worked.

But not nearly fast enough. The inland provinces raised a clamor of protests about the "unfair" advantages of the coastal areas. Not only did they establish their own industries in competition with the established manufacturers of the coast, they also retaliated by embargoing shipments of raw materials outside their own borders, by levying a production-support fee on outside buyers of scarce goods, and by demanding payment in foreign exchange for their materials. They even moved some of their factory operations to Guangdong to take advantage of the generous investment provisions available in the SEZs.[65]

In the late 1980s, Guangdong in fact surpassed Shanghai, formerly the leading industrial province in China, in exports.[66] Shanghai's relative decline was traceable in large part to raw material and power shortages that stemmed from decentralization and the decision of the supplying areas to use their materials themselves. It was reported, for example, that despite state plans obliging other provinces in 1988 to provide 2200 tons of raw silk to Shanghai, they actually provided only 13 tons. Shanghai was consequently forced to spend nearly $900 million on the free market buying raw materials, compared with virtually no free-market purchases in 1985. Even so, one-third of Shanghai's cotton mills were idle because no cotton was to be found.[67] Shanghai was also hampered by the fact that its economy was dominated by state-run companies, which were less entrepreneurial and flexible and more subject to state production allocations and low state-set prices than the vibrant collective and private enterprises that mushroomed in Guangdong.

State Sector

Although reforming state enterprises to make them more efficient lay at the heart of China's economic reforms, the country had barely started to tackle the problem in the 1980s. The nonstate sector in which guaranteed employment did not prevail grew rapidly, but, at the end of the decade, it provided less than one-third of the jobs in the urban labor force; the great preponderance of workers was employed in state enterprise.

Resistance to labor reforms was sharp. Workers in state enterprises gave little evidence of any strong desire to give up lifetime job security for the risks of the contract system. Wage reform, too,

China's Economic Reforms

which was intended to reward workers for higher productivity by providing bonuses out of enterprise profits, was widely resented and thought unsuitable for a socialist society. In fact, social pressures on enterprise managers were so strong that equal bonuses were widely distributed to all employees. Beijing, moreover, recognized that the existing distorted price system meant that profits or losses did not reflect efficiency; thus, bonuses that were tied to recorded profits were not capable of achieving their goal.

In addition, Beijing's apprehension about permitting loss-making enterprises to go into bankruptcy – a bankruptcy act was passed in 1988 – meant that failure to improve efficiency was not penalized.[68] At the same time, enterprises in the innovative private and collective sectors of the economy could go bankrupt and constantly did. Thus, at the end of the decade, profits and losses of state enterprises – therefore, of the preponderant part of the Chinese economy – reflected primarily success or failure in bargaining about taxes and low-priced inputs. It was ironic that the state sector, protected to a large degree by its monopoly position, low input, and high product prices managed to lose money despite apparently having the rules of the game rigged in its favor, while the collective and private sectors, competing in high-priced markets, thrived and grew. In fact, domestic demand and supply conditions had changed so drastically since the time when prices were originally fixed that even the sole producer of a product had trouble showing a profit.

The dual-price system was extended into foreign exchange trading – first, in 1986 in a limited form in 3 SEZs, then in 1988 in 5 (out of 29) municipalities, provinces, and autonomous regions – when auction markets in foreign exchange were authorized.[69] In these markets, convertible currencies trading at a large premium in RMB above the official exchange rate provided a cheap source of local currency for diverting goods from less-favored provinces. Even Fujian, where such a foreign exchange trading center was located, complained that Guangdong traders bought Fujian goods with cheap RMB and exported them at lower prices.[70] The introduction of an official dual exchange-rate system brought complaints from the International Monetary Fund (IMF), which China had joined early in the decade.

Cut-throat competition in inputs, insofar as it sprang from a dual-price system grounded in distorted relative prices, did not serve China well. In some cases, it diverted scarce materials from more efficient, established industries to new, inexperienced small factories

42   *China, Hong Kong, Taiwan and World Trade*

in the inland provinces, thereby reducing productivity growth below its potential. It created overcapacity in industry that aggravated raw material shortages and diverted scarce capital away from more productive uses in infrastructure and raw material development. In diverting scarce materials to the artificially more profitable export markets, it exaggerated latent inflationary forces and the budget deficit, adding to demands for higher wages (through bonus payments) that enterprise managers found hard to resist. These distortions, in combination with enormous consumption demands in China and the legacy of equality (the importance of "keeping up with the Jones's"), provided a high-powered motor to inflation and retarded improvements in quality as well.

Worsening raw material shortages produced higher inflation rates and shorter periods of expansion as growth continued. Increasingly severe controls were necessary in periods of retrenchment to bring inflation down. In the future, if pressures for growth continue and if the bottleneck sectors continue to lag, the shortages will become more intense, periods of austerity and retrenchment will last longer, and periods of expansion will be shorter until the economy settles into a prolonged "stagflation" (i.e., inflation combined with low or zero growth). The dual-price system would then have impaled the economy on the petard of Stalinist bottlenecks.

These ills will linger so long as the dual-price system persists. In fact, China's economic reform will only be completed when all prices – controlled and free market – reflect Chinese internal scarcities. When and if this happens, the dual-price system will disappear; those forms of corruption traceable to price distortions will also disappear. If, at that time, inadequacies in transport and communications still cause market segmentation in China, differences in prices among regions could still prevail, but they would be no more than a reflection of the (expensive) cost of moving goods from one region to another.

As the PRC moves forward with its economic reform program, it is probably unnecessary for optimum resource allocation that relative prices in China reflect world market prices. The internal Chinese market is large enough in most cases to permit economies of scale where these are important, unaided by access to foreign markets. Thus, a relative price system reflecting the relative scarcities of Chinese inputs and the preference pattern of Chinese consumers would maximize the productivity of Chinese resources. It would also maximize the contribution China could make to world economic development as the Chinese economy becomes more and more open. If, however, administratively controlled prices of important inputs like fuel, power, or labor are maintained at levels that do not reflect internal scarcities, distortions in resource allocation will persist, and productivity and growth will be hampered.

Corruption stemming from personal venality, whether in politicians or business executives, will always be present in China, as elsewhere. In China, the special political role of the Communist Party and traditional social philosophy will make the problem of corrupt politicians more difficult to correct.

INFLATION, CORRUPTION, AND THE FUTURE OF PRICE REFORM

Even before the 1989 shift to a conservative regime in Beijing, the completion of price reform was not yet in the foreseeable future. Much, very much, remained to be done.

In the first decade of reform, China clearly succeeded in stimulating in rural areas collective and private enterprises whose rapid growth provided the main engine of advance for the Chinese economy. State enterprise remained the main drag on rising productivity and economic activity. In part, the relative lethargy of state enterprise may have been a statistical illusion: While private and collective enterprises sold their output primarily at high free-market prices, state enterprise was constrained by lower state-fixed prices. Nonetheless, state enterprise typically was overstaffed, and its workers were typically under-employed, with consequent low productivity. Although state industry provided 60 percent of industrial output, for example, it required 70 percent of the country's nonpeasant work force to do so. Chinese officials estimated that in early 1989, 20 percent of the work force in state enterprise – 20 million people – were redundant.[71]

The state sector, moreover, comprises large-scale enterprises, frequently behemoths, which are typically sole producers of particular products in the People's Republic. Throughout the decade of reform, China displayed little interest in breaking up these monsters to introduce or further stimulate competition.

Within the state sector, the operation of banks and financial institutions was of crucial importance to the success of economic reform. Market socialism was to replace centralized controls with

44 China, Hong Kong, Taiwan and World Trade

market controls, but the operation of the entire economy was to be directed from Beijing by manipulating financial and fiscal levers of indirect control. "The state regulates the market, the market guides the enterprise" was the Chinese description. Instruments of indirect control included taxes and government spending on the fiscal side, interest rates and money supply on the financial side. With taxes subject to bargaining at the local level and widespread evasion as well, Beijing had lost control of revenues; with no enforcement of bankruptcy laws, Beijing could not control expenditures. Similar impotence existed in financial controls, with deadly serious implications.

Financial Sector

In the pre-reform years, the financial sector in China played a strictly limited role in the tightly controlled economy. Its function was to execute and monitor plan fulfillment through control of financial flows. Allocations from the treasury for working capital and investment requirements were transferred to the enterprises through the banking system, and enterprise profits were similarly transferred back to the treasury. Resource requirements were mandaged by the annual plan and the budget. Separate accounts were maintained and monitored for each authorized use of funds – wages or capital construction, for example.

Until the 1980s, the People's Bank of China (PBC) was the country's sole banking institution, a vast enterprise with thousands of branches throughout the country. Money in circulation depended primarily on wage payments by enterprises to households and on household saving decisions. Both enterprise and individual accounts were maintained in the PBC. With few opportunities for spending, the value of individuals' savings accounts mounted.

Economic reform entailed enormous changes in the role of banking in China. Specialized banks were established to cater to the requirements of different sectors of the economy (e.g., the Agricultural Bank or the Construction Bank), with the role of the central bank assigned to the PBC. A wider range of interest rates was established, and the level of interest rates was raised several times so that interest might become the indirect instrument of the government for limiting and allocating the demand for borrowed money. The banking system was to replace the budget as the decision-making authority for financial resource distribution,

China's Economic Reforms

extending credit to those enterprises that could use it profitably, denying credit to those enterprises that could not service or repay their loans.

Even after a decade, reform in the financial sector was incomplete – necessarily so because the budget continued to reimburse the losses of state enterprise and because local and central officials continued to intervene in the lending decisions of banks. Lending decisions, in other words, continued to be perceived as risk-free and, in the state sector, were in fact so. In consequence, every relaxation of direct controls over credit was followed by excessive credit creation and inflation, the excesses becoming more extreme as further decontrol and pressures for growth expanded the opportunities for making money and as differentials between controlled and market prices widened.

Indeed, because of the failure of official interest rates to reflect the level of inflation, banking itself became a profitable opportunity for private enterprise in China. Although technically illegal, private banks were reported to be thriving in Zhejiang Province (on the coast south of Shanghai) and especially in the capital Wenzhou. There private banks were said to provide up to one-third of enterprise credit requirements at rates far in excess of official rates. By offering twice the official rate for deposits and charging even more for loans, the private banks prospered.[72]

The virtually risk-free investment environment caused China's money supply (currency and bank deposits) to expand much more rapidly than real output. Until 1984, while budget deficits were relatively small, inflation remained about 2 percent annually. With the money supply increasing by 30 percent or more after late 1983, inflation rose to more than 10 percent in 1985. Retrenchment in 1985–86 brought the state budget into surplus (the only surplus in the first decade of reform) and a drop in inflation to roughly 6 percent.[73] In 1988, however, the budget deficit reached 8 billion yuan, and the money supply instead of falling by 20 percent, the official target, jumped about 40 percent, spurring industrial output to its highest growth rate ever (more than 20 percent), but raising inflation even more.[74] Bank runs and panic buying in the summer of 1988 were followed by yet another period of retrenchment.[75] This time, however, skepticism about the central bank's ability to control the money supply was widespread.

In Western industrial countries, a budget deficit is financed by the sale of government bonds to the private sector, thereby permitting

46 *China, Hong Kong, Taiwan and World Trade*

the government to tap the savings of individuals and corporations. Thus, aggregate purchasing power is kept to the level of goods' availability and inflationary pressures avoided. In China, in contrast, the central bank financed the budget deficit by crediting the bank accounts of the loss-making enterprises and agencies with state subsidies, thus creating money and monetizing the deficit.

China's financial problems were aggravated by its virtual lack of a bond market, especially for treasury bonds. Before 1988, although a minuscule bond market existed in China, the borrowers included enterprises, financial institutions, and government projects; treasury bond issues were for project finance, not deficit finance.[76] In February 1988, the State Council authorized an issue of 9 billion yuan ($2.4 billion) of one to three-year treasury bonds, one-third to be sold to enterprises, the remainder to be sold to individuals as a deficit-financing device.[77] Treasury bond purchases, however, had come to be viewed as compulsory, their cost being automatically deducted from wages, and a thriving black market had developed. A limited legal secondary market was sanctioned in midyear for 1985 and 1986 treasury bonds owned by individuals (not those held by enterprises), but it did little to curtail illegal trades of all treasury issues. The main difficulty was that the bonds paid 8–10 percent, less than half the inflation rate. The bonds sold at a discount in the black market, but at a premium in the official market maintained by the banks. Thus, the bonds moved through the black market to the banks, thereby negating their deficit-financing function.[78]

China's mishandling of its domestic finances during the first decade of reform was *not* due to inadequate advice from its own economists or foreign advisers. The World Bank, other foreign bankers, and Chinese economists all recommended limiting money supply growth, raising interest rates, curtailing credit, and limiting the budget deficit – yet none of these steps was taken, or taken only in inadequate measure. As Li Yungi, an economist with the People's Bank of China wrote in late 1988, "China's problem is that it [the PBC] does not enjoy . . . independence. It is directly controlled by the State Council and monetary policy thus completely reflects the behavior of the government."[79] In August 1988, after bank runs and panic buying gave a further push to inflation, the PBC raised interest rates by less than 2 percent to nearly 9 percent, with inflation well into the double-digits. Speculation in Beijing at the time was that the central bank had to accept a much lower interest rate increase than it wanted, having lost the battle with the industrial ministries who wanted to keep their operating costs down.[80] In the spring of that year, moreover, the head of the central bank, Chen Muhua, a skilled negotiator who had won the respect of foreign lending institutions, was replaced by a Soviet-trained chemical engineer with no previous financial experience. The foreign community in Beijing opined that the leadership wanted a weak central bank chief.[81]

By early 1989, despite inadequate interest rates, tight banking controls had created a serious shortage of currency throughout China, generating fears of a collapse of production and the worst of both worlds – stagflation. Both bank loans and deposits of enterprises were frozen, and many farmers were not paid for their sales to the state. Even foreign investors, who had been assured that they would not be affected by austerity, were unable to get bank credit for domestic purchases.[82] With bank funds unavailable, cash became precious. Traders demanded cash in payment, and factories were unable to pay their bills. Scattered reports suggested that the most acute shortages of funds occurred in rural areas, although all of China was affected.[83]

Such draconian measures were necessitated by the fact that, for whatever reasons, the authorities felt able to use only one instrument of control – the money supply (bank deposits and currency). Interest rates and fiscal policy remained *ultra vires*. Further, to make currency control effective, the autonomy of localities had to be restricted, with Beijing taking back into its own hands through administrative measures many of the freedoms previously extended to provinces and municipalities.

Thus, foreign borrowing and foreign exchange expenditures were again centralized and investment projects in the SEZs were canceled or postponed.[84] Nonetheless, because local governments were largely responsible for their own finances, local interests were still able to work around Beijing's orders. Beijing would have needed armies of skilled and uncorruptible bank examiners, accountants, and tax authorities to enforce its control over localities. Whether exhortations to obey orders and act in the national interest would be sufficient was dubious.[85] Draconian measures did succeed in slowing industrial growth in early 1989, although evidence of progress against inflation had yet to appear.[86]

The impact of repression on the ability of localities to ignore Beijing's orders after mid-1989 was uncertain. The central government still lacked skilled bank examiners in requisite numbers. Party

48   *China, Hong Kong, Taiwan and World Trade*

members existed in plenty, but whether they were uncorruptible was a question. Beijing had been condemning corruption for some time, and some minor party functionaries had been prosecuted. Corruption was practiced, however, at all levels of the party and by family members of those at the top of the hierarchy. Loyal cadres could, nevertheless, frighten local authorities sufficiently to make Beijing's commands effective in the environment of fear that appeared to grip much of China in late 1989.

Inflation and Corruption

The renewed burst of inflation at the end of the 1980s, at a rate unprecedented for the PRC, was a source of grave concern throughout the country. The destructive hyperinflation in China of the late 1940s had been perhaps the most important factor in the success of the Communist revolution. The ruling Nationalist government's inability to control inflation at that time, together with the prevailing high level of corruption within the government, caused the Nationalists to be totally discredited in large segments of Chinese society. Moreover, in the late 1980s, many people were still alive in China who remembered the horrors of the last stages of that inflation and its accompanying anarchy. Then, the moral authority of the government had disintegrated, law and order had been replaced by lawlessness. When, in mid-1988, rumors of imminent price reform swept the country, the consequent panic buying, hoarding, and bank runs were, in fact, a manifestation of that memory. Inflation properly remained of great concern to Chinese authorities.

China's strengthening propensity toward inflation clearly was demand-driven in the late 1980s, but it was also traceable to supply limitations. In the consummate analogy of the eminent British economist Alfred Marshall at the turn of the century, supply and demand were compared to two blades of a scissors in determining prices; neither one blade nor the other could be said to do the cutting, it took both together. (The endless arguments of Chinese and foreign economists about whether Chinese inflation was demand-caused or supply-caused would benefit from a reacquaintance with Marshall.) In China, limitations on the growth of rawmaterial and infrastructure-services supply, because these sectors were effectively open only to state and local government investment, set a ceiling on the rate of noninflationary growth of industrial input. Thus, if economic development in China were to be inflation-

China's Economic Reforms 49

free, demand growth – thus, money supply growth – would have to be limited to the 5 to 7 percent growth rates in these bottleneck sectors, plus the rate of productivity growth. In contrast, during the years 1979–89, China's money supply grew at an average rate of more than 20 percent, while GNP climbed by 10 percent and industrial production by 12 percent. The share of raw material and mining industries in China's industrial output slipped from 14 percent and 15 percent in 1981 to 9 percent and 11 percent in 1985, for example.[87]

More rapid growth without inflation would have required an acceleration of investment and output in raw materials, fuel and power production, and transportation. The leadership appeared reluctant to make the commitment of resources necessary to alleviate these bottlenecks, despite its awareness of their existence and its emphasis on these as priority sectors in its 1978 plans. Such reluctance probably was the outcome of an industrial bias on which socialism in both the USSR and China was based: Economic development and expansion of manufacturing were equated.[88] If the regime had been more concerned with pressing for competition for the large state monopolies by breaking them into smaller competing units and permitting bankruptcy of state enterprises, efficiencies in raw material use would have been furthered, and the bottlenecks would have been less severe, even with lagging investment in raw material production and infrastructure industries. In this regard, the regime was impaled on the Leninist petard of guaranteed employment.

The austerity program introduced in late 1988 was based on a drastic pruning of investment projects (a 21 percent cut). Although in the original formulation key sectors like energy, transport, and raw materials were to be exempt from the slowdown, by the spring of 1989, construction projects in these sectors too were subject to termination.[89] "Indispensable" projects were confined to agriculture, chemical fertilizers, and education. The shift was a recognition of mounting problems in agriculture and the rural areas,[90] and the decline in the quality and quantity of education throughout China.

Such willingness to sacrifice investment in the bottleneck sectors reflected not only the intractability of the budget deficit and the regime's fear of social unrest, but also the inherent bias against infrastructure investment. The budget for 1989 contained an increase of 17 percent for subsidies to state enterprise and a huge

50 *China, Hong Kong, Taiwan and World Trade*

increase of 29 percent in subsidies to consumers to compensate for rising prices.

A reduction of the total budget deficit of 1 billion yuan (12 percent) seemed a pious hope.[91] Tax laws in China had been routinely ignored. In Shanghai, a tax-avoidance rate of 86 percent among registered business executives was discovered by the tax authorities.[92] Throughout China, the number of unlicensed individuals was legion, and an estimated 70 percent of all industrial and commercial enterprises practiced tax evasion.[93] In addition, new and higher taxes to raise revenues were aimed particularly at the productive private and collective sector, and loans to such enterprises were to be eliminated. Even before the ascent of the conservative regime later that year, the outlook for controlling inflation was bleak. Repression seemed likely to eliminate any productivity gain and, probably, to reduce productivity, while the political need to assuage the restive population implied the likelihood of wage increases and further agricultural subsidies. With many foreign investors frightened away and foreign credits contracting, China's economic planners and the Chinese people were in an unenviable position.

A large part of China's difficulties in controlling inflation resulted from the time that was required to lay the groundwork essential for the operation of a market mechanism, while the Chinese were uncharacteristically impatient. It took time to train the appropriate specialists required for implementing China's reforms – from plant managers to bank examiners and tax officials. It also took time to establish competition and break the monopolies prevailing in many industries, a step necessary before administrative controls could be effectively replaced by a market mechanism there. China had been much too cavalier in its attitude toward monopoly. It took time to develop the money market instruments and institutions necessary to implement indirect financial controls. China was making progress in all of these areas when time – at least temporarily – ran out.

With the benefit of hindsight, it would perhaps have been more effective if China's implementation of economic reforms had been based on a phased plan. In the first phase, while building the body of skills, specialists, and institutions necessary for the effective operation of market socialism, China should have confined growth to what was supportable by the existing raw material supply and infrastructure and limited decontrol to agriculture. Thus, the establishment of the minimum body of supervisory skills and the financial

China's Economic Reforms

structure needed to replace government controls of industry with a market mechanism regulated by indirect financial and fiscal controls would have been in place to stem the pressure for more rapid growth rates beyond the capacity of the infrastructure.

In the second phase, expansion of industry and decontrol would be initiated, while expansion of the bottleneck sectors would continue. Supervised and monitored by a growing body of financial skills, the regulation of the economy and curtailment of corruption would be facilitated.

After a decade of attempting to do everything at once, however, China did appear to be turning toward the course of slower, noninflationary growth within the range of that supportable by its bottleneck industries. Further major decontrol measures were postponed until inflation should have been brought under control. By the spring of 1989, however, it was too late.

In any event, control of inflation through ruthless sustained suppression of demand, like that practiced under Mao, was probably no longer possible in China. It had been successful for three decades largely because corruption was perceived to have been eliminated. Not only did the iron rice bowl make everyone equal, but political officials and members of the Communist Party also lived at the same level of well-being as peasants and workers. Only those at the top of the party received special perquisites, and they were nonostentatious. Under Mao, the party had more moral authority and won more widespread admiration than any previous Chinese dynasty. Party and workers labored together to build a better China; all were imbued with an idealism that sustained the system.

The great sin of the party in the late 1980s was widely perceived to be its members' participation in corrupt, self-serving activities. The distintegration of party members' moral standards during the first decade of reform was properly as much a source of concern to the Deng regime at end of the 1988 as was inflation.[94] The great tragedy of the bloodshed in Beijing in 1989 lay in the fact that the leadership itself had recognized and condemned corruption before the students occupying Tiananmen Square demanded an accounting of party leaders' incomes. Their actions, however, did not match their words.

The march of the students through Beijing in the spring of 1989 for "democracy" and the enthusiastic support they received from a throng of bystanders were originally an expression of deep dissatis-

52   China, Hong Kong, Taiwan and World Trade

faction, not with the government, the party, or economic reform, but with corruption and the disintegration of moral standards. In first seeking a financial accounting from party officials, the students sought to identify the sources of corruption; then, in seeking freedom of the press, they sought to publicize these sources and their own efforts at correction because the media ignored their efforts. There were no calls from the students for freedom of choice, no criticisms of the economic reforms or even of inflation. There was a cry for dialogue and for the leaders to listen. The students, in fact, gave little indication of understanding the implications of "democracy" beyond an association of democracy with honest, efficient government.

Corruption, however, which made millionaires out of those in high position while the people suffered from inflation and austerity, was something the students did understand and resent. China's management of the corruption crisis was more important to the students than the management of inflation. Beneath the corruption crisis lay the dual-price system and general mismanagement of the Chinese economy.

Observers of the repression in Beijing in mid-1989 were quick to draw the generalization that economic freedom was impossible without political freedom. Indeed, the case can be argued that freedom of choice in the economic realm will inevitably be followed by demands for freedom of choice in the political realm. Reports from China beginning in 1988 indicated that dissident groups of intellectuals were arguing with increasing passion for greater political freedom in China; the students in Beijing and elsewhere were exposed to these arguments. Further, the discipline and organization displayed by the student demonstrators in Beijing in 1989 suggested that they may have been following a carefully prepared strategy of demonstrating in favor of eliminating corruption, a goal with universal appeal, while planning subsequently to broaden their goals to include political reform – but that is reading between the lines of available facts.

It is tempting to compare the political constraints on China's economic reform in the late 1980s with the political potency of populist policies in newly democratic Brazil or Argentina at the same time. In each case, uncontrollable budget deficits produced economically destabilizing inflation. In each case, the budget deficits were uncontrollable because of the size of the state sector in the economy and the amount of employment there. In each case, state enterprise was used as a repository for the otherwise unemployed or the politically faithful. Costs were consequently bloated, and productivity telescoped. Throwing that many people out of work by permitting these loss-makers to go bankrupt was not something the regimes could contemplate; in each case, those in power had a bear by the tail.

Whether a democratic China would be a populist China and force its elected officials to follow full employment policies while aiming at higher living standards than the country's economic capacity could produce is not knowable. Whether a ruthlessly authoritarian government in China can achieve the growth necessary to produce higher living standards for a sufficient number of Chinese to enable it to be democratically electable (i.e., popular at home) is the challenge facing Deng Xiaoping and his supporters in the Communist Party. Until the party regains the respect it once had, or until a more efficient and law-abiding regime takes the helm, the outlook for China is bleak.

FOREIGN TRADE AND INVESTMENT[95]

China's decision in the late 1970s to participate extensively in world trade electrified the world business community. European, American, and Japanese business representatives rushed to China to establish early ties. All too many were attracted by the vision of a market of a billion consumers, with no realistic conception of how poor and backward that market was.

Their grossly exaggerated hopes were encouraged by China's willingness to accept project bids from all sources, by widespread speculation in the Western media about China's oil wealth – at a time when oil prices seemed to have no ceiling – and about the rates at which China's trade could grow.[96] In early 1979, for example, the *Journal of Commerce* speculated that by 1985, two-way trade between China and the United Kingdom (U.K.) could reach $30 billion.[97] In fact, in 1985, two-way trade between China and the entire twelve members of the European Community amounted to little more than $8 billion, and that with the United Kingdom to about $1 billion.[98]

There were voices of caution, however. The U.S. Department of Commerce suggested in early 1979 that U.S. exports to China during the next five years would amount only to $12–15 billion (in

54   *China, Hong Kong, Taiwan and World Trade*

1979 dollars); in fact, they aggregated nearly \$12 billion, but in then current, inflated prices. *The Economist* in 1979 guessed at \$40–50 billion of Chinese exports by 1990; China's exports reached \$40 billion in 1987.[99]

Formal diplomatic relations with the European Economic Community had been opened in September 1975, although formal relations with each of the (then) nine Community members had been established in the previous three years.[100] Sino-European trade, although small, was growing at an estimated 30 percent annually by the mid-1970s. Trade with the United States had resumed following President Nixon's 1972 visit to China, and trade with Japan followed shortly, although formal diplomatic relations were not established with the United States until late 1978. In the interim, China's imports from the United States were largely agricultural – grains and soy beans – and its exports primarily textiles and local products.

Thus, by 1978, China's foreign trade was already expanding rapidly, and the Chinese were even then experimenting with a variety of techniques in paying for imports. Nonetheless, in 1978, trade growth leapt forward: Imports jumped by an estimated 56 percent, exports by 26 percent, and the combined total amounted to \$21 billion.[101] Negotiations for billions of dollars of imports – complete plants, machinery, equipment, technology, and services – exploded in a frenzy of activity, although contracts actually signed amounted to only \$8 billion.[102]

Wild optimism was not confined to foreigners in the late 1970s. The Chinese themselves overestimated the capacity of their country to overcome bottlenecks in infrastructure, materials, labor skills, and experience, while expanding production and exports. At the end of February 1979, however, China abruptly suspended more than \$2 billion in contracts for Japanese equipment as the Chinese undertook a more realistic reappraisal of their economic policy and scaled back production plans. These developments and delays in concluding contracts with European Suppliers provided a healthy deflation of the previously excessive expectations of Chinese and foreigners alike.[103]

The successive periods of retrenchment, which marked the first decade of China's economic reform, all had an effect on foreign trade. Mounting trade deficits after 1978 were corrected by the first period of retrenchment in 1980–81, but after a short interval of trade surpluses, they reappeared even more sizably in 1985–86 (see Table 2.2). The second slowdown in 1985–86 brought only a decline

China's Economic Reforms

TABLE 2.2 *Foreign Trade and Investment (in billions of current U.S. dollars and percentages)*

Year	Exports	Rate of growth	Imports	Rate of growth	Balance	(Exports+imports)/ national income
1952–65	1.61	7.4%	1.57	4.3%	+0.04	10.0%
1966–78	4.72	11.5%	4.64	12.9%	+0.08	9.0%
1979	13.66	40.1%	15.67	43.9%	−2.01	13.6%
1980	18.27	33.8%	19.55	24.8%	−1.28	15.3%
1981	22.01	20.5%	22.01	12.6%	0.00	18.7%
1982	22.32	1.4%	19.28	−12.4%	+3.04	18.1%
1983	22.23	−0.4%	21.39	10.9%	+0.84	18.2%
1984	26.14	17.6%	27.41	28.1%	−1.27	21.3%
1985	27.35	4.6%	42.25	54.1%	−14.90	29.4%
1986	30.94	13.1%	42.91	1.6%	−11.97	32.7%
1987	39.44	27.5%	43.21	0.7%	−3.77	33.1%
1988	47.54	20.5%	55.25	27.9%	−7.7	33.2%

SOURCES: State Statistical Bureau (PRC), *Zhongguo Tongji Nianjian: 1988 [Statistical Yearbook of China]* (Beijing: Chinese Statistics Publishers, August 1988). Data for 1988 *Beijing Review,* March 6–12, 1989, p. 26. (Data from Robert F. Dernberger, "The People's Republic of China: A Historical Introduction," *Asia Pacific Report 1989—Focus: China in the Reform Era,* Charles E. Morrison and Robert F. Dernberger, eds. (Honolulu: East-West Center, 1989), p. 60.

in the deficits (not a reappearance of surplus) in 1986–87, but deficits again surged in 1988.[104]

Despite the stop-and-go policies, however, and the absolute declines in the value of China's imports in 1982, foreign trade expanded rapidly during the first decade of reform. Trade turnover rose by a compound rate of 10.5 percent, with imports growing at an annual average of 9.6 percent, exports at a healthy 11.3 percent.[105] Because these growth rates exceeded those of world trade, China's relative importance as a trading nation rose. According to the General Agreement on Tariffs and Trade (GATT), China in 1988 was already sixteenth in the list of world exporters, up from twenty-first in 1973; China was the fourteenth largest importer, up from the twenty-second position during the same period.[106] China's imports exceeded those of South Korea and Sweden in 1987; in exports, it followed those of Sweden. China's exports accounted for only 13 percent of its gross domestic product (GDP) – large for a continental economy, but small for an ambitious developing country.

56 China, Hong Kong, Taiwan and World Trade

Further, China was the third largest exporter of textiles in 1987, although if reexports through Hong Kong had been included in its figures, it would have been at least a close second to West Germany, the world leader. Its exports of textiles, moreover, were the most rapidly growing in the world.[107] China's exports of clothing were similarly among the world's largest and most rapidly advancing, as were its exports of chemicals and electronics. By 1988, China had become the fifth or sixth largest arms exporter.[108]

Between 1987 and 1988, China's trade jumped by nearly 17 percent, exports by 15.5 percent, and imports by 17.7 percent. With exports at more than $40 billion, China met its target for the seventh Five-Year Plan for 1990 two years ahead of schedule. By 1986, China's trade sector amounted to more than one-quarter of its GDP.[109] China's potential as a significant factor in world trade was becoming evident; it had already become a driving element in China's growth, contributing an estimated 20 percent of industrial growth in 1987.[110]

China's trade in services also was expanding. Tourists from the West flocked to see the ancient land so long closed to them. Revenues from tourism rose from $263 million in 1978 to $1.5 billion in 1986. In an unprecedented move for the PRC, early in the reform era, China began providing labor services for large construction projects especially in the Middle East and Africa, earning an additional $1.2 billion by 1988 from such services. Expanding capacity in China's merchant fleet was also a source of additional revenues.[111] China's trade in services, on balance, provided increasing foreign exchange receipts through the decade, rising from $400 million in 1981 to $1.7 billion in 1987.[112]

The composition of China's trade changed dramatically in the first ten years of economic reform. Energy exports escalated until 1985, with crude oil providing one-quarter of the country's export earnings in that year. After 1985, with the exception of 1987, the drop in oil prices and China's own escalating energy requirements brought a decline in both the volume and value of energy exports.[113] In 1988, exports of fuels accounted for only 8 percent of total exports. Meanwhile, exports of industrial products were mounting well beyond their 55 percent share of 1978 to nearly 70 percent in 1988. Textiles remained the largest Chinese export item, but higher value-added categories of textiles, especially clothing, achieved increasing importance. In addition, chemicals, machinery, and electrical appliances grew in significance.[114]

China's Economic Reforms

Changes in imports were less sharp. Imports of foodstuffs that had been important in the 1970s and early 1980s (more than 20 percent of total imports in 1982) dropped sharply with the early success of rural reform and, by 1986, accounted for only 4 percent. After that, the dual-price system caused farmers to shift production from the controlled staples to more profitable uncontrolled foods, resulting in a rise in imports of grains and sugar. Despite mounting imports of durable consumer goods (radios, televisions, refrigerators, and such) imports for industry – chemicals, synthetic fibers, rubber, and particularly machinery – continued, as they had under Mao, to comprise about 80 percent of China's much larger import bill. Machinery and equipment, however, grew in importance as China sought foreign technology.[115]

In contrast to the 1950s, when the Soviet Union and Eastern Europe accounted for three-quarters of China's trade, by 1989, their share was only 8 percent. In the late 1980s, the nonsocialist countries of the Pacific Basin made up more than two-thirds of China's total trade. Although growing absolutely, China's trade with Western Europe declined as a share of the total, from 18 percent in 1978 to 13 percent in 1988. China's major trading partners – Hong Kong, Japan, and the United States, in that order – were all part of the Pacific Basin (although the European Community, if treated as a single trading partner, would rank third in China's total trade, ahead of the United States). Until 1987, Japan was in the top position (accounting for nearly one-quarter of trade turnover in 1986), but was outpaced by Hong Kong in that year.

In the history of the People's Republic, the geographic distribution of China's trade had always reacted to changes in the climate of political relations with its trading partners.[116] The early orientation of trade toward the Soviet Union and Eastern Europe reflected ideologically based "socialist solidarity" and the U.S.-led embargo of trade with China. After the Sino-Soviet split of the mid-1960s, trade between the two Communist giants dropped sharply to very low levels, where it remained until bilateral relations began to thaw in the early 1980s under Deng. Between 1982 and 1986, trade grew so rapidly that the USSR became China's fifth largest trading partner (after Hong Kong, Japan, the United States, and West Germany), where it has remained.[117]

Geographic proximity and the complementarity of the two economies provided the basis for Japan's quick assumption of first place in the list of trading partners after economic relations were nor-

58   *China, Hong Kong, Taiwan and World Trade*

malized. By 1984, Japan held more than 30 percent of China's trade.

Trade relations, however, have not been smooth, reflecting a basic Chinese mistrust of Japan, which is founded on historical enmities as well as Chinese complaints about the large bilateral trade imbalance in Japan's favor, inadequate Japanese investment in China, Japan's failure to transfer technology, and what the Chinese viewed as Japan's attempt to rewrite history to soften the account of Japanese atrocities against Chinese during World War Two.[118]

After the rapid appreciation of the yen in 1985 and the consequent depreciation of the U.S.-dollar-based Hong Kong currency, Hong Kong replaced Japan as China's prime trading partner. Stimulated by exchange rate changes, Hong Kong boomed as manufacturers from Japan, the United States, Europe, South Korea, and Taiwan sought to keep costs down by importing components and finished goods from sources with lower costs. Hong Kong's trade with China mushroomed, with imports primarily from Guangdong flooding into Hong Kong for use there or, increasingly, for reexport to the rest of the world. In 1987, Hong Kong accounted for nearly one-third of China's total trade, compared with 18 percent for Japan.[119]

Trade relations with the United States, too, were colored by political relations, especially in regard to Taiwan; however, the acerbity of Chinese reactions to alleged U.S. offenses was less sharp than in the case of Japan. After the opening of trade relations in 1972 when trade was almost nonexistent, its volume shot up so rapidly that, by 1982, the United States was China's third largest trading partner. A bilateral trade agreement signed in 1979, Most-Favored-Nation (MFN) treatment in 1980, eligibility for U.S. Export-Import (Exim) Bank credits, Overseas Private Investment Corporation (OPIC) insurance, and almost continuous relaxation of U.S. export controls all contributed to the rapid expansion. In 1988, when trade between the two countries reached $10 billion, the United States remained in the third position in China's total trade. U.S. exports of high technology products increased in importance in Sino-U.S. trade.[120] Chinese officials and U.S. business executives complained that trade was impeded by such things as U.S. export control regulations on high technology exports to China, the failure of U.S. tariff policy to treat China as a developing country, and expanding U.S. import controls on Chinese textile and clothing products.[121]

China's Economic Reforms

Chinese authorities vehemently protested U.S. import quotas on Chinese textiles.[122] In retaliation for tighter U.S. textile controls in 1983, China embargoed purchases of U.S. soybeans and wheat, as well as cotton and synthetic fibers. The Chinese also complained that, despite their many requests, the United States had not extended its Generalized System of Preferences (GSP) – that is, duty-free treatment – to Chinese imports. According to the 1974 U.S. Trade Act, such preferences for less developed country (LDC) exports to the United States could only be accorded to GATT members.

Unofficially, China pushed especially hard to be freed from the discriminatory treatment of "nonmarket" economies in U.S. trade law. Nonmarket economies were subject to higher U.S. import duties and more restrictive antidumping provisions, for example, than other countries.[123] It apparently rankled China to be categorized as something less than a first-class member of the world trading community by the world's largest market, although the United States had accorded MFN treatment to China and required that a "dumped" Chinese product injure a domestic industry before an antidumping duty was imposed.

The Chinese supported, although not with direct funding, a lobbying effort organized by a professional U.S. lobbyist to work for the repeal of "outmoded and discriminatory U.S.-China trade laws" and against protectionist trade legislation affecting China.[124] This effort not only created a China caucus in the Congress, but also was successful in inducing the Congress to incorporate into the 1988 Trade Act a provision requiring the Department of Commerce to study China's new market orientation to determine whether U.S. law should be changed to treat China more fairly. (U.S. law assigned to the Commerce Department the authority to define and develop the list of countries to be treated as nonmarket economies. Thus, the Commerce Department possessed the authority to move China to the list of market economies.)

The required study had not yet been completed at the time of the bloodshed in Beijing. Congressional outrage about China's blatant disregard of human rights was so sharp, however, that there is little likelihood of any immediate step toward improving China's position in U.S. trade.

Nonetheless, China had clearly learned the importance of an organized lobbying effort.[125] In addition to the Committee for Fair Trade with China, in cooperation with other textile exporting

60 *China, Hong Kong, Taiwan and World Trade*

countries, China had organized an International Textile and Clothing Bureau to lobby for less restrictive trade in Western Europe and the United States.[126] China can be expected to use this instrument increasingly in the future as its preoccupations once again turn to growth.

Foreign Investment

Throughout the pre-reform period, China's trade with the West was strictly pay-as-you-go. China's determination not to be victimized by foreigners was a consequence both of its history and ideology. Ideologically, Communist regimes feared entrapment by imperialist bankers; in addition, China's experience in the mid-1960s, when its split with the USSR resulted in an abrupt cessation of Soviet credits to China, added to Chinese apprehension about the dangers and vulnerabilities created by foreign borrowing.

At the start of the reform period, China's apprehension about foreign borrowing was still in evidence. In an August 25, 1978 report from Tokyo, Japanese reporters who had met with Chinese officials wrote that China, although still adhering to a self-reliance policy, would accept private loans, but not government loans.[127] By November of that year, nevertheless, China was negotiating with the Japanese Export-Import Bank for credits and, in early December, China signed its first major agreement, a low-interest line of credit from the official French export credit agency, COFACE.[128] After that, trade contracts and credits from public and private sources were negotiated more rapidly than the scope and details of the modernization program could be agreed upon by Chinese authorities. In late February 1979, China abruptly suspended nearly $3 billion in Japanese contracts to give its policymakers time to take stock. International bankers who had earlier speculated that China might borrow as much as $100 billion to finance technology imports during the next seven years revised that estimate downward to $20 billion or $30 billion.[129]

Despite the pause, in the 1970s, China continued to pursue lines of credit with Western banks, bargaining hard over terms, and it began discussions about membership with the World Bank and IMF. The Bank of China also began to develop extensive links with its counterparts abroad. In the late 1970s, Western bankers commented on the financial innocence of Chinese banking officials, noting that their years of isolation had left the Chinese ignorant of

China's Economic Reforms   61

even the most basic Western financial practices. By the end of 1979, China had not only signed $13 billion in government credits plus $9 billion in commercial loans, but the Bank of China had even joined Western Banks – cautiously – as an international lender.[130]

In succeeding years, China continued to pursue foreign investment in all forms – foreign direct investment vigorously, especially in joint ventures, and foreign loans and credits more cautiously. Many of the credit lines negotiated with foreign commercial banks were used only in part, if at all. Despite China's enthusiasm for joint ventures, foreign direct investment lagged, for reasons discussed below.

Despite its original mistrust of intergovernmental credits, the economic reformers quickly recognized the advantage of low-interest concessionary rates offered by foreign government agencies and the international institutions. A soft loan with Japan, as well as numerous other credit agreements, was negotiated in 1979.[131] In mid-1979, China ended two decades of statistical secrecy and once again commenced publication of detailed annual reports on the economy in what proved to be preparation for a move to join international lending institutions.[132] The PRC had assumed the China seat in the United Nations (UN) in 1972, but did not seek aid funds from UN agencies until 1979. Early in 1980, China formally applied for seating in the IMF and World Bank, and, as soon as the spring of the same year, the PRC replaced Taiwan, first in the Fund, then in the Bank in May 1980.[133]

Despite pressures for rapid growth based on modernization and thus on imports, China's sense of fiscal prudence prevailed until 1985 and led to minimum reliance on foreign short-term credits, with emphasis rather on medium and long-term debt maturities. Credits from private lenders were buttressed by a guarantee from foreign public agencies like export-import banks, thus reducing interest charges.

China's use of IMF resources was infrequent and quiet. Only two drawings had been made by July 1989. One, in 1981, repaid in 1983, appeared to have been as much for the purpose of testing the mechanism as for balance-of-payments support. A second for $760 million occurred during the retrenchment of 1986. China was considerably more active in the World Bank, however. World Bank (including the International Development Association) loan commitments to China totaled $8.5 billion through May 1989. World

62 China, Hong Kong, Taiwan and World Trade

Bank officials worked closely with the Chinese, offering detailed technical advice on all aspects of economic policy.[134]

Borrowing jumped in 1986, and, by the end of 1988, total foreign investment in China had more than doubled, reaching $47 billion according to official sources. (See Table 2.3. China does not publish detailed loan information; therefore, data should be treated with caution. Especially after 1985, when local entities became active borrowers abroad, the records are probably of dubious accuracy.) More liberal financial policies allowed a multitude of new Chinese borrowers to become active, including provincial and municipal enterprises with little or no previous experience in international finance. Although approval of foreign borrowing by the PBC was still required, the requirement was widely ignored. Many of the foreign loans were short term and rolled over several times. Late in 1988, as part of the general retrenchment, Beijing once again limited borrowing authority in an effort to regain control. The number of entities allowed to borrow abroad at their own discretion was reduced from more than 100 to 10.

Direct investment rose continuously through the decade, although less rapidly than borrowing. By the end of 1988, direct investment amounted to nearly $12 billion. Joint ventures were the most popular form of direct investment, accounting for nearly $5 billion at the end of 1988, with cooperatives close behind at nearly $4 billion. Most direct investment projects were small, averaging less than $2 million each.[135]

Meanwhile, China also was becoming active as an international investor. Between 1979 and the end of 1988, China invested at least $5 billion in a variety of countries and industries around the world. (Estimates of total Chinese investment abroad range as high as $25 billion.)[136]

The China International Trade and Investment Corporation (CITIC), created to facilitate China's trade and investment, probably was the largest Chinese investing entity, having invested at least $1 billion outside of China by the end of 1988. As a result of astute management of its assets abroad, however, their value in mid-1989 in Hong Kong alone was estimated at nearly that much. Hong Kong was by far the most popular site for all Chinese investors, especially the Hong Kong real estate market. In addition to state and provincial trading and investment companies, subsidiaries were established to do business on the side by a variety of Chinese

TABLE 2.3 *Utilization of Foreign Capital (in billions of yuan)*

	1979–82	1983	1984	1985	1986	1987	1988	1979–88
Total	12.46	1.98	2.71	4.65	7.26	8.45	9.84	47.35
Loans	10.69	1.07	1.29	2.69	5.01	5.81	6.58	33.14
Percentage of Total	85.80%	54.00%	47.60%	57.80%	69.00%	68.80%	66.90%	70.00%
Direct Investment	1.17	0.64	1.26	1.66	1.87	2.31	2.68	11.59
Percentage of Total	9.40%	32.30%	46.50%	35.70%	25.80%	27.30%	27.20%	24.50%
Other*	0.60	0.27	0.16	0.30	0.38	0.33	0.58	2.62
Percentage of Total	4.80%	13.60%	5.90%	6.50%	5.20%	3.90%	5.90%	5.50%

*Other = Total − (Loans + Direct Investment).

SOURCES: State Statistical Bureau, *Zhongguo Tongji Nianjian: 1988* [*Statistical Yearbook of China*] (Beijing: Chinese Statistics Publishers, August 1988). Data for 1988 *Beijing Review,* March 6–12, 1989, p. 26. (Data corrected from Robert F. Dernberger, "The People's Republic of China: A Historical Introduction," *Asia Pacific Report 1989 – Focus: China in the Reform Era,* Charles E. Morrison and Robert F. Dernberger (eds) (Honolulu: East-West Center, 1989), p. 60.

64 *China, Hong Kong, Taiwan and World Trade*

enterprises and individuals. Especially in the late 1980s, making money by speculating in the Hong Kong property market was a favored pursuit of many Chinese Communist Party members, some of whom set up intricate webs of Hong Kong companies to avoid scrutiny.[137] Even the People's Liberation Army and Xinhua, the state news agency, were active. Some part of the accelerated foreign borrowing activity in the second half of the 1980s apparently was directed toward speculation in Hong Kong real estate.

Although China's foreign indebtedness was modest both in relation to GNP (about 11 percent) and to exports (a debt service ratio of about 10 percent), and although its foreign exchange reserves at the end of 1988 were estimated at more than $18 billion, the international financial community found several causes for concern.[138] The debt's foreign currency mix relied heavily on Japanese yen, with 40 percent of China's external debt being yen-denominated. Because Chinese foreign exchange receipts were primarily in dollars, volatile yen-dollar exchange rates meant that the debt service burden was at the mercy of exchange fluctuations.[139] In addition, the ability of the PBC to exercise effective control of debt management – in the face of extensive decontrol and political meddling and the large proportion of short-term high interest loans in the debt – worried experts at home and abroad.[140]

More basic, China had never developed a long-term debt strategy. Despite years of planning, including foreign trade planning, China had never developed an explicit five or ten-year balance-of-payments plan, even during the reform period, and thus was not in a position to develop a debt strategy. The maturity profile and currency mix of foreign borrowing were the consequence of project finance and the lender's terms, as well as the uncoordinated borrowing activities of local entities. In 1987, when more than one-half of China's debt was denominated in currencies other than the U.S. dollar; China's foreign debts increased by $4 billion (15 percent) solely because of the depreciation of the dollar in that year.[141]

In addition, China's definition of foreign debt excluded short-term trade credits, borrowing by joint ventures and foreign-owned enterprises, and compensation trade. These omissions accounted for some of the differences between Chinese and foreign-debt estimates.

Chinese officials had made some progress in tackling a number of these problems by mid-1989, aided by expertise from the World

Bank and the IMF. Currency risks had been diversified somewhat and some of its borrowings refinanced with cheaper money. A debt management office was established.[142] One potentially serious ambiguity remained: Of China's total foreign debt, how much, if any, was non-sovereign? Although foreign lenders perceived most borrowing by Chinese enterprises as sovereign debt, the status of borrowing by provincial agencies was not clear. In addition, loans incurred by Chinese companies registered in Hong Kong technically were not sovereign debts of China.

The 1989 Beijing demonstrations and consequent crackdown brought a prompt reaction in foreign financial markets. Of immediate concern was whether interest due in the next few weeks would be paid. Trading abroad in Chinese paper essentially stopped because of a lack of buyers, and Chinese borrowings already scheduled had to be postponed. Bond-rating agencies said that a downgrading of the credit rating of Chinese borrowers was inevitable.[143]

Throughout its history, the PRC had been scrupulous about meeting its international financial commitments on time and at par. In fact, during the 1960s, China paid off its debts to the USSR ahead of schedule and despite many economic problems at home.[144] Similarly, during the economic reform period and especially during the difficult months immediately after the repression in mid-1989, the PRC continued to honor its international financial obligations.

Possessed of a strong sense of national honor and "face," it is unlikely that the PRC will do otherwise in the future, at least for those obligations that it perceives as its sovereign debt. Meeting its obligations, however, may not be easy for China.

Estimates of the amount of interest and principal due in the early 1990s on China's outstanding debt varied. All estimates agreed that such payments would peak in 1992, but those amounts ranged from $4.2 billion to $10 billion.[145] China's foreign currency reserves (excluding 12.7 million ounces of gold) at the end of April 1989 were put at $19.1 billion. During the first half of 1989, China's foreign trade deficit amounted to nearly $12 billion annually. After June 1989, foreign exchange receipts were expected to decline both because of domestic constraints (the impact of scarce materials, fuel, and transport on exports and the consequences of political turmoil on export availability), and foreign reactions to the June repression. Fearing for the security of their supply, foreign customers were likely to shift some of their orders to other countries.

66   *China, Hong Kong, Taiwan and World Trade*

Also, foreign direct investment and tourism in China that had contributed $5 to $6 billion in foreign exchange in 1988 were expected to fall off sharply as were receipts from foreign loans.

Thus, with $15–20 billion in aggregate debt service payments due in the next three and a half years, China could be expected to clamp down on imports, push exports, and possibly to depreciate the foreign exchange value of the renminbi. The impact of depreciation, however, on costs – and thus on prices or subsidies – was a concern. Any attempt at debt restructuring would be taken reluctantly because China would face higher interest rates than it had been paying. China will probably have to seek additional foreign loans; real per capita incomes will decline seriously in all probability. Nonetheless, China's national pride would require that it meet its obligations.

Obstacles to Foreign Trade and Investment[146]

Pressures for growth in the 1980s led China to importune foreigners to expand direct investment in China, especially those who provided technology transfers. Although foreign direct investment – largely in the form of joint ventures – rose during the 1980s, its pace was slow, impeded by a variety of obstacles stemming largely from China's ignorance of Western business concepts and practices. Western businesses sought the security and guidance of laws and regulations that would spell out, for example, what they could and could not do, how disputes would be resolved, and what taxes and fees they would pay to whom. China's legal system, in the Western sense, was totally undeveloped.

Chinese laws and regulations governing foreign investment evolved slowly in response to pressures from Western business. Even after a decade, however, foreigners still complained that operating in China was full of unexpected difficulties. Rules and regulations were frequently changed with no public announcement, let alone explanation, of the change. China might cease enforcement of laws once strictly monitored, or having ignored laws on the books for years, might commence their enforcement without warning. Some new laws were made retroactive; rarely was legal recourse against the Chinese government available. It was often extremely difficult to determine who was in charge of which subjects, which bureaucrat's agreement was final, how many officials in which agencies had to agree. Some bureaucrats were knowledgeable, efficient, and helpful, others quite the opposite.

China's Economic Reforms

67

Foreign business executives complained about their ability to hire and fire Chinese employees and their inability to pay incentive wages. Chinese employees were sent to them by the central employment agency. If they proved unsatisfactory on the job and the employers complained, the employee was likely to be replaced by an equally (or more) unsatisfactory substitute. Only a small fraction (10 percent) of the wages paid by the foreign employer was received by the Chinese employee, the bulk going to the state agency.

Maintaining an office in China was enormously expensive for foreign businesses, as well as uncomfortable, and many businesses operated out of hotel rooms. In fact, the expenses were so high that many businesses chose to maintain their China headquarters in Hong Kong where, even in the inflationary boom of 1988, rents were low by comparison and living conditions incomparably more pleasant.

Despite the many difficulties of operating in China, a number of foreign business executives in China were exhilarated by the challenges, the opportunities, and the vibrancy of the Chinese scene. Others, however, were depressed, cynical, and caustic.

The differences appeared to be in part differences in personalities, in part the industries in which they operated, and in part the nature of the agreement they had with China. (Technology transfer contracts might or might not involve foreign investment.) Those producing (or selling) something of high priority to China (e.g., high technology machinery or equipment) and maintaining an active program of technology transfer, supported by a training program for Chinese workers on imported machinery and equipment, generally fared well. They had ready access to high officials; negotiations were tough but reasonable; they made money. Others producing something of lower priority to the Chinese program were not so fortunate.

Ready access to and cordial working relations with top Chinese officials meant that favored foreigners were informed earlier than others of changes in rules. It meant that they were assigned more highly skilled employees. Investors in joint ventures were permitted to pay incentive wages; employees of noninvestors received wages only a little higher than the average Chinese worker.

High rents in China for foreigners, set at the official perception of what the market would bear, were evidence that the market mechanism was operating. Buildings having the amenities that

68 *China, Hong Kong, Taiwan and World Trade*

foreigners expected (heat, air-conditioning, elevators, and the like) were scarce, although construction in Beijing and other cities important to foreigners had progressed at such a rate that, in late 1988, foreign business executives expected rents to fall in a year or two.

All foreign business executives producing and selling to China were under constant pressure for "offset agreements" – agreements to purchase Chinese-made goods for export with payment to China in convertible currency. Until late 1988, China required about 15 percent of any foreign sales contract to be "offset" by the purchase for export of some Chinese product. In general, however, Chinese quality was so poor and availability of offset products so limited, foreigners had difficulty locating Chinese products that were exportable. Even technologically simple products like forgings were difficult to market abroad because of quality. The 15 percent requirement was manageable, however, because foreign businesses could build into their own selling prices to China the difference between the price they paid for the offset product and what that product would bring on the world market.

In 1988, in the face of mounting inflation, trade deficits, and accumulating infrastructure and raw material bottlenecks, the Chinese raised the offset requirement to 50 percent of the value of their contract, a requirement foreigners said was impossible for them to meet. Negotiations on the new offset requirement were still in progress in mid-1989, when martial law and turmoil caused many foreigners to leave the country. Their enthusiasm to return to China will in part reflect their perception of how reasonable they believe the Chinese will be about offset requirements.

In fact, before the crackdown, Chinese officials had been reasonable about the new offset requirement, at least with favored foreign businesses. They had indicated a willingness to allow plenty of time – a decade or two – for meeting the requirement, meanwhile urging more technology transfer to improve Chinese product quality. The issue and its resolution, however, remained ambiguous.

The requirement for offset agreements stemmed from China's chronic foreign exchange shortage. Like all rapidly growing developing countries, China's imports tended to exceed exports, resulting in balance-of-trade and balance-of-payments deficits. In fact, these were a reflection of foreign borrowing and foreign investment; in addition, China's push toward modernization meant a push to import. Also China's distorted internal price structure and

China's Economic Reforms

overvalued exchange rate both led to depressed exports and exaggerated imports. With no meaningful prices to guide resource allocation, much investment was inefficient, depressing productivity and output growth. Offset agreements succeeded only in reducing China's terms of trade and raising the price of imports in relation to export prices, thus correcting to some degree exchange rate overvaluation.

Many of the problems and frustrations that harassed foreign investors in China also plagued foreigners buying and selling there. The opaqueness of rules and regulations and the abrupt changes in taxes, fees, tariffs, surcharges, quotas, licenses, inspection certificates, issuing authorities, and multilayered bureaucracy were a constant complaint of foreign importers and exporters. A Chinese adviser, Chinese or Hong Kong employees, or consultants helped to ease the problems, but could not eliminate them.

Differences among various provinces and municipalities in the degree of authority for contracting with foreigners for imports and exports meant that import duties and export fees depended on the location of the port through which the goods moved. Similarly, the degree of authority possessed by any one Chinese official varied and was greater in the provinces doing the most foreign trade.

The deviousness of officials in their dealings with foreigners was considerably less in small towns than the urban centers like Guangzhou. Officials in Guangzhou, for example, when asked about cash incentives for exports, replied that they did not exist, although notice of such export subsidies had been published in the official *South China Daily*. At the same time, officials in small towns revealed a refreshing openness in discussing costs of producing for export in a state factory. Thus, the production of $1 worth of export goods was reported to cost about 11 RMB when the official exchange rate was less than 4 RMB to $1, clearly an expensive way to earn foreign exchange.

In general, import constraints and the difficulties of selling to China mounted in periods of retrenchment, both in terms of variety and burden. Protection lessened as the level of foreign exchange reserves recovered. Protectionism also varied among industries, mirroring the attitudes of the ministries in charge. The chemical industry was reported to be one of the most protectionist in China. Similarly, the Ministry of Machine Building was said to be one of the most bureaucratic and protective of its turf, as well as protectionist.

70   *China, Hong Kong, Taiwan and World Trade*

China was aware of the complaints of foreigners and, in many cases, attempted to improve conditions and to make China a more attractive place for foreign business. Laws and regulations affecting foreigners continued to evolve, if slowly. Indeed, many thoughtful Chinese were coming to the conclusion that a rule of law in China must replace rule by the Communist Party if economic reforms were to be successful. The multilayered bureaucracy, including the dual-price system, was perceived by many Chinese as a transitional phenomenon, a necessary evil for negotiating the path from administrative to market control. Interference from the bureaucracy with decision making by enterprise managers was a complaint of Chinese as well as foreign business executives. The deviousness of Chinese officials, especially in Guangzhou, was explained by foreigners as a case of the Chinese having learned quickly from Hong Kong executives. Changes in import and export controls were largely the consequence of Beijing's inability to control foreign trade by any except direct means. Chinese officials were aware of the obstructionist tactics of certain Beijing ministries. They attempted to control and alleviate the consequences by ministry mergers in an effort to subordinate the obstructionists to those supporting reform.

Still, many Chinese officials remained basically suspicious of foreigners, were apprehensive of once again being exploited by them, and saw no wrong in indulging in a bit of exploitation themselves. In some officials, Chinese national pride verged on arrogance. In dealings with foreigners, the Chinese – at home and abroad – continuously sought exceptions in their favor from foreign law or custom.

CONCLUSION

The record of China's first decade of economic reform was mixed. Accomplishments were sizable and obvious – a surge of production, a rise in living standards, an explosion in foreign trade. Techniques of production were modernized, primarily by employing more advanced technology, but also, to some degree, through more efficient managerial techniques. The private and collective sectors experienced rapid growth, displaying vibrant and innovative entrepreneurial talents as well as a tendency to "outgrow the plan." In general, results varied by industry and geographic location. Some improvement in productivity occurred, although Nicholas Lardy

China's Economic Reforms

71

concludes that such gains in total factor productivity as may have taken place were probably the result of eliminating the most obvious sources of inefficiency inherited from the Maoist era. They were the consequence of a one-time catching up that is not likely to be repeated, unless the many remaining severe distortions in the economy are corrected – especially the domestic price structure.[147]

Crises of mounting intensity were evidence of basic weaknesses in the reform program, increasingly aggravated by growth and the inheritance from the pre-reform era. Even in agriculture – the original success story – rising unemployment, declining grain production, deteriorating irrigation systems, and rising costs boded ill for the future. In industry, bottlenecks in infrastructure and raw material supply resulted from both the price structure and the failure of authorities to assign sufficient priority to expanding capacity in the bottleneck industries. At the same time, state enterprise was trapped by inefficiency because of its need to serve as the employer of last resort. Uncontrolled growth of credit and the money supply were the consequences of the price system, political meddling, and the lack of adequate accounting and supervisory skills. Political waffling at the highest level on issues of growth versus control of inflation, moreover, would have made fiscal and monetary policy ineffective regardless of enforcement capabilities. A dual-price system and a tax system implemented at the local level, with revenues passed to the next higher governmental unit, encouraged the spread of corruption and resource misallocation.

Foreign trade and investment both supported and led the growth of output. The foreign sector aggravated basic weaknesses in the economy and the reform effort, and was inhibited from alleviating them by the level and volatility of administrative controls. The foreign sector exacerbated the basic shortages in infrastructure caused by the distorted price system and inadequate investment. At the same time, the managerial talents brought by foreigners, their emphasis on efficiency and quality, the training they provided, and the knowledge of foreign markets that they imparted all helped to raise productivity, growth rates, and foreign exchange receipts. The foreign sector's contribution to the reform effort was far more positive than negative.

How Chinese economic reform would have progressed had it not been interrupted by political repression after its first decade can only be guessed. Stalinist price distortions and Leninist employment guarantees were incompatible with the efficiency and productivity that were the goals of the reform; both required revision. What does apear certain, however, is that the economic reform was only interrupted.

Chinese people at all levels agree that China must resume its rightful place in the world, and that place is a position of power. They are aware that their present position of power will deteriorate if their relative economic strength is not enhanced and maintained. They are aware that China has become irrelevant in many international forums; the fact of irrelevance for China is not one the Chinese are willing to accept with comfort. Thus, to achieve the position in the world that they regard as rightful, the Chinese will have no choice but to continue the economic reform and modernization effort in some form – sooner or later.

3 China and the World Trading System

INTRODUCTION

The world economy that China undertook to join through its participation in the world trading system was itself in the process of dramatic accelerated change during the 1980s. The changes were so comprehensive that nearly every aspect of the trading system was affected. All of the changes have had, and will continue to have, implications for China.

The very fact of accelerated change in the world economy and world trading system meant that the goal of catching up was much more difficult than it would have been in earlier decades; the target itself was receding. China's previous isolation had made even a slowly moving goal difficult of achievement. In seeking to modernize its technology during the 1980s China learned the hard way that a leap to a new technology without having gone through the intermediate stages complicated and delayed the catching up process. By the late 1980s, in many cases China was willing to settle for a transfer of less than state-of-the-art technology.

Acceleration of technological change had stimulated accelerated changes in patterns, practices, instruments, and institutions throughout the world trading system. Evolving patterns of comparative advantage among countries, for example, meant that the allocation of resources in China which would yield maximum output for China's labor, capital, and materials was by no means self-evident. What China could produce most efficiently, what China could import most cheaply in terms of its own real resource content, could only be determined and adjusted as it engaged in trade with its neighbors and the rest of the world. In a world with prices and exchange rates in a constant state of flux, flexibility of China's own internal prices as domestic demand and supply conditions changed became even more important. By the same token China's attempt partially to stabilize prices was certain to frustrate its goal of maximizing productivity and therefore to retard the catching-up process.

74   *China, Hong Kong, Taiwan and World Trade*

In terms of sheer volume, world trade in the 1980s had recovered smartly from lower growth rates in the early years of the decade and at the end of the decade was once again leading world output. Meanwhile the product composition of trade and also its geographic distribution were shifting. Trade in manufactured goods was once again the most dynamic component of merchandise trade, growing more rapidly than trade in agricultural or mineral products. Within the manufactured products component, important shifts toward goods embodying higher technology occurred; trade in electronic products rose more than twice as fast as total world trade in manufactures, for example, while world trade in steel declined in absolute terms.

Underlying all international commerce and characterizing all international transactions was intensified competitiveness among products, markets, and regions.[1] Successful development programs in a number of developing countries had made them formidable competitors of the older industrialized economies. The pattern of comparative advantage among countries and regions could no longer be perceived as stable; rather, it had become another economic variable subject to the control and direction of government policy. Economic growth and development in all countries implied competition for technological advance. Among developing countries, including China, "technology transfer" had become a prime goal and anthem. To keep up with shifting product markets as well as to catch up with the west, China's prime need was for technology.

Although expanding markets in industrialized countries continued to provide the main impetus for world trade growth, import demand in the developing countries accelerated sharply after 1987. Important shifts also were occurring among countries and regions within these broad aggregates. Japan's imports abandoned their lethargic growth and started to rise steeply in the second half of the decade in response to exchange rate and domestic policy changes. At the same time Japan's export growth became much more subdued. The Asian developing countries became not only the most rapidly growing economies in the world but also the countries whose imports as well as exports were growing most rapidly. In consequence Asia's share in world trade expanded. Western Europe too seemed energized in the late 1980s with growth rates regularly surpassing expectations. By 1987 the share of Asia and Western Europe in world trade had risen to over two-thirds.

China and the World Trading System 75

China had the good fortune to be located in the most rapidly growing area of the world. Because its neighbors' markets were expanding, China's exporters could benefit from lower transport costs in serving those markets. At the same time the dynamism of the area and similarities in structures of production meant that the degree of competition among producers there was intense both for markets within the area and outside – especially in Europe and the U.S. The perception on the part of China's foreign customers of a *possible* supply interruption as a consequence of the shift to a more conservative regime in China led many to consider transferring their purchases to other suppliers in the area; intense regional competition meant that such a transfer could be accomplished with ease.

Heightened competition throughout the world helped to bring new patterns of bilateral or regional economic relationships into existence toward the end of the 1980s, all of which were a challenge to China to some degree. Worried by their own sluggish growth rates, high unemployment levels and the emergence of strong protectionist sentiments in the U.S. Congress, members of the European Community agreed to a program, "EC 1992," that sought to eliminate within Europe all barriers to the movement of goods, capital and people by the end of 1992. For similar reasons Canada sought a bilateral free-trade agreement with the U.S. Such developments alarmed East Asian countries who feared that each of these new regional arrangements was devised to limit their access to European and North American markets. Various initiatives in the Asia-Pacific region were a collective reaction by these countries to the perceived threats elsewhere. At the end of the 1980s, however, only one initiative, the Pacific Economic Cooperation Conference, a loose forum of private and public sector leaders from Pacific rim countries, included China as a member. The others, including Australia's proposal for an Asia-Pacific economic cooperation organization, excluded China because of the delicacy of the Taiwan-Hong Kong-China relationships (see Chapter 4) and because of the sensitivity of the smaller countries to the inclusion of a large socialist power. Such developments served to make membership in the multilateral trade organization, the GATT, even more attractive to China.

Merchandise trade, however, represented only one component of the world trading system. Trade in services – for example, banking, insurance, accounting, engineering, tourist, and such services as well as services of labor and capital – had grown in importance; despite

76   *China, Hong Kong, Taiwan and World Trade*

data inadequacies, it was clear that trade in capital – borrowing and lending across national boundaries – had come to swamp trade in goods in the 1980s in terms of value. The *daily* volume of foreign exchange trading world-wide amounted to more than $500 billion in the spring of 1989, having doubled in just three years.[2] By comparison the *annual* volume of world merchandise trade in 1987 amounted to $2.5 trillion. Bankers estimated that 80–90 percent of foreign exchange trading represented banks' trading for their own account rather than for importers, institutions engaging in direct investment abroad or other such trade or investment reasons. It thus represented a short-term transfer of banking funds, or "hot money" lent abroad in highly liquid form and subject to further international movement at any time.

The enormous and rapidly growing volume of liquid funds moving across national boundaries had revolutionalized the character of the world's trading system by the end of the first decade of China's economic reform. Although the volume of international capital movements had been growing since the 1960s, technological change, decreased financial regulation, and increasing competition among financial institutions caused the international movement of liquid funds to mushroom in the 1970s and 1980s. The effects on the world trading system were momentous. Where in earlier decades exchange rates were primarily influenced by merchandise trade volumes, by the 1980s huge and highly mobile volumes of capital had become a more important determinant of exchange rates, at least in the short-term. Exchange rates became more volatile, changing with greater frequency and amplitude. Even developing countries like China, which normally linked the value of their currency to that of a major developed economy or to several of these, were not immune. Changes in exchange rates had major and usually unpredicted effects on their commodity trade, capital inflows, and indebtedness levels.

In no sector of the world trading system had practices and patterns changed more dramatically than in finance. During the 1980s changes in international finance were revolutionary and ongoing. The debt crisis in Latin America and other developing countries early in the decade had diverted the flow of international capital away from the debt-laden LDCs. The appearance of sizable balance of payments deficits in the U.S. and the appearance of counterpart surpluses in Europe, Japan and some of the NICs had substantial implications for China. The U.S. became a new and

China and the World Trading System

powerful competitor for capital and a less willing and able contributor of development funds for the developing world including China. China, however, benefited from the fact that the debt-laden LDCs could no longer compete for development funds. The strength of U.S. competition raised interest rates worldwide and the costs of debt service. The dollar exchange rate became more volatile as the outlook for the U.S. demand for funds shifted and all currencies were affected. Meanwhile the rising affluence of Japan brought a new aid donor and source of international capital to the forefront of the list creditors. China benefited from the new strength of Japan both because of its proximity and because of the previous checkered history of its economic relationships with Japan. China also benefited somewhat from the new affluence of Taiwan, whose international reserves at the end of the 1980s were second only to those of Japan.

Interest rate levels around the world also had become more volatile in the 1980s, responding to and causing additional international capital flows. Developing countries found to their dismay that the service charges on their outstanding international debt could vary significantly with exchange rate and/or interest rate shifts without any change in the level of their debt. In brief, international transactions of all kinds had become subject to a much larger degree of risk than had previously been the case and managing risk became a prime goal of banks and businesses.

Astonishingly these enhanced risks did not appear to depress the growth of world trade. On the contrary, the globalization of economic activity proceeded apace, stemming from the same causes as the globalization of capital and finance – technological change, deregulation, more intense competition, and rising affluence.

The heightened degree of competition throughout the world inevitably affected institutions. The International Monetary Fund, originally established to manage a regime of fixed exchange rates, lost its original mission with the introduction of variable exchange rates in the early 1970s. Through astute aid in managing the LDC debt crisis in the early 1980s, however, it gained a new de facto mission in debt management and economic development. The World Bank, originally established to support long-term development efforts found its mission being encroached upon by the IMF and groped for a new or revised goal. The GATT, originally established to reduce barriers to merchandise trade, had been so successful in lowering tariff barriers that it found much of its original

78   China, Hong Kong, Taiwan and World Trade

mission largely accomplished. In the meantime, however, non-tariff barriers had multiplied, non-merchandise trade had grown in importance and the relationship between trade and capital flows had become much more intimate. In the Uruguay Round the GATT was attempting to cope with areas over which it never had exercised any authority. The three major international economic organizations were out-of-date and badly in need of modernization. Each of the three was important to China, especially its pending application to return to membership in the GATT.

CHINA'S INTEREST IN THE WORLD TRADING ORGANIZATION

Early in the reform period, when the Chinese authorities had concluded that it would be in their national interest to participate fully in world economic institutions, they moved quickly. Although the PRC had been in the United Nations since 1972 and thus formally qualified to seek membership, it only applied to the IMF and World Bank in 1980. Its applications were accepted with alacrity.[3] During the rest of the decade China drew on the IMF for funds only to a very limited degree, but used World Bank resources extensively. Although the Bank was an important source of loans for China, even more important was the Bank's expertise in problems and practices of economic development. China came to rely extensively on World Bank advice during its first decade of economic reform.

Early in the 1980s, China also informally indicated an interest in rejoining the GATT. While for a number of years after that its interest in the multilateral trade agency appeared to wane, the PRC in fact was preparing itself for a formal application by studying in detail the operation of the agency. Its UN representatives in Geneva enrolled in courses offered at GATT headquarters there and a small body of GATT expertise developed among trade officials in Beijing.[4] China joined the GATT-sponsored Multifibre Arrangement regulating world textile trade in 1983 and obtained observer status in the GATT the following year.[5] Both steps were widely viewed as precursors to an application for GATT membership. During 1985, at informal discussions in Geneva and elsewhere, Chinese representatives attempted to convince the United States and EC that China's application for GATT membership should be judged in the broad context of its foreign policy rather than on narrow commercial terms. In every other applicaiton for membership, the GATT had judged the applying country's eligibility solely on the basis of the adjustments to its trade policy required for compliance with GATT rules.[6] These efforts to have China's GATT membership handled as an exceptional case came to nought. In July 1986, resigned to negotiating its GATT membership on traditional terms of commercial policy, the PRC formally applied to resume its status as a contracting party to GATT.[7]

The status of China's economy in transition from central control to primarily market control was equivocal and changing continuously, a fact that led to forecasts of a prolonged period of negotiations between China and GATT members over the terms of China's resumption. There were many potential points of inconsistency between GATT rules and the facts of China's economic life. First, according to GATT practices, the facts had to be ascertained and actual points of inconsistency determined and then resolution of the inconsistencies negotiated.

China's eventual return to the GATT was never in doubt. Although many LDC GATT members looked with some apprehension on China's emergence into the world economy, concerned about China as a competitor in Third World markets and for bilateral and multilateral aid funds, these concerns were somewhat assuaged by the hope that China would also provide a new market for their exports and political support for their position in GATT councils. Similarly industrialized members worried about China's potential for flooding their markets with cheap exports but were attracted by the possibilities for their own exports in a market of over 1 billion people.

All GATT members agreed, however, that China's integration into the world economy was of momentous importance and that China should be represented in the GATT in order that the General Agreement be a truly worldwide trade organization. All were aware that throughout its existence the General Agreement had remained a technical, narrowly focused trade organization, increasingly representative of world trade and free from the degree and kind of politicization that had characterized the UN. A new member, a superpower, already an important trading nation and with enormous potential, could change the nature of the GATT dramatically. And it could do so for good or for ill.

A country of China's resources and potential, committed to maximizing the productivity of its own economy through reliance on

80 *China, Hong Kong, Taiwan and World Trade*

market forces and participation in the world economy on the basis of its own evolving comparative advantage, could boost world trade and world economic growth as well as its own. By participating in the GATT, China could legitimize its economic reform program and strengthen the domestic political support for that program at home. By participating in the GATT, China could also strengthen and fortify that organization through its compliance. Basing its commercial policies on GATT precepts, it would bring an increasing share of world trade into accord with the GATT. It would make the GATT a more potent organization through its use of GATT mechanisms and also through the force of its example. And the more it supported the precepts of the GATT, the more benefit it would get from its membership. With more of world trade conducted under the same rules, the more orderly and predictable each country's trade would become and the greater would be the benefits of trade accruing to all members.

Not only would the stature of the General Agreement be raised, but so would be China's. China was large enough and powerful enough to make a significant difference to the rest of the world and to the GATT. China's influence in the world would be enhanced both through its own greater economic strength and through its role in expanding and supporting world trade and development. With powerful new support the GATT would become more powerful. The opportunity for betterment offered to the world by China's application for GATT membership was too large and important to be denied.

There were, however, risks. If a country of China's power and potential were to accede to the GATT with cynicism or with a commitment having only low priority, it would have the capacity for troublesome mischief or destructive misuse. Since China was applying as a developing country, it would receive all of the benefits of GATT membership, but be free from most of the obligations. Thus China would be in a position to push exports aggressively while limiting imports tightly. If China were to use its power to gain every possible short-term advantage while yielding a minimum of benefits to its trading partners, the benefits to the rest of the world could be negligible. Such a course would limit the longer-term benefits China itself could derive from the GATT and thus serve to enhance its cynicism. Its trading partners would themselves come to doubt China's commitment and would also become cynical. In seeking to protect themselves from aggressive or disruptive Chinese export

China and the World Trading System
81

tactics, they would be more likely to adopt extra-GATT measures. Trade disputes and bitterness would multiply, the GATT would be weakened and the promise and opportunity implicit in China's membership would be lost. And if China were to attempt to use the GATT to further its own non-economic goals, the resulting politicization of the formerly technical organization could effectively demolish its usefulness to all. Such were the hazards to be avoided.

Because the stakes involved in China's membership in the GATT were so large, the terms according to which it took up its membership were crucial. Negotiations were approached with care.

The speed with which China provided answers to GATT members' questions of fact attested to the seriousness of Chinese purpose and the importance the PRC attached to GATT membership. Literally hundreds of probing questions were answered by China in only 18 months. By the spring of 1989 the fact-finding phase was completed and China prepared to undertake actual negotiations for the terms of the protocol of its resumption.

China's pressure for an immediate return led many observers to speculate over the reasons for the urgency China so clearly attached to becoming a GATT member. The reasons adduced by both Chinese and foreigners were several. Chinese officials stressed the fact that GATT membership would anchor their modernization and reform effort to the world trading system and would thus add legitimacy to their economic reform program at home, giving it a firmer domestic foundation. Others stressed economic reasons – GATT membership would bring China wider and more secure access to Western markets and would permit its access to the Generalized Special Preference (GSP) program of the United States, giving many Chinese goods duty-free treatment in the U.S. market. Access to GATT's dispute settelement mechanism would ease the resolution of trade disputes. Because, it was opined, the Chinese realized that the window of opportunity for export-led growth like that enjoyed by Japan, Korea, and Taiwan was closing as foreigners became impatient with the way the world trading system had operated, China felt some urgency in taking advantage of that window while it was still open, and in being in a position to influence any change in the rules that might be in train in the GATT. For whatever combination of reasons, speedy GATT membership clearly was important to China.

PROBLEM AREAS OF CHINA IN THE GATT

Concerns of GATT members of the consistency of China's commercial practices with GATT rules of proper trading procedures centered on two basic sets of GATT rules and the mechanisms designed to ensure that the rule would be followed in practice. These were the rule of non-discrimination and the associated mechanisms of transparency and reciprocity, and the rule defining fair trade with the associated mechanisms for defense against unfair trade practices contained in GATT articles on safeguards, subsidies, and dumping.

Non-discrimination, Transparency, and Reciprocity [8]

The GATT from its intiation has insisted that every member give equal treatment to any traded commodity regardless of its source or destination by according Most Favored Nation (MFN) status to all products.

> Any advantage, favor, privilege or immunity granted by any contracting party to any product originating in or destined for any other country shall be accorded immediately and unconditionally to the like product originating in or destined for the territory of all other contracting parties.

The above quotation is the phrasing of the non-discrimination, MFN clause, of Article I. It clearly refers to all duties, fees, rules, and formalities affecting both imports and exports. No trading country can legally discriminate against the product of any GATT member in any regard.

The MFN principle has served both as a mechanism for making multi-nation bargaining sessions operationally manageable (e.g., the original "principal supplier" basis for negotiations) and as the ethic for endowing the world trading system with moral legitimacy. As Article I of the GATT it commands more reverence than any other GATT principle, yet it too is sinned against. The GATT itself permits as exceptions customs unions and preferential duties for the exports of the LDCs, both obvious forms of discrimination.

In addition the drafters of the GATT recognized that GATT members might be tempted to adopt or maintain discriminatory trade procedures (and also to avoid reciprocity) if they were permitted to conduct their trade in secrecy. The GATT therefore requires transparency of trade matters by requiring that its members

China and the World Trading System

make information on trade practices and results available in both written form and through consultations.

Despite such farsighted precautions members have avoided MFN treatment through various extra-GATT techniques primarily involving non-tariff barriers to trade. Because Part IV (and other relevant Articles) for all practical purposes essentially waive for the LDCs (which represent two-thirds of all members) almost all of the basic obligations of the GATT, the sins against the MFN principle are widespread.

Those who drafted the General Agreement recognized the intertwining of trade and finance and therefore the necessity for insuring that GATT non-discrimination and reciprocity goals not be frustrated by inappropriate international financial practices of its members. To this end provisions were made (Article XV) for cooperation between the International Monetary Fund and the GATT. Indeed, membership in the IMF became a prerequisite for accession to the GATT or, failing IMF membership, a special agreement with the GATT on the subject of foreign exchange rates and convertibility consistent with the rules of the IMF. The experience of the 1930s had clearly demonstrated that exchange controls were an effective means of discriminating among products and countries as well as among currencies.

The intent of these provisions has been largely ignored. Collaboration between the GATT and the IMF has been minimal, in large part because balance of payments stringencies have resulted in widespread use of exchange controls, inconvertible currencies and exchange rate changes. In addition the carte blanche given by the GATT to the LDCs meant that trade flows diverged widely from the Pareto optimum because of trade controls as well as exchange controls. The GATT itself, moreover, has not used its instruments of surveillance and consultation nearly to the extent that it might have.

Starting in 1974 the principal mechanism of the GATT for using the MFN principle to expand world trade lay in reciprocal tariff concessions negotiated periodically by its members in the course of seven GATT-sponsored negotiating "rounds" as well as in the Uruguay Round (1987–90). The General Agreement was built on the assumption that trade flows respond to price changes, that trade could therefore be increased by a reduction in tariffs and that reciprocal tariff concessions could be negotiated in such a way that a balance of mutually advantageous gains could be achieved by both negotiating partners granting substantially equivalent concessions.

84 *China, Hong Kong, Taiwan and World Trade*

Despite the importance of the principle of "mutually advantageous" and "substantially equivalent" concessions, no criteria have been developed for measuring reciprocity. The conceptual problems of defining the value of a concession, and the empirical problems of acquiring the requisite data once a definition is settled, all remain formidable. In addition all negotiators prefer to return home with their own calculations to show that the export concessions they obtained were greater than the import liberalization they conceded. A country's private negotiating agenda might aim to maximize domestic employment opportunities through trade negotiations or to maximize its export proceeds or to minimize the impact of trade negotiations on its balance of payments position, or other specific goals. An undefined concept of reciprocity accommodates a variety of negotiating agendas. It has been politically useful to permit reciprocity to remain ambiguous.

The principle of reciprocity was successfully challenged by the developing countries (LDCs). Claiming that they could not afford to pay for the trade concessions made by the rich countries and that they should be treated differently, the LDCs succeeded during the Kennedy Round (1962–67) in adding to the General Agreement a new section (Part IV) stating that the developed countries cannot expect to receive reciprocity from the LDCs. (This is only one of a list of commitments on the part of developed countries toward the LDCs contained in Part IV.)

Despite its ambiguity (and in many ways because of it) the reciprocity principle is perhaps the main reason for the success of the GATT-based world trading system during the post-war years. The system did reduce world tariff barriers dramatically (from over 40 percent in 1947 to an average of 5–10 percent at the start of the Uruguay Round) through a series of bargaining sessions conducted on the basis of "mutually advantageous" concessions. The reductions were politically saleable at home because they were perceived to be reciprocal.

Safeguards, Subsidies, and Dumping

The major derogations from the GATT of the past decade or so have primarily been the consequence of mounting discomfort with the still widespread application of the non-discrimination principle required by the GATT. The escape clause of the GATT (Article XIX) which permits safeguards (protective devices) against injurious imports has been interpreted to require non-discriminatory import controls. If a member's automobile industry is being injured by imports, for example, higher import duties must be levied against all automobiles regardless of their source. Moreover, a country that undertakes such import-limiting action must compensate its trading partners either in the form of reduced import barriers on other of their export products or by accepting heightened import duties against its own products.

The first major derogation from the GATT safeguard mechanism materialized in regard to textile imports from the LDCs in the markets of the developed countries. In response to acute domestic political pressures the United States and Europe in 1961 negotiated under GATT auspices a Long-Term Cotton Textile Agreement with major LDC suppliers limiting the rate of growth of imports of cotton textiles. That agreement and its successors, the Multi-fibre Arrangements (MFA) of 1973, 1977, 1982, and 1986, were negotiated to provide for an "orderly" expansion of the world's textile trade. The MFA, which essentially defines the terms by which importers may restrict textile imports, has been referred to as "GATT Aberration No. 1."

Surging LDC resentment over the MFAs has effectively eliminated the use of similar sectoral arrangements within the GATT to limit the growth of developed country imports in other sectors of industry. Nonetheless, quasi-sectoral arrangements have arisen outside the GATT as Europe and the United States have employed such devices as voluntary export restraint agreements (VERs) to limit their imports of automobiles, steel, and consumer electronics, all of interest to LDCs. LDC experience with the textile agreements also is the source of their suspicion and doubts concerning any amendments to the Article XIX safeguard mechanism.

Despite their unanimous condemnation of the MFAs, the developing countries unofficially admit that the textile agreements have had certain advantages. In limiting export growth the agreements thwarted the development of cut-throat competition among producers in any one country and among exporting countries and thus prevented a severe collapse of textile prices that might otherwise have happened. The agreements also accelerated structural adjustments in LDC economies, shifting resources into higher valued-added industries earlier than might have been the case absent the MFAs. Nonetheless the fact that the agreements became more and more inclusive of all textiles and textile products with

86 *China, Hong Kong, Taiwan and World Trade*

each successive MFA was perceived as a restraint by the LDCs and deeply resented.

In the 1970s Europe and especially the United States were confronted with a new phenomenon, highly targeted export selling based on efficient production and marketing techniques and plentiful long-term finance. Such export targeting practiced first by Japan was perfectly legal under the GATT, but frequently proved highly disruptive in the targeted markets. The success of the Japanese practice, moreover, captured the attention of the emerging, newly industrializing countries (NICs) who clearly profited by emulating Japan's experience.

European countries especially have long complained that the safeguard mechanism is out-of-date. In contrast to dumping or export subsidies which the GATT treats as unfair competition and against which import-limiting tariff increases do not require compensation, disruptive surges in imports resulting from export-targeting are treated as legitimate sales, although they are typically concentrated on one country and one sector. The Europeans argued that in such cases the GATT should permit selective safeguard action; a targeted import country, injured by a sudden inundation of legal imports, should be able to limit imports from the single disruptive source. In addition they claimed that compensation should not be required – that disruptive targeting, in other words, should be made illegal. The issue was argued in the Tokyo Round but left unresolved. It was on the agenda of the Uruguay Round where negotiating difficulties continued.

The major opponents of change in the GATT escape clause mechanism were the LDCs which feared selective safeguard action would be used primarily against their exports. The United States supported the LDC position, although it attempted unsuccessfully to find a compromise. The United States proposed, for example, "consensual selectivity" (GATT jargon is indomitable) according to which a country could selectively limit imports if the supplying country agreed, if the agreement were subject to GATT scrutiny and if a time limit were set on the new controls.[9] The British also suggested a compromise that would involve a GATT inspection team (à la the IMF) for countries using safeguards, with a three-year grace period before compensation would be required and a public hearing to ensure equity and transparency.[10] By mid-1989 progress toward a resolution of the dispute in the Uruguay Round was by no means assured.

China and the World Trading System

If the country injured by targeting were to seek redress through the GATT, it would be compelled to limit imports from all sources of the targeted product. Rather than this course, the United States and Europe have chosen to go outside of the GATT to negotiate VER agreements bilaterally with Japan and certain NICs or to wield some other extra-GATT form of non-tariff barrier.[11] To be sure, the short-run best interests of the LDCs were served by the U.S.-Japan VER in automobiles because the automobile exports of Korea, Brazil and other LDCs remained at least unaffected or more probably increased as a consequence of the bilateral agreement.

Every solution to world trade problems that is sought outside of the GATT weakens the authority of the existing system and encourages further derogation. The NICs and the LDCs would be among the chief losers if the GATT should become impotent; their opposition to a revision of GATT safeguard rules is short-sighted.

In contrast to an injurious surge of imports, defensive action against which requires payment of compensation, dumping, and subsidies are not legal practices and importers subject to dumping or export subsidies by their trading partners may take defensive action without paying compensation.

Dumping is defined as a sale for export at less than fair value ("normal value" is the GATT language of Article VI) which in turn is defined as an export price, with appropriate adjustments, lower than the domestic selling price of the product or, if that is not available, the cost of production of the product. If a product is sold at a lower price abroad than at home or at a price below its cost of production, of necessity, there must be some element of "bounty" or subsidy in its export sales price. By including reference to subsidies and their remedy (countervailing duties) in the same Article the GATT implicitly recognized the intimate relation between dumping and a subsidy. In the same paragraph, Article VI(5), the use of both an anti-dumping and a countervailing duty to compensate for the same trade act is forbidden, again recognizing that dumping involves a subsidy. In addition, although both dumping and subsidies are illegal according to GATT, defensive action in the form of anti-dumping duties or countervailing duties is permitted only if the dumping or subsidization causes serious injury to a domestic industry.

The Subsidies Code of the GATT, negotiated during the Tokyo Round (1973–79), addressed the intractable problem of dealing with dumping and subsidies on the part of non-market economies by

88 *China, Hong Kong, Taiwan and World Trade*

mandating the use of a "surrogate country" approach. This permits the prices of a like product from a third country to be used as the basis for determining the fair value of exports from a non-market economy. It was a Rube Goldberg approach to an admittedly difficult problem.[12]

Reconciling the trading practices of a centrally controlled economy with the rules and mechanisms of the GATT proved to be an extremely difficult chore throughout the GATT's history. Although Poland (in 1967), Rumania (in 1971) and Hungary (in 1973) were admitted to the GATT after they had become centrally-controlled economies (Cuba and Czechoslovakia had been founding members in 1948 before their economies were centrally controlled), and although their protocols of accession entailed contentious and prolonged negotiations, no one was happy with the results. Determining whether the trade practices of these countries were non-discriminatory and fair proved to be an intractable challenge. These countries were small and their actual and potential trade insignificant in the total of trade among market economis. In addition because GATT members were permitted to retain previously existing quantitative restrictions on their imports from the centrally-controlled GATT members, they perceived themselves protected from any trade losses that might be the consequence of limited reciprocity.[13]

China's size and its potential for trade, however, made it a very different case. The trade benefits denied to China's trading partners, should its trading practices to be non-reciprocal, discriminatory or unfair, could be significant. As a consequence the transparency of China's trading practices as well as of its internal economic policies, and especially the degree to which internal prices were market-determined and permitted to affect trade were of major importance to GATT members.

In bilateral and multilateral discussions, Chinese representatives noted that the precedents of the East European protocols of accession were not appropriate models for its resumption. They pointed out that the chief apprehension of GATT members concerning the possibilities of discrimination in the trade practices of Eastern European applicants had stemmed from the fact of the preponderance of their trade with other centrally controlled economies. With those countries trade was centrally planned, bilaterally balanced and conducted essentially on the basis of a form of barter. Prices in intra-East European trade were controversial and required

China and the World Trading System

prolonged bilateral negotiations which for major contracts could take years. Transparency was non-existent; MFN treatment was impossible to guarantee or monitor.[14]

In China's case trade with Eastern Europe and the USSR was conducted on the same basis of planning and barter, but it amounted to only 15 percent of China's total trade turnover and consequently aggregate access to the Chinese market for GATT members was not an issue as it had been in the East European cases. China stressed that GATT membership would facilitate economic reform and thus itself would insure increasing market access in China. Most GATT members accepted this argument.

Concerns About China's Import Regime

China's claim that its tariff structure was, or would become, its chief instrument of import control was not as readily accepted by GATT members. China's frequent resort during the first decade of reform to quantitative restrictions in periods of retrenchment suggested a future pattern of reliance on the balance of payments exception (Article XII) to the GATT ban on quotas. As a developing country China would be permitted to raise its duties and employ quantitative restrictions when experiencing severe balance of payments deficits.

By the time of the Uruguay Round, the almost continuous reliance of many developing countries on the exceptions permitted them in the GATT was being questioned in many quarters. The drafters of the General Agreement had anticipated substantial collaboration between GATT and IMF officials in advising on and monitoring exceptions employed by GATT members for balance of payments reasons. Through the years, however, collaboration between the two agencies had become entirely pro-forma rather than substantial. Notification to the GATT and the IMF occurred after the import restraints were put in place and was rarely questioned. Because developing countries as capital importers had chronic balance of payments deficits, such laxity in implementing GATT provisions made it easy for them to rely on import restraints in pursuit of rapid growth often to the detriment of the productivity of their own economies.[15]

The subject was to be discussed in the Uruguay Round. No changes in the GATT, however, were required to make cooperation between it and the IMF effective, but only a more serious, conscientious approach by officials of the two agencies especially the

90 *China, Hong Kong, Taiwan and World Trade*

IMF. Also under discussion in the Uruguay Round was a program of surveillance by the GATT to monitor the trading practices of its members. A similar program in the Organization for Economic Cooperation and Development (OECD), where member countries confronted by other OECD members had to justify their economic policies, was highly effective. Surveilance by the GATT of all exceptions to its rules, in focusing publicity on these abuses, could go a long way toward alleviating them.

If surveillance becomes GATT practice and if cooperation between the GATT and IMF becomes substantial, China would face challenges should it attempt to rely unduly on balance of payments deficits as an excuse for maintaining high tariffs and quantitative import restraints. Already impatient with LDC import restraints, its trading partners would be likely to exhibit less patience with China. It is after all in the nature of a developing country to experience chronic balance of payments deficits as a recipient of aid, foreign loans, and investment from abroad. A balance of payments deficit per se is not evidence of a necessity for import restraint. Further probing is needed for justification.

In addition to the role of tariffs in China's import regime, GATT members were concerned over the role of government. The preponderance of state enterprise in China's industry meant that monopoly still characterized segments of the economy important in China's imports. The central government directly purchased most of the large import items of plant and equipment. In the case of smaller contracts, although a number of state trading companies were active in China's foreign trade and did compete with one another, the State remained in a position to use its monopoly power when in the view of the top leadership the situation so required. Thus in the past it was rumored that China denied large contracts to the Japanese in the 1980s to punish Japan for failure to transfer technology. In 1983, when bilateral negotiations with the United States for textile quotas failed, China banned all further imports of American cotton, soybeans and chemical fibers.[16] As a consequence GATT members worried whether in the future Chinese purchases might discriminate among suppliers on non-price grounds.

GATT members also worried about China's pricing policies. The continuing pervasive role of the central government in price determination for basic inputs – labor, capital, fuel, and power – made it impossible for the foreign trade mechanism to serve as a guide to efficient resource allocation. The priority given to technology

China and the World Trading System

91

imports by Beijing authorities, for example, might also have appeared if the market had been driving import demand, but the mix of technology-embodying items would have been different (e.g., more mining, transportation, and power-generating equipment). Misallocation of resources would limit China's growth and thus its ability to import, thereby restricting the degree of reciprocity China accorded its trading partners. Further, the fact that social benefits – housing, health, education – were tied to the workers' place of employment meant that achieving enough labor mobility for domestic scarcities to be reflected in wage levels would require a long-term effort. The transition to a primarily market-based pricing system would be a prolonged process.

Concerns About China's Export Regime

Chief among the concerns of GATT members about China's trading policies was export pricing. During the first decade of economic reform China's exports, primarily labor-intensive products, had been sold at very competitive prices especially compared with other countries' exports of the same goods. China made no secret about the urgency of its quest for foreign exchange in order to finance technology imports. Nonetheless its terms of trade (export prices in relation to import prices) were low. China was willing to accept a less favorable price for its labor in terms of imports of machinery and equipment than most other developing countries. China's unfavorable terms of trade could have reflected the relatively poor quality of Chinese goods, the cost advantage of its sizable labor force or its productivity. They could, however, have reflected an administratively controlled economy's ability to offer more labor per unit of foreign exchange than more market-oriented economies did.[17]

The pervasiveness of subsidies in Chinese industry and the differences between domestic prices, cost of production and export prices worried China's trading partners both because of their potential for market disruption (in association with high Chinese export expansion) and because of their potential for engendering bitter disputes over unfair trade practices.[18] Between 1980 (when the first case was filed) and mid-1989, sixteen anti-dumping investigations had been initiated in the United States against Chinese goods, compared with twenty-four launched against Taiwan for the same interval.[19] By the end of 1988 there were ten anti-dumping orders in

92   *China, Hong Kong, Taiwan and World Trade*

effect in the United States against China, covering findings against Chinese products starting in 1983. At the same date eleven anti-dumping orders were active against Taiwan, covering findings from 1971.[20] In 1985, U.S. imports from Taiwan were more than four times larger than U.S. imports from China; in 1988 imports from Taiwan at $25 billion were three times larger than those from China. China's capacity to generate trade disputes was clearly huge.

Whether or not China would follow a mercantilist trading policy was a continuing source of concern. Statements of Chinese leaders that China's opening to the West was necessary for China to resume its rightful place in the world, but only one step on its road to socialism might have been a technique for selling the economic reform to reluctant party members. It might also have been a sincere statement of long-run goals implying immediate import replacement, long-term self-sufficiency and a position of power in world forums like the GATT for pressing China's perceived national interests.

The Chinese argued that although government ownership dominated their industry, China had separated ownership from management of enterprise and in such a system prices could operate as they do in a market economy. Price reform, moreover, was a continuing process. The "two-tier" price system, a major source of concern to GATT members, would be gradually eliminated and only commodities of vital importance would remain under central control. Already in 1989, they pointed out, for export-oriented industries only 30 percent of material inputs was supplied at the low state price, 70 percent at market prices.[21]

They stated that China's economic reform would accelerate domestic growth by allowing China to build on its comparative advantage in international trade. They argued that China's import and investment controls were not evidence of a mercantilist policy, but rather a consequence of foreign exchange shortage. They pointed to China's imports of automobiles and an array of consumer goods as evidence that the Chinese system was increasingly open and offered an opportunity to the world for growth. They stressed their interest in fair, non-discriminatory trade and insisted that China not be subject to discrimination.[22]

China recognized GATT members' concerns over the transparency of its system as justified. It indicated that matters were improving as China's legal system evolved and that the basic problem stemmed from technical inefficiencies rather than lack of willingness to provide information.

China and the World Trading System

Chinese representatives constantly objected to the discriminatory treatment that was practiced against them in the European Community (EC) and the United States. The EC's quota restrictions on imports from China were repeatedly and vehemently stressed as out of compliance with the GATT. Similarly the failure of the United States to extend unconditional MFN treatment to China was a constant source of complaint as was U.S. denial of GSP treatment to China. (U.S. trade law permitted MFN treatment to a country "controlled by international communism" only as a special annual exception requested by the President who was required to determine each year that progress had been made toward a system of free emigration from that country.)

In 1983 the U.S. textile industry initiated a case against Chinese-made textile apparel, charging unfair competition in the form of subsidies, and asking the imposition of countervailing duties. This was the first such case brought against a non-market economy. The Chinese formally complained about the case and suggested that they might retaliate against U.S. grain imports if the United States applied countervailing duties. After considerable public comment and behind-the-scenes activity the case was withdrawn. No other countervailing duty case had been brought in the United States against China by mid-1989.

In the United States the difficulties of determining whether dumping or subsidies existed in the case of exports from a non-market economy produced bizarre laws and judicial decisions. The use of a "surrogate country" for dumping cases in the GATT has been mentioned; in the United States a "constructed cost" for this purpose involved an intricate attempt to estimate cost of production based on the surrogate country approach.[23] In the case of subsidies, after prolonged legal wrangling over a charge of subsidized steel imports from Poland and Czechoslovakia, a U.S. Court of Appeals finally decided in 1986 that the countervailing duty law did not apply, essentially denying that subsidies could exist in a centrally controlled economy. At the same time, however, it ruled that the dumping law was applicable. The decision was an easy way out, but it flaunted the basic conceptual and legal identity between a "bounty" and selling at less than fair value. The 1986 decision was at least one reason why no countervailing duty cases were brought in the United States against China after that date.

The United States in particular confronted one legal problem based on its own domestic legislation with China's application for

94 *China, Hong Kong, Taiwan and World Trade*

resumption of its GATT membership. The Jackson-Vanik amendment in Title IV of the Trade Act of 1974 prevented the United States from extending unconditional MFN treatment to communist countries. Section 406 of the same Act, in addition, provided for selective safeguards in the case of communist countries. Because of this legislation the United States would be required to "opt out" (refuse to consent to the application) of any new GATT accession agreement with a communist country that did not contain provisions in accord with its own existing legislation. Because Article XXXV, the "opt-out" provision, applied only to new entrants to the GATT and not to returnees, it could not be used by the United States in the case of China's application for *resumption* of membership.[24] If the protocol of China's resumption contained a selective safeguard provision, one difficulty would be overcome, but the problem of China's emigration policy still remained.

GATT members, and especially the United States and the EC, accepted many of China's arguments, but remained apprehensive about the ability and willingness of China to meet GATT obligations during its transition to a primarily market-based economy. Transparency seemed to be a problem for Chinese as well as foreign officials. Decentralization in China intentionally and unintentionally had given local authorities much more control over prices, production, trade, and investment (as discussed in Chapter 2). In addition, the coastal provinces and SEZs had much greater authority over foreign trade and investment than the rest of the country. Further, local authorities everywhere wielded more influence than Beijing intended. It was not at all clear that Beijing was fully informed; its "technical inefficiencies" were deep-seated.

China had no equivalent of the *Federal Register* in the United States to announce officially new laws and regulations; consequently, the shifting legal regime was opaque, especially to foreigners. Not only did China change tariffs unilaterally and without warning, but surcharges, quotas, licenses, and such appeared abruptly. Whether they were non-discriminatory in operation was usually impossible to judge.

Similarly, subsidies, the dual price system and the artificial exchange rate made any meaningful comparison between Chinese internal and export prices impossible. Thus it was impossible to judge whether China was in fact trading on a basis that would enhance its own productivity as well as whether China was practicing fair trade.[25] Further, since the opaqueness of China's trading

China and the World Trading System

practices was in large part rooted in the transitional devices China had chosen to employ on its way to a primarily market-oriented economy, it would endure throughout the transition period. Finally, while GATT members were aware that China's incorporation into the IMF and World Bank structure had been relatively smooth and that China had mostly accepted the existing structure of rules, they were also aware that joining the GATT would require many more adjustments on China's part. They were not convinced that China would be both willing and able to make those adjustments.[26]

Such concerns caused the United States and Europe to insist that China's protocol of resumption contain a selective safeguard provision. Such a provision had been included in the protocols of admission of certain East European countries as the only exception to MFN-based safeguards condoned by the GATT. The Chinese representatives were adamantly opposed. They claimed that as a developing country China was entitled to preferential treatment in every regard. They also alleged that acceptance of a discriminatory clause would inhibit China's growth by diverting Chinese exports away from those products where it had a comparative advantage and thus endanger the success of China's outward-looking economic reform program.

This was the main point of contention between China and its trading partners in the bilateral discussions that had been held prior to mid-1989. Just before the shift to the conservative Deng regime in Beijing, rumors had appeared in the American press that the Chinese had agreed in principle to selective safeguards in bilateral discussion with the United States,[27] but these were not confirmed.

Before mid-1989 most GATT members were willing to give China the benefit of the doubt in many areas of concern to them. This attitude toward China stemmed in part from geo-political considerations. China was a huge country, a superpower geographically and politically in a position to serve as a counterweight to the USSR. The attitude also had an ideological base, although in many quarters the ideology was viewed through rose-colored glasses. China appeared to be well launched on its way to capitalism and while not yet having abandoned socialism, was often perceived as likely to do so. The favorable attitude toward China also mirrored a genuine admiration for Chinese capabilities, their capacity for hard work, their dedication and their ingenuity. Finally, it also reflected the success of a mounting, well-designed lobbying effort by China in the capitals of its major trading partners.

96   *China, Hong Kong, Taiwan and World Trade*

The ruthless suppression of the student demonstrations in June 1989 demolished much of the good will from which China had benefited. Prior to June 4 that good will might have made possible some change in U.S. legislation permitting the United States to agree to unconditional MFN treatment that China's resumption of GATT membership would imply. After mid-1989 such a change did not seem feasible. Europe was even more demoralized by and resentful of China's abrupt use of power than the United States. Japan was politically constrained by the history of its relations with China in expressing its repugnance and by the dominance of commercial considerations over much of its foreign policy. China's pride was unlikely to permit it to push for admittance to the GATT as long as there was doubt about its success. Thus it was likely that China's application for resumption of GATT membership would essentially lie dormant until such future time as China's governing regime might once again gain favor in the eyes of its important trading partners. Trade would undoubtedly continue in the interim, but its rate of growth, like that of the Chinese economy, would slow for the reasons to be discussed in Chapter 5.

4 "Greater China": The Special Problems of Hong Kong and Taiwan

INTRODUCTION

For Hong Kong and Taiwan, relationships with mainland China were uniquely important; they had been so historically and would continue to be so into the future. Despite their differing relationships to the PRC, during the 1980s the people of Hong Kong and Taiwan had been both hopeful and doubting, optimistic and pessimistic about the future of their relations with mainland China. For each the best and the worst seemed the same. The best-case scenario was an eventual conquering of the PRC by their economic system, already planted in the mainland and flourishing there through the efforts of their traders and investors. The worst was an overwhelming of their own economies by a diehard Communist occupation.

Hope and optimism in Hong Kong and Taiwan were exemplified in the spring of 1989 by public discussion of a potential "Greater China" economic alliance that would extend and formalize the growing triangular trade in goods among the PRC, Hong Kong, and Taiwan. The idea originated with a proposal by a Taiwanese businessman-professor of economics for a Greater China Common Market that would begin with the establishment of direct trade between Taiwan and the PRC in 1990. A common market would be set up by 2000 and a "democratic United States of China" would be achieved by 2050. The idea generated excitement and considerable enthusiasm, especially in Taiwan, while being totally consistent with the PRC policy of encouraging Hong Kong and enticing Taiwanese trade and investment on the mainland. The idea of a Greater China articulated the form and feasibility of the romantic vision of the conquering of the mainland by a few million people through economic prowess alone.[1]

Economically it was a sensible proposal, recognizing the complementarity that was the basis for thriving trade and investment

98 *China, Hong Kong, Taiwan and World Trade*

between Hong Kong and China directly, and between Taiwan and China indirectly via Hong Kong. It would combine the marketing skills and financial strength of Taiwan, the infrastructure, service, and manufacturing skills of Hong Kong and the ample labor and raw materials in China into an area already generating $300 billion of foreign trade. Presumably a free flow of labor would not be contemplated until living standards on the mainland were much closer to those of Hong Kong and Taiwan. It set a time limit of a decade for the PRC to make a phased adjustment in prices and indirect controls necessary to its own goals. It would do so with the active aid of thousands of entrepreneurial expatriate countrymen who were skilled and experienced in managing business and who not only could communicate directly with the mainland labor in local dialects but who had many relatives on the mainland. It would unite China, carrying "one country, two systems" to its logical conclusion.

The shift to a conservative regime in Beijing in mid-1989 killed all hope for the best, leaving fear and depression in an expectation of the worst. Fear was the dominant reaction in Hong Kong, depression in Taiwan.

China had been separated from both Hong Kong and Taiwan over a century earlier in the humiliation of a military defeat by an outside power that produced lasting resentment over the loss of what the Chinese viewed as traditional parts of imperial China. Neither was of any economic significance at the time of its loss.

Hong Kong had only a small fishing population in 1841 when it was ceded to Britain after the first Opium War. Because the island of Hong Kong was threatened by instability in the Kowloon peninsula only one mile away, Britain extracted from China possession of the peninsula in 1860 and in 1898 was given a 99-year lease of the adjacent New Territories. (The leased Territories accounted for 90 percent of the area of the British colony of Hong Kong.) The Japanese occupied Hong Kong for three and a half years during World War Two, after which an influx of Chinese into Hong Kong from the mainland began.

China first occupied Taiwan during the Manchu period and during the seventeenth century the island came to be reckoned as part of the Chinese empire. China ceded the island to Japan in 1895 but, because of objections by the Chinese there, Japan was able to occupy it only by force. Japan developed the island as a colony dependent on the homeland for manufactured goods and supplying it with food and raw materials. Taiwan was returned to China in

"Greater China": Problems of Hong Kong and Taiwan 99

1945 after Japan's defeat in World War Two when the Nationalist government was in nominal control of the mainland. The only territory remaining under Nationalist control during the intensifying civil war of the next four years, the island was converted into a military stronghold. In late 1949 Chiang Kai-shek and the Nationalist forces retreated to Taiwan at which time the People's Republic of China was established by Mao Tse-tung's victorious forces on the mainland.

HONG KONG

After World War Two the people of Hong Kong became well accustomed to operating in a "one country, two systems" context. As a British Crown Colony, Hong Kong had no parliament and its people could not vote. At the same time, while the British economy was subject to much government ownership, control, and interference, Hong Kong operated a free enterprise, free-trade system that was arguably the most private-sector oriented economy in the world. Blessed by a magnificent natural harbor and an economically strategic location, it flourished. To its natural and institutional advantages were added a sustained inflow of skilled, ambitious, hard-working people and a world environment that encouraged growth, market expansion, and world trade. The people of Hong Kong made good use of these advantages and out of a ruined outpost of the British empire at the end of World War Two they created a thriving, throbbing city-state based first on entrepôt trade, then on manufacturing, then increasingly on services.

Relations with China

Despite having economic systems that were diametrically the opposite of each other, the PRC and Hong Kong were important trading partners even in the Mao period. China was the largest source of Hong Kong's imports. Nearly half of the food and fresh water required by Hong Kong came from the mainland. Banks, retail, and trading enterprises owned by the mainland operated in Hong Kong and even during Mao's more radical experiments, cooperation between China and Hong Kong continued. Mutually agreed border controls over emigration to Hong Kong were maintained by China and food and water flows were never interrupted.

100   *China, Hong Kong, Taiwan and World Trade*

During the pre-reform period Hong Kong first developed into an export-oriented industrial economy and after the late 1960s a leading financial center. Its average annual real rate of growth was nearly 9 percent and in the late 1970s nearly 12 percent. It achieved the highest per capita income of the developing countries.[2]

Hong Kong's relationship with China deepened and quickened during the economic reform period. The Colony's own (domestic) exports to the PRC leaped upward (an average annual rate of over 100 percent, 1978–84), but even more important Hong Kong once again became an entrepôt for China as well as for many other countries. After 1980 the PRC became the largest market for Hong Kong's re-exports as well as the largest source of goods re-exported through Hong Kong.[3] Hong Kong's entrepôt trade, including products processed from Hong Kong materials in Hong Kong-owned plants in the PRC, became the most dynamic part of its dynamic economy. Re-exports accounted for more than 50 percent of GDP, with nearly half of that trade involving goods coming from China in 1988.[4]

Neither the course of Hong Kong's relationship with the PRC nor of its economic growth was smooth. In 1982 Hong Kong experienced two blows: The world economic recession brought a decline in the volume of the colony's exports. More ominously, China's demand for sovereignty over all of Hong Kong, long rumored but officially confirmed in that year, and a resulting row between China and Britain, shattered confidence in Hong Kong's future. The real estate and stock markets collapsed (prices fell by 50–70 percent), business and bank failures multiplied and growth plummeted to 1 percent from 9 percent the previous year. The Hong Kong dollar sank as capital started to leave the colony.[5] In 1983, in the face of a severe financial crisis, the government announced a stabilization plan that involved tightly linking the Hong Kong dollar to the U.S. dollar. Equally important, both Britain and China, chastened by the Hong Kong panic, became more accommodating. Britain agreed to cede sovereignty over all of Hong Kong and negotiations toward the goal of a 1984 bilateral agreement concerning the details of the transfer moved forward. Irrepressibly the Hong Kong economy recovered smartly, aided by an upturn in the U.S. and world economies.

For the rest of the decade, except 1985 when world trade stumbled, Hong Kong's economy boomed. Real GDP grew at nearly 10 percent in 1984, at 12 percent and 14 percent in 1986 and

"Greater China": Problems of Hong Kong and Taiwan   101

1987, at 7.5 percent in 1988.[6] Relations with China played an increasing role in Hong Kong's prosperity. Commencing in early 1985 the depreciation of the U.S. dollar to which the Hong Kong dollar was tied made Hong Kong exports more competitive in Europe and Japan. Between 1985 and 1988 the Hong Kong dollar fell 16 percent against the yen and 20 percent against the deutschmark. Then, as the Taiwanese and Korean currencies, under pressure from the U.S., appreciated in terms of the dollar, Hong Kong's competitive position further benefited.

Relations with the GATT

Underlying Hong Kong's booming economy was the sustained expansion of world trade after World War Two to which the operation of the GATT had contributed so significantly. Represented by the UK, Hong Kong had been a GATT member from the beginning and regarded the General Agreement as the cornerstone of its commercial policy. Hong Kong maintained no import quotas and levied no duties on imports (except for revenue levies on liquor, tobacco, cosmetics and some petroleum products from all sources, domestic and foreign); it subsidized nothing and thus was in no position to practice discrimination in trade. Hong Kong also signed the special GATT codes, with the exception of the aircraft agreement which was irrelevant for Hong Kong.[7] It was a member of the MFA (textile) agreement in its earliest form; indeed these agreements were originally modelled on a 1959 bilateral agreement with the UK restricting Hong Kong's cotton textile exports to Britain.[8] Hong Kong lived up to its obligations, used the GATT appeals mechanism when it believed other members were not doing so and was generally perceived to be a model GATT member. Indeed Hong Kong was a staunch and active supporter of the GATT whether acting indirectly through Britain or on its own behalf, as it did in the MFA.

Because of the importance to Hong Kong of trade and its membership in the GATT, the colony was greatly relieved that the Sino-British 1984 agreement specified that after 1997 Hong Kong could continue to participate in international economic and trade organizations and would remain a free port and a separate customs territory. It pressed the UK to negotiate separate GATT membership for Hong Kong both with China and with the GATT itself. In April 1986, under the sponsorship of the UK and with the support

102 *China, Hong Kong, Taiwan and World Trade*

of the PRC, Hong Kong became a full member in its own right, the 91st GATT contracting party.[9] The fact that China, only an observer at the GATT, not only supported this move but simultaneously announced that in 1997 Hong Kong would become a separate administrative region, strengthened its standing in the international community.[10]

Growth in the Late 1980s

After 1985, expanding world trade and exchange rate changes boosted not only exports of Hong Kong's goods but they did even more for its entrepôt trade. Aided by intermittent devaluations of the Chinese currency, Hong Kong's trade and investment in China flourished. Increasingly Hong Kong business set up shop across the border in China to produce or process goods destined for export. Foreigners, too, established bases in Hong Kong for doing the same thing. Three-way joint ventures between Hong Kong, foreign, and Chinese business grew in popularity.[11] In addition foreign businessmen establishing operations in China sought the advice and aid of the experienced entrepreneurs of Hong Kong. And because Hong Kong had the only deep-water port in South China capable of handling container cargo as well as a wealth of financial and trade services, much of China's escalating foreign trade was funneled through the colony.

Hong Kong's expanding business and investment with the neighboring parts of China was propelled by growing demand for its exports and the pressure of rising rents and wages in its cramped homeland. Growth rates well over 10 percent in 1986 and 1987 forced office and residential rents to jump by 40 percent or more while wages in some sectors went up by more than 20 percent, and the consumer price index approached double digits.[12] Manufacturing activity found room to expand across the border where rents were negotiable and labor costs one-third or less than those of Hong Kong. The service sector in the colony itself boomed with hotels, banks, investment and trade services increasingly sought out by foreigners doing business in Hong Kong, China, or other parts of Southeast Asia.

Meanwhile the ties between Hong Kong and China – and especially Guangdong province – had become broad and deep. Personal contacts between Hong Kong businessmen with friends and relatives across the border were many and often provided the

"Greater China": Problems of Hong Kong and Taiwan 103

basis for the joint ventures or processing agreements. In either case the Hong Kong partner typically provided equipment, training, capital; the Chinese partner, the plant and labor. In addition Hong Kong businessmen financed roads, factories, schools, and hospitals in China and sent funds to relatives in the north.

By the end of 1988, Hong Kong had established some 2500 joint ventures in China and was employing about 1.5 million Chinese there – in contrast to a manufacturing labor force at home of less than 900 000. Everyday an estimated 25 000 trucks crossed the border carrying components and materials to China and returning with processed goods for Hong Kong. About one-third of China's foreign currency earnings came from or through Hong Kong, and Hong Kong investment in China had provided nearly two-thirds of total foreign investment there by the end of 1988.[13]

Beyond trade and investment, cooperation at the government level for public utility development was many-sided. In the field of transportation, road, rail, air, sea, and river traffic between Hong Kong and the mainland was regulated by long-standing agreements, joint planning and frequent contacts. Also, linked electric power grids permitted a sharing of power during periods of peak demand. After 1979, the power flow was primarily from Hong Kong to Guangdong, through an interchange in Shenzhen which alleviated somewhat the chronic Chinese power shortage. The Shenzhen facility was operating at close to capacity in 1988; plans were under way to increase generating capacity on both sides of the border. Water flowed in the other direction under a 1980 agreement, with China providing about two-thirds of Hong Kong's total supply in 1988.[14]

Joint Declaration and Basic Law

On 26 September, 1984, the UK and PRC initialed the Joint Declaration on the Question of Hong Kong, an agreement spelling out the principles on which the PRC's policy toward Hong Kong would be based after 1997. It stated that Hong Kong would become a Special Administrative Region of China, enjoying a "high degree of autonomy" and maintaining existing econonic and trade systems for 50 years; human rights and private property rights would be protected by law. Hong Kong could participate in international economic and trade organizations, establish economic and trade missions in foreign countries and regions under the name "Hong

104   *China, Hong Kong, Taiwan and World Trade*

Kong, China." The agreement also outlined Hong Kong's form of government. It left the details to be negotiated between Britain and China, commencing in 1988, after which a "Basic Law" was to be enacted by China that would, in effect, be a constitution for Hong Kong.

The agreement was more detailed and reassuring than most had expected and although there were many ambiguities and some unanswered questions, a continuation of the status quo was reaffirmed for thirteen years. Since Hong Kong had always possessed a short-time horizon, expecting all investments even in real estate to be fully amortized over an interval of five years or so, there was still plenty of time for its people to go about their business.

Nonetheless, after its 1983 panic, Hong Kong remained tense and jittery, reacting to any actual or perceived change in China or elsewhere that might conceivably affect its status after 1997. The legal departure of Jardine Matheson, a long-established, highly respected British trading company that shifted its ownership to a holding company in Bermuda in 1984,[15] was a jolt to confidence and the stock market. Although the colony was relieved by its 1986 admission to the GATT as a full member, any perceived shift of power in Beijing away from the reformers, like the 1986 silencing of student protests or the dismissal in 1987 of Hu Yaobang from the chief party position, caused tremors in Hong Kong. More and more citizens decided to emigrate.

Despite the tension, however, Hong Kong remained largely an apolitical community. Hong Kong people were satisfied with the administration. Although they lacked self-government the British provided a rule of law that respected human rights, offered plentiful economic freedoms and maintained social and political stability. A pragmatic people, they were concerned more with performance than principle and the performance of the existing government drew high marks. They trusted the professional knowledge and technical skills of the bureaucrats and the system that had enabled them to make a decent living. Thus, they showed little interest in the Sino-British negotiations concerning the details of Hong Kong's system of government after 1997, believing that the proof of the pudding would come with the eating.[16]

The 1984 Agreement had promised self-government for Hong Kong but left it undefined. A small but active corps of Hong Kong residents believed that full democracy and universal suffrage were necessary to ensure Hong Kong's autonomy after 1997. This group

"Greater China": Problems of Hong Kong and Taiwan   105

was upset by the appearance in early 1989 of the second draft by China of the Basic Law for Hong Kong that proposed full democracy only after the year 2011 and by Britain's agreement that only 15 out of the 55 members of Hong Kong's legislature, the Legislative Council, would be directly elected in 1995 and in office in 1997 when China was to take over.[17] Between the end of February and the end of July 1989, the second draft would be discussed intensively and then its final form prepared for action by the People's Congress early in 1990.[18] Although most in Hong Kong agreed that the second draft of the Basic Law contained a number of improvements over its first draft, especially in important areas of Hong Kong's judicial and administrative autonomy, the provisions for elections were a disappointment.

The active democratic lobby periodically attempted to attract public notice and support for its cause and to combat the apathy that infected the majority of the population. Hunger strikes, burned copies of the first draft of the Basic Law, and student demonstrations brought out only small numbers, however.[19]

Apathy and inactivity evaporated in late May 1989 during the height of the student demonstrations in Beijing. In what was probably an unprecedented degree of voluntary public participation in a street demonstration anywhere, one million people out of Hong Kong's total population of 5.5 million turned out in support of the Chinese students. The Hong Kong stock market followed a roller-coaster course, plunging with martial law, soaring with an apparent weakening of Li Peng's position and collapsing again with rumors of gains by the hardliners.[20] When, after the weekend of bloodshed in Beijing, Hong Kong markets opened on June 5, Chinese-owned banks were beseiged by residents seeking to withdraw their deposits, and the stock exchange fell 400 points on opening. During the day security trucks replenished cash supplies drained by the runs on Chinese banks and by the day's end the stock exchange had lost 22 percent of its value.[21] Although activity was frenetic, there was no panic as the government acted successfully to provide liquidity and maintain confidence in the system.

Citizenship and Emigration

Hong Kong's reaction to the events in Beijing was heightened by a long simmering quarrel with Britain over the citizenship of its people. In 1981 London had finally removed the right of abode in

106 *China, Hong Kong, Taiwan and World Trade*

Britain from British subjects in Hong Kong. Affected were 3.3 million Chinese born in the colony who therefore held – or were eligible to hold – British Dependent Territories passports. The Hong Kong government had argued that some, or preferably all, of these people should have an ultimate right of abode in Britain, but London remained adamant. It claimed that an influx of that many people would produce intolerable economic and social strains in Britain. Lack of residency rights had contributed to the emigration of Chinese from Hong Kong; emigration had contributed to the growth-generated labor shortage there in the late 1980s.

Even the British agreed that the emigration would lessen if Hong Kong people had the right to live in Britain. Nearly 46 000 people emigrated in 1988, despite sharply higher wages and salaries, up from 30 000 in 1987 and an average of about 20 000 in the earlier years of the decade.[22] Even before the events of June, numbers were expected to rise in 1989 to 45–50 000. Most went to Canada, U.S., and Australia; about half were employed and about one-quarter of the total were professional and managerial workers. After establishing citizenship elsewhere, at least some émigrés returned to Hong Kong to work and add to their coffers.

After the Beijing repression, the number of applicants for emigration permits swamped consulates all over the colony, and Hong Kong officials and businessmen increased pressure on Britain to change its position. The Chinese in Hong Kong, whether entitled to a British National (Overseas) passport, which was no more than a travel document, or to a British Dependent Territories passport were, in Chinese law, ethnic Chinese and therefore Chinese nationals. After 1997, none would qualify for British consular protection. A British passport, however, would enable these Chinese to leave Hong Kong without problem even after 1997 and live at least temporarily in Britain while they rearranged their lives.[23]

The Future of Hong Kong

In the summer of 1989 the outlook for Hong Kong was bleak; even the professional optimism of civil servants was subdued. The soaring hopes for a considerably more democratic People's Republic that had dared to appear at the height of the Beijing student demonstration collapsed into anguish and despair after blood was shed. Where before the crackdown Hong Kong's fears were concentrated on the impact of Chinese control on the colony's economy and on whether

"Greater China": Problems of Hong Kong and Taiwan   107

its business might wither under Chinese bureaucratic interference, after June 4 the fear was of the presence of the People's Liberation Army. Where earlier it was largely the business community that feared a post-1997 invasion of bureaucrats, after June 4 the entire population feared a military invasion. The Sino-British agreement, after all, permitted PLA troops to be stationed in Hong Kong. Although there had been fears in Hong Kong about the future since the first Chinese demand for sovereignty in 1982, it had also been possible to hope for the best and to agree with the businessmen who said, "we must trust Beijing." In the summer of 1989 that trust was difficult to summon. References to Beijing's broken promises in Tibet were frequent.

Fears about post-1997 Hong Kong took many forms. The antipathy of hard-core Chinese communist ideologues for capitalism concerned many Hong Kong people. Many of the Chinese party cadres found vulgar and repulsive the greed and opportunism of the SEZs; the ability of such party members to accept an unchanged Hong Kong that they already viewed as the essence of unbridled capitalism could lead to future troubles, even if economic reformers were once again to come to the ascendancy.

Worry about the dangers of mismanagement of Hong Kong under Chinese sovereignty took on a sharper edge, even on the assumption of a well-meaning regime in Beijing. Corruption in business dealings with China had been common but corruption in Hong Kong had been kept under control by the colony's Independent Commission Against Corruption as well as other bodies. Could this success continue under the Chinese regime?

Then, too, Hong Kong was already flooded by many officials from the mainland. No one knew how many PRC-owned or PRC-controlled organisations already existed in Hong Kong. No count had ever been attempted by the Hong Kong government. Everyone was aware, however, that they were many in finance, trade and other services. The influence of the PRC in Hong Kong's daily life, moreover, had become increasingly evident, creating worry and resentment. PRC-owned businesses "played by different rules," being able to count on a government subsidy if they were inadvertently or purposefully mismanaged. Since after a decade of economic reform Beijing had taken no meaningful steps to eliminate subsidies or control corruption, there was little hope that it would do so in the next eight years.

Hong Kong's dependence on the mainland for food and water had always been an underlying source of concern both in terms of

108   *China, Hong Kong, Taiwan and World Trade*

security of supply and price. Runs on grocery stores in the colony had occurred whenever relations with Beijing became tense. China had never shut off the flow of food or water, but neither had the Chinese People's Liberation Army turned its guns on the Chinese people before 1989.

The impact of 1997 on Hong Kong's trade was always a primary concern and it, too, became sharper and more fearful in the summer of 1989. Hong Kong's economy had become much more dependent on the mainland than ever before and hence more vulnerable to any withdrawal of China into commercial isolationism. A China only marginally interested in trade with the West meant a withering of Hong Kong's role as an entrepôt and of Hong Kong's hopes of becoming the main international financial and service center of a rapidly growing China. If China reversed its "open door" policy, most of Hong Kong's industry would be seriously injured, dependent as it had become on labor-intensive operations on the mainland. Worse, a repressive authoritarian regime in Beijing could become an outcast of the world community subject to trade sanctions. As a part of China after 1997, Hong Kong would be likely to be included in these sanctions; if it were not, pressures from the mainland for aid in evading them could become irresistible. In either case Hong Kong's economic life as it had existed would be dead.

Hong Kong worried too about its continued membership in international organizations and especially the GATT after 1997. Membership in GATT was based on the ability of the member government (the relevant GATT article for Hong Kong's membership, Article XXVI, specified "government" not country) to differentiate its exports from those of any other source, and on the willingness of importers to accept the differentiation. Under usual conditions a stamp reading "made in Hong Kong" would be sufficient. After 1997 it was not inconceivable that unscrupulous mainland Chinese might stamp exports made on the mainland with the Hong Kong mark. Such misuse of the mark would continue to be a criminal act under Hong Kong law after 1997, but whether it would be prosecuted was a worry. Textile exports were always a special concern because of their importance to Hong Kong and because of the quota system imposed by the MFA. Even if China maintained a rigorous visa system of recording its textile exports after 1997, a soft textile market could lead producers abroad to agitate for combining the Chinese and Hong Kong quotas.

The announcement from Beijing, in July 1989, that "we will not allow people to use Hong Kong as a base for subverting the central

"Greater China": Problems of Hong Kong and Taiwan 109

people's government. Not engaging in activities to overthrow (the Chinese government) is a precondition for allowing (Hong Kong) to retain its capitalist system,"[24] added to Hong Kong's concerns about its immediate future as well as its position after 1997. Hong Kong residents had been active in collecting money to help the dissidents in China and in aiding activists to flee from the mainland. Deng Xiaoping had always made it clear that Hong Kong could maintain its own system after 1997 provided it did not attempt to replace the socialist system on the mainland. The draft of the Basic Law, moreover, gave Beijing the right to declare a state of emergency and impose its law on Hong Kong when it considered there was "turmoil" there as well as when China was at war.[25] And even if before 1997 Hong Kong were to attempt to outlaw support by its people for Chinese dissidents (which was highly unlikely), it would not be able to enforce such a restriction.

The previous complacency of Hong Kong about the period prior to 1997 evaporated in the summer of 1989. The growing labor shortage, partly the consequence of a flow of emigrants, was expected to jump and to cause further upward pressures on wages. In addition, a survey of industrialists taken in late June by the Federation of Hong Kong Industries indicated that about three-quarters of those questioned said they were now considering or planning emigration, up from about one-third in May.[26] The Hong Kong economy was already feeling a chill. Hotel occupancy rates were down, rents of apartments were declining and sales were becoming sluggish.[27] Signs of capital flight accumulated. Brokers reported that part of the rise in the Singapore stock exchange reflected transfers by Hong Kong investors looking for a safe haven.[28] Reports that Hong Kong investment and production companies were setting up overseas offices accumulated.[29]

Hong Kong's customers around the world, aware of the colony's deep dependence on the mainland for its manufacturing activities, had become concerned over whether Hong Kong businessmen could continue to fill their contracts. Guangdong's production had been largely unaffected by the turmoil in the north of China, but overseas buyers, anxious for secure sources of supply, were talking about shifting their orders away from Hong Kong.[30] Confidence in the Chinese-owned businesses in Hong Kong was hit especially hard as foreigners worried about their ability to meet commitments. Companies headed by Chinese with ties to Zhao Ziyang and the liberal faction of the Communist party were especially suspect.[31]

110 *China, Hong Kong, Taiwan and World Trade*

Rising wages, falling investment and business activity and a flight of entrepreneurs could deprive Hong Kong of the one attraction its system held for Beijing: its ability to aid China's economic development and exports. If, in 1997, the Chinese were to take over a depressed, run-down and inflationary economy, their excuse for "meddling" would be strong. Pessimism would feed on itself.

Optimistic voices heard in Hong Kong in the summer of 1989 now had a hollow ring for most residents. Nevertheless, the old arguments that had provided the basis for hope still adhered. As long as China continued to regard Hong Kong as a vital entrepôt, a door to the world, a source of management, marketing and financial skills, and a learning center, it was in China's self-interest to maintain confidence in Hong Kong and to maintain Hong Kong's system intact. Hong Kong itself could help in sustaining confidence. The shock of the June events was deep, but if Beijing's words and actions moderated and if Beijing acted to buoy confidence in Hong Kong, the shock would dissipate. Confidence could be rebuilt at least to some degree although the risk of doing business in Hong Kong would command a greater premium than before.

The Hong Kong government itself undertook a variety of confidence-boosting measures. Not only did it push the British on the passport and right-of-abode issue, it went ahead with plans for a new airport, a new port and an expansion of the transport network leading into China.[32]

The flexibility of the Hong Kong economy, moreover, and its ability to bounce back had been well demonstrated many times. Confidence had been jolted before, causing investment in Hong Kong to drop off, but rising returns to investment eventually brought the capital back. Most of the economic fundamentals of Hong Kong remained unchanged. First, there was still time for at least one more cycle of investment. Hong Kong had always looked for full amortization in the short run and recently many projects had offered full returns in three to five years. Although Beijing might be placing a lower priority on its "open door" policy than previously, economic growth was still important to the leadership and in the party's self-interest. Hong Kong could play an important role in helping to maintain growth rates on the mainland, providing technical, financial and professional expertise in addition to its complete trade infrastructure.[33]

Second, Hong Kong remained a superb geographic location for many activities and the only deep-water port south of Dalian in

"Greater China": Problems of Hong Kong and Taiwan   111

northern China. Hong Kong was the chosen location of foreign business for overseeing their interests elsewhere in Southeast Asia. It was an entrepôt not only for China but for most of the area. As a free port it was a shopping heaven for the Japanese and a shopping attraction for foreigners worldwide. These advantages were not likely to change quickly. There was, moreover, no immediate alternative to Hong Kong as a financial center. Singapore was most often mentioned, but its regulations were tighter than those of Hong Kong and far less predictable under its aging President Lee Kuan Yew. Hong Kong's high technology communications network, its unrestricted foreign exchange flows and low taxes were hard to replicate.[34] Certain foreigners in Hong Kong observed, moreover, that the Basic Law accorded them more rights than they were then enjoying, since British laws favored the British in Hong Kong over other foreigners.

Hong Kong's high quality work force was leaving in larger numbers and getting more expensive, true. Still the emigration drain was limited by the fact that receiving countries were at, or close to, their immigration quotas and waiting periods for would-be emigrants were getting longer. International companies were coping by rotating some of their employees through their foreign offices or hiring foreigners. At least one-third, possibly much more, of the population was unable to leave, lacking money, family abroad or the skills required by immigration quotas. Some, having established foreign residency requirements, returned to work in Hong Kong. Also, as Ronald Skeldon of the University of Hong Kong pointed out,[35] emigration might be part of the solution to Hong Kong's continued prosperity. Despite emigration Chinese communities being set up around the world were likely to retain contacts with Hong Kong and each other; their business interests were likely to involve Hong Kong, China and Southeast Asia. Thus as emigration increased so did the number of these expatriates whose experience and contacts would lead to business with Hong Kong. Emigration could be a stabilising factor as 1997 approached, rather than a destructive one.

In addition, government policy had been aiming at a slowing of Hong Kong's frenetic growth rates. Inflation had reached the double digits in late spring of 1989 and a decline in property values was viewed as overdue. The government's response had been an increasingly tight fiscal policy and a sizeable budget surplus (that later would be available for financing large infrastructure projects).

112   *China, Hong Kong, Taiwan and World Trade*

Thus the blow to confidence in early June in economic terms had a silver lining. Further, the fact that the Hong Kong dollar had remained steady in the immediate aftermath of the Beijing bloodshed suggested that the confidence level was retrievable.

Finally, it had long been argued that China's goal of a reunification of Taiwan with the mainland underlined the importance to China of proving that its "one country, two systems" policy could work. The Taiwan issue gave high priority in Beijing to the maintenance of confidence in Hong Kong. If the Hong Kong economy should wither, China's hopes for peaceful reunification of Taiwan would be indefinitely postponed.

Thus there were logical reasons against allowing despair in Hong Kong to become all-consuming. Hong Kong could still hope (and fervently did) for a return of the moderate economic reformers to control in Beijing. All Hong Kong could realistically do meanwhile was attempt to make the best of a bad situation by keeping itself a viable economy of value to China. In the short run that might not be sufficient; a diaspora might be inevitable. Still that, too, had happened before, during the Japanese occupation of World War Two. Then, after the Japanese defeat, the people had returned to Hong Kong to go on to bigger and better things.

TAIWAN

For the people of Taiwan, who were ecstatic supporters of the demonstrating students in Beijing, the events commencing on June 3–4 brought a stark realization of the preposterous futility of their claim to represent all of China. For although they now had improved circumstantial evidence to support that claim, they could do nothing about it. Deep and bitter frustration was the prevailing reaction in Taiwan. For forty years the Taiwan people had harbored a dream of one day returning to the mainland to the tumultous welcome of the assembled multitudes. The dream had faded in recent years, but events in May had reawakened it. Taiwan, however, had less than 20 million people; there were sixty times that number on the mainland. And the dream had no longer included a military invasion of the mainland against opposing forces.

Originally it had. For a decade or two after their 1949 retreat to Taiwan, the Nationalists spoke bravely but vaguely about recapturing the mainland. At the same time Communist dogma talked about

"Greater China": Problems of Hong Kong and Taiwan   113

conquering Taiwan by force. Neither side attempted to put its words into action, powerfully dissauded by the presence of the US Seventh Fleet and a formal mutual defense treaty between the US and Taiwan.

In the meantime the people on Taiwan had gone about the business of making the island strong, militarily and economically. The mainlanders – those living in Taiwan (and their children) who moved to the island between 1945 and 1950 – concentrated on defense and politics. The Taiwanese – those others born and raised in Taiwan, speaking Chinese, whose ancestors had migrated from the mainland 300 years earlier – concentrated on business. The mainlanders dominated the government, whose legislature represented all Chinese provinces and most of whose members therefore were those elected on the mainland in the 1940s. The Taiwanese, representing only one province, held only a sprinkling of seats (less than 12 percent). The Nationalist Party, the Kuomintang, led by President Chiang Kai-shek, was preoccupied with military matters and returning to the mainland.

The party turned over the management of the economy to technicians, chose a highly skilled and competent group of economic planners and set in motion a land reform program that distributed the large Taiwanese estates to landless peasants. Landowners were compensated in the form of stock in the formerly Japanese-owned industry. In addition, reflecting traditional Chinese reverence for education and scholarship, the Nationalists established a system of high quality schools and colleges, access to whose higher levels was on the basis of merit. Equality of educational opportunity was never questioned by the regime's critics.[36]

The Economic Miracle

The economy taken over by the Kuomintang was almost entirely agricultural. The Japanese had established utilities on Taiwan and permitted sugar mills and some light industry, but even textiles were of negligible importance in 1945. The land reform program sponsored by the Kuomintang in the 1950s was hugely successful and frequently cited by economists and sociologists as a model for establishing a prosperous and stable rural community. It was essential to the economic miracle that started in the 1960s. It produced the crops that fed the growing cities and earned the foreign exchange to finance industrialization. The previous owners

114 *China, Hong Kong, Taiwan and World Trade*

of the landed estates, moreover, now owned the island's industry and turned their attention to business.

The economic planners first concentrated Taiwan's industrialization on labor-intensive goods for export markets while working to improve the island's infrastructure, extending its transport and communications systems and constructing an environment favorable to investment and growth. Later the emphasis shifted from raw and processed farm goods and light textiles to increasingly sophisticated products involving more capital and higher value-added by manufacture. The success of the program was supported by high savings patterns (one-third of GNP) and a tax system that enabled the island to become self-sufficient in capital in the 1970s while maintaining an equality of income distribution on a par with that of the U.S., Japan, and Western Europe. U.S. economic aid (a total of $1.7 billion) helped in the early years, but it ended in 1965. U.S. military aid and especially its mutual defense treaty with Taiwan were essential to the security and stability required to attract investment.[37]

During its first two decades after the advent of the Kuomintang the economy of Taiwan grew at an average annual rate of more than 8 percent; during the 1970s GNP grew at over 9 percent and exports at over 30 percent. Investment grew even more rapidly than GNP, rising from less than 12 percent of GNP in the early 1950s to more than one-quarter at the end of the 1970s. Moreover the importance of foreign capital in domestic capital formation dropped sharply from 40 percent during the 1950s to an outflow of capital in the 1970s as loan repayments exceeded new foreign investment. Under the Japanese Taiwan's average per capita income had never reached $100; at the end of the 1970s it was approaching $1,500.[38]

The data give no indication that the 1970s was a decade of shocks for Taiwan. The decade started with Taiwan's being voted out of the UN in 1971, to be replaced by the PRC. The visit of Secretary of State Kissinger to Beijing in that year, followed by the 1972 visit of President Nixon to China, its concluding Shanghai communique establishing direct relations between the U.S. and the PRC, and the Japanese switch of diplomatic recognition to the PRC in the same year, represented a series of rapid seismic thrusts at Taiwan. Then the oil crisis of 1973–74, at a time when three-quarters of the island's energy needs was being met by imports, brought a pause in economic growth and a deepening awareness of the island's many vulnerabilities.

"Greater China": Problems of Hong Kong and Taiwan   115

Although the Shanghai communique had foreshadowed the shift of U.S. recognition from Taiwan to the PRC, derecognition, when it was announced at the end of 1978, came as another shock. The island was incredulous and indignant. A large part of the shock and dismay stemmed from the awkward and undiplomatic fashion in which the U.S. State Department handled the affair, but still the loss of U.S. diplomatic recognition and the ending of the mutual security treaty represented the cutting of an umbilical cord after three decades of support and protection.

Despite Taiwan's worries about the impact of derecognition on trade, investment, its international legal status and the possibility of a Chinese invasion, the economy did not hiccup. The Chinese, moreover, ceased shelling the islands of Quemoy and Matsu (which they had been doing regularly with propaganda leaflets every other day) and began a series of friendly overtures to Taiwan.

During the 1980s the island's economic progress was in many ways more spectacular than that of the 1970s. Per capita income quadrupled to over $6000 by 1988, putting Taiwan in the same league as Spain and Israel and just behind Hong Kong and Singapore among the LDC's. Its international currency reserves, the second largest in the world, amounted to $4000 for every human being on the island. In 1987 it was the 13th biggest trading country in the world and the 11th biggest exporter, losing to Belgium-Luxembourg for a place in the top ten. While its average growth rate (1980–88) was just under 8 percent, this was a decline from double-digit growth earlier caused in large part by a restructuring of the economy and a tightening of monetary policy as inflation became a threat in the booming domestic market.

The Role of Trade

Taiwan's economic growth was propelled by foreign trade. After the mid-1970s exports represented more than half of GDP on the average, up from 11 percent in 1960. While industrial products accounted for less than one-third of exports in 1960, they rose even more rapidly than total exports to make up 94 percent of the total in 1987. The remainder was agricultural or processed agricultural products. Imports grew only somewhat less rapidly, from just under 20 percent of GDP in 1960 to 46 percent in 1988. Raw materials always dominated imports, remaining at about two-thirds of the total. Capital goods ranged from 25 percent to 30 percent of imports while consumer goods remained flat at less than 10 percent.[39]

116 *China, Hong Kong, Taiwan and World Trade*

Trade with Japan and the U.S. always dominated Taiwan's foreign commerce, increasingly so for exports as time progressed, but less so for imports. Together the two top trading partners provided just under one-half of Taiwan's export markets in 1960 but 57 percent in 1987; in contrast their import share dropped from 73 percent to 56 percent over the same period. Meanwhile the U.S. share of Taiwan's export market rose from less than 12 percent to nearly 50 percent in 1988 while Japan's dropped from 38 percent to 14 percent. The opposite shift occurred in the U.S. role in imports. In 1960 the United States had provided 38 percent of Taiwan's imports, but it supplied only 22 percent in 1987. Japan's share of Taiwan's imports remained about the same, however, at approximately one-third. For the rest, Taiwan's trade was spread over a large number of trading partners, the share of no one country ever achieving as much as 10 percent.

In the 1960s Taiwan had an import surplus with both Japan and the United States, a consequence of the net flow of foreign capital into Taiwan. Taiwan's trade with Japan was in deficit consistently throughout the post-war years with a sole exception in 1955. In contrast Taiwan's trade with the United States shifted from a deficit to a surplus in 1968 and remained so through the 1980s. The shift in the U.S. position reflected the ending of U.S. aid and Taiwan's transformation from a debtor toward a net creditor internationally.[40]

The spectacular export surpluses generated by Taiwan in the 1980s, which at their peak in 1986 represented more than one-fifth of GNP, produced a variety of economic and political problems for the island. They grew out of an increasingly undervalued exchange rate.[41] Productivity in Taiwan was increasing much more rapidly than that of its major trading partners in the U.S. and Europe. Wages on the island lagged farther and farther behind productivity advances and in addition after 1983 Taiwanese wholesale prices declined. The resulting cost advantage was not reflected in the foreign value of its currency. Taiwan's foreign currency reserves mounted, the money supply rose, but businesses and individuals had few outlets for their surplus funds. Booming equity and real estate markets absorbed some of the liquidity but with imports tightly controlled, resource allocation concentrated on exports and the banks unwilling to lend to any except sanctioned borrowers, the dangers of inflation became awesome.[42]

The trade imbalance also was the source of considerable friction in Taiwan's relations with its major trading partner, the United

"Greater China": Problems of Hong Kong and Taiwan 117

States. Taiwan responded to a variety of pressures from embittered U.S. officials for liberalization of imports and currency appreciation. Between mid-1986 and early 1989 its currency, the New Taiwan (NT) dollar, appreciated by more than 40 percent and its import regime was dramatically changed. Import duties were slashed and requirements for licenses reduced. Average tariff rates of 27 percent at the end of 1986 (a significant understatement because of the importance of prohibitive rates) fell to about 12 percent by late 1988 with the rate on American imports put at about 5 percent.[43] In 1988 Taiwan spent at least 50 percent more on imported goods than it had in the previous year as prices of imports in NT$ collapsed.[44] U.S. consumer goods were especially popular in the booming Taiwanese market. Exports meanwhile started to decline causing the trade balance to drop and business to worry about losing markets to cheaper sources in China and Southeast Asia.

The accomplishments of the Chinese on Taiwan, in converting a feudal, agricultural, sleepy community into a modern industrial state in two generations, were remarkable and often remarked upon. Like Hong Kong, Taiwan was fortunate in its timing. It commenced its drive for growth when world markets were expanding, trade barriers falling and economic growth worldwide being propelled by trade expansion. Unlike Hong Kong, however, Taiwan did not maintain an open market; the role of the government in its economic development was active not passive. Until the late 1980s imports were strictly controlled by licenses and tariffs, many prohibitively high. Industrial development was guided by the economic planners through rigid controls over all parts of the financial sector.

The Financial Sector

All banks were government-owned or government-controlled, and their number limited to sixteen. Foreign banks were narrowly confined in the functions they could fill.[45] Not only were banks required to operate according to rigid lending regulations but they were often ordered to extend "policy" loans at below prevailing interest rates to industries that the government wished to encourage. Interest rates were subject to ceiling and floor limits.[46] Capital movements similarly were strictly controlled and the foreign exchange rate for the NT dollar maintained at a level that encouraged exports. In short, free enterprise on Taiwan was controlled and directed by the economic planners who took full advantage of an hospitable world environment for growth.

118   *China, Hong Kong, Taiwan and World Trade*

Imports were not the only area of liberalization in the late 1980s. Controls over the financial sector were loosened, at first in response to pressure from the U.S. and then because of internal anomalies. The ceiling was raised, for example, on the amount of loans foreign banks could make in Taiwan and the issue of U.S. credit cards was permitted.[47] A limited number of U.S. insurance companies was permitted to do business in Taiwan (other foreign firms were still excluded). Most foreign exchange controls were relaxed in 1987 and within limits capital allowed to leave the island.

The increased liquidity of the banking system as bank loans lagged far behind accumulating savings brought a torrent of criticism of domestic banks from business and professional sources in Taiwan. Liquidity in some banks was so high, in fact, that they refused to accept large new deposits.[48] Yet lending regulations were so rigid (loan officers in some cases were held personally responsible for bad loans) that many small businesses had to turn to the unregulated gray market for funds where they paid extortionist interest rates. One estimate indicated that private enterprise relied on the gray market for nearly one-third of its funds, with bank loans accommodating less than half of borrowing requirements.

At the end of the decade a new banking bill was signed into law permitting new private banks to be established, foreign banks to accept savings deposits, offer longer-term loans and engage in a trust business. It also removed controls on interest rates.[49] It further contained provisions that would permit regulators to eliminate or control the lending operations of the gray market which had been allowed to flourish because of its strong political connections.[50] Although the markets still remained highly restricted, Taiwan had taken the essential first steps toward open financial sectors.

Political Change

The 1980s also brought a staggering degree of liberalization in the political life of the island. With the aging of the Kuomintang migrants, their children took over leading positions in the party and government. The younger generation was mostly Taiwan-born, well educated and more flexible and pragmatic than its elders. "Indigenization," the process of bringing more and more Taiwanese into positions of control, started under President Chiang Ching-kuo, the Generalissimo's son and progressed apace under his successor, President Lee Teng-hui, thus diffusing tensions that had built

"Greater China": Problems of Hong Kong and Taiwan   119

between Taiwanese and mainlanders during earlier years. President Lee himself, who assumed office in January 1988 upon "CCK"'s death, was Taiwanese.

In mid-1987 martial law was lifted – for the first time in thirty-eight years – and the island changed from a repressive authoritarian fortress to a much more open society. Some human rights were still abridged – most notably political representation. The press was no longer controlled, however; demonstrations were permitted, strikes and collective bargaining were legitimized and the Kuomintang was no longer the sole legal political party. Political pluralism was permitted and to the relief of many the chief opposition party (Democratic Progressive Party) came under the control of moderates who opposed advocating independence for Taiwan. In 1988, for the first time, the policymaking body of the Kuomintang, the Central Standing Committee, had among its members a majority who were Taiwanese.[51] Independence, long a sensitive issue, was close to becoming a non-issue on Taiwan.[52] Independence was sensitive because implicitly it would deny the legitimacy of Kuomintang control. It implied that reunification with the mainland was not a goal for Taiwan and hence that Taiwan did not claim to represent all of China. Ever since 1949 both Beijing and Taipei had insisted that there was only one China and that Taiwan was a province of China. Only eight months before the bloodshed in Tiananmen Square, President Lee in reviewing his troops on Taiwan's national day had told them that their mission was still the "recovery of the mainland."[53] Further, Beijing had long stated that it would invade and take Taiwan by force if Taiwan should declare independence. Recommending independence always had been legally a seditious act, as it continued to be after martial law was removed. After 1987, however, the law was no longer enforced.

Liberalization also extended to Taiwan's relations with China, although at a much more modest pace. Ever since 1949 Taiwan's policy toward the mainland had been summarized as the "three noes" – no contact, no negotiation, no compromise. Step by step the three noes were loosened in the late 1980s. In 1987 Taipei first permitted mail to be sent directly to the mainland through the Red Cross in Taipei. Further its citizens were legally allowed to travel to the mainland, to visit relatives there. Forty years of unrealizable curiosity about the mainland and especially about relatives on the mainland immediately brought a flood of applications for permission to visit.[54] A total ban on visits to Taiwan by people from the

120   *China, Hong Kong, Taiwan and World Trade*

mainland was loosened somewhat in 1988 to permit mainland Chinese to visit sick relatives or attend a funeral on the island. The more restrictive treatment of visits from the mainland was probably less due to a concern over security than to worry over an inundation of defectors larger than the crowded island could absorb. Denying sanctuary to mainland defectors was unthinkable; hence the only solution was to limit the number of visitors.

Although trade with the mainland had been totally banned until 1988, a small but rapidly rising amount of goods moved between the two places, indirectly through Hong Kong, Japan, or elsewhere. The flow picked up steam after exchange rate changes beginning in 1985 made competitiveness in the U.S. market a matter of increasing concern to Asian suppliers. In the late 1980s Taiwan, like Hong Kong but to a lesser degree, faced a shortage of industrial land and labor.[55] The land shortage was partly artificial, due to legal protections for agricultural land, but the island's average population density was exceeded in the entire world only by Bangladesh.[56] Labor shortages and rising wages attracted illegal immigrants from low-wages Asian countries and generated a national debate over labor imports.[57] Taiwan businessmen in high labor-intensive industries noted Hong Kong's advantages in trading with and investing in China and sought to replicate them. Aided by skilled Taiwanese lawyers, they established Hong Kong companies to trade with or produce in China. Others set up plants in China with Hong Kong partners.[58]

Taiwan's two-way trade with the mainland amounted to less than $1 billion before 1985 (according to Hong Kong data) and was predominantly a flow of Taiwan's manufactured goods to the PRC. In the early 1980s, seeking to improve relations with its claimed province, Beijing had admitted goods from Taiwan free of customs duties, treating them as internal trade. The flow of mainland goods to Taiwan was much smaller consisting primarily of herbal medicines, tolerated by Taiwan officials. After 1985 trade volume rose rapidly, but from a very small base. Re-exports through Hong Kong to Taiwan of PRC merchandise became more than twice as large as the reverse flow in the late 1980s. Two-way trade through Hong Kong reached $1.5 billion in 1987 and $2 billion in 1988. Taking account of other shipments through Japan and Singapore probably raised the total exchange with the PRC to something approaching $3 billion, still a small fraction of Taiwan's total trade of $110 billion. Estimates of Taiwanese investment in the PRC which was concen-

"Greater China": Problems of Hong Kong and Taiwan   121

trated in Fujian province across the straits varied from $200 million to $400 million.[59]

Trade and investment with the PRC received a vigorous push in October 1988 when the Nationalists at a Party Congress endorsed more liberal trade and travel policies toward the mainland. Indirect imports of thirty important industrial and agricultural raw materials were to be permitted legally as was investment in China through third countries. In addition visits in both directions of journalists, intellectuals, students, artists, entertainers and such would be allowed after government screening.[60]

The looser party position was an acknowledgement of reality. It recognized the deterioration of Taiwan's competitive position in world markets and the necessity for its industrialists to lower costs in the face of rising wages and land scarcities at home. It also recognized that Taiwan's arch competitor, South Korea, was expanding its ties with the PRC and would benefit from lower costs on the mainland; thus to avoid being left behind in the competitive race, Taiwan had to react.[61]

The necessity for trading indirectly with the mainland added to Taiwan's costs. Not only was the trade route circuitous and thus transport costs higher than need be, but goods had to be off-loaded in the third port, although they might subsequently be loaded again on the same ship, further inflating costs. Nonetheless mainland prices were so much lower than those in alternative markets that indirect trade was still profitable. Late in 1988 the off-loading requirement was lifted, although the necessity for stopping at a third port remained.[62]

Trade and investment were also encouraged by a series of overtures from the mainland. In July 1988, just prior to the meeting of the Nationalist Party in Taiwan, Beijing announced that Taiwanese investors could put money into any project on the mainland, in contrast to foreigners who were limited to industries targeted for development. The Taiwanese could appoint the Chairman of the Board of a joint venture, and Beijing promised to speed their investment application process, guaranteed that there would be no nationalization of Taiwanese-owned assets and that secrecy would be maintained.[63] Beijing also hinted that it might be willing to renounce the use of force, to abandon its "Four Cardinal Principles" of Communism, and share power with the Kuomintang if Taiwan would give up any claim to independence.[64]

122 *China, Hong Kong, Taiwan and World Trade*

Foreign Policy

The economic and political liberalization of Taiwan commencing in 1987 was official recognition of the increasing anomalies of the island's existence. In 1985, for example, *The Economist*[65] had commented that if Taiwan were a person it would be in the hands of a psychiatrist; in 1986 the *Financial Times* (London) referred to the island's "obsessive paranoia."[66] The government claimed to represent all of China and yet ruled only one province; the government's legitimacy was based on that claim which was recognized by only a handful of countries abroad and had diminishing support at home. Taiwan was becoming increasingly wealthy, increasingly important in international commerce, and yet increasingly isolated and an object of mounting impatience in most of the rest of the world. Meanwhile the government's nemesis, the Communist regime on the mainland, was impressing the world with its reasonableness, its peaceful intentions and its patient overtures toward its renegade province. Taiwan's intransigent rebuffs were increasingly perceived as nihilistic and irascible. Something had to be done.

Basic to the anomalies confronting Taiwan had been the leadership's sterile view of the island's future: the passive hope that eventually Taiwan's example might convert the mainland to democracy and free enterprise. Further, the opposition had nothing better to offer. Its demand for "self-determination" was viewed in Beijing and in parts of Taiwan as a code for independence. Beijing had long made it clear that a declaration of independence on Taiwan, like "turmoil" there or a Taiwanese-Soviet pact would occasion the use of military force against the island. Many in Taiwan, meanwhile, both in the opposition and in the Kuomintang, had been agitating for more economic, social and cultural contacts with the mainland. The October 1988 loosening of restrictions on contacts with the mainland initiated a new active foreign policy by Taiwan.

The new policy was two-pronged. First, it sought to use Taiwan's political and economic development actively as a model to influence the pace of reform on the mainland through more personal contacts and trade. It still endorsed the "three noes," but now "no contact" meant "no official contact." The goal was the same, but now many more people would be directly exposed to the very different levels of living between Taiwan and the mainland.

Visitors from Taiwan would see the scarcities, feel the restrictions, observe the immobility and learn through personal experience

"Greater China": Problems of Hong Kong and Taiwan   123

of contrast to value their own system more. Visitors from the mainland would in the same way learn what a difference the system makes. They would see first-hand what a per capita income twenty times their own means and how much greater the rewards to their own efforts would be if their system were to be changed. Thus it was hoped that the base of support for the Kuomintang at home would be broadened and strengthened while that for the communist conservatives abroad would be weakened and dissipated.

Second, the new policy also sought to use Taiwan's economic strength to end its isolation from the world community and to improve its foreign relations. It set up a $1 billion economic aid program to help developing countries friendly to Taiwan and another smaller fund to sponsor international educational conferences, academic exchanges and such. It sought to increase the number of countries granting diplomatic recognition to Taiwan as well as to expand its informal relations with other countries.[67]

Taiwan's new "flexible diplomacy" sent a high-level delegation, headed by its President, to visit Singapore, a country having diplomatic relations with neither China nor Taiwan. The new diplomacy allowed its President to be referred to as "from Taiwan," rather than from "the Republic of China" on which it had always previously insisted.[68] It allowed its Finance Minister to head a Taiwanese delegation to the Annual Meeting of the Asian Development Bank in Beijing under the name "Taipei, China."[69] It endorsed a concept of "one China, two equal governments" that would effectively recognize the legitimacy of the communist government on the mainland while giving the government on Taiwan an equal status.

Taiwan and the GATT

Taiwan's new pro-active foreign policy also sponsored a campaign to gain entry into the major international organizations from which the island was excluded. Because the Nationalists were in nominal control of the mainland during the immediate post-war years when the major international economic organizations were established, they had represented China in the IMF, the World Bank and the GATT and had held the China seat in the UN even after their retreat to Taiwan. With the exception of the GATT they retained their membership in these organizations until they were voted out to be replaced by the PRC or until the PRC was admitted.

124 *China, Hong Kong, Taiwan and World Trade*

In some cases the organization's procedures would have permitted Taiwan to continue as a member, but the Nationalists had adamantly refused to be present at any gathering containing representatives of the Chinese Communist Party or to accept any change in legal status that implied that Taiwan was subordinate to the Beijing government. The IMF, in particular, was flexible in its criteria for membership and the United States sought to have Taiwan's association with the Fund continued after its executive directors voted in 1980 to make the PRC a member. Taiwan refused, however, to accept any name implying that it represented something less than all of China.[70]

In the case of the General Agreement on Tariffs and Trade the Nationalists, as representatives of China in 1947–48, had been a leader in the original drafting group of efforts to ensure that developing country interests were adequately covered.[71] At the first round of tariff negotiations under the new agreement in Geneva in 1950, the Nationalist representatives formally withdrew China from the General Agreement, explaining that their government could no longer insure that all of China would abide by the rules of the GATT. The Nationalists were aware that the negotiated tariff concessions would apply to all exports from China, and that the beneficiary would be primarily the mainland. Since Taiwan's interest in foreign trade in early 1950 was negligible and since it was then considering a policy of import substitution rather than export expansion, withdrawing from the GATT as a preclusive move against the mainland must have been perceived as in the short-run and long-run national interests of the Kuomintang.[72]

By 1965, however, having entered upon a program of rapid economic growth based on export expansion, Taiwan sought and obtained observer status in the GATT. As the island's economy was highly protected from import competition and the authorities saw few benefits from full GATT membership, observer status permitted Taiwan to attend all meetings but exempted it from all obligations. It remained as an observer until 1971 when the PRC was admitted to the UN as the sole representative of China. While not technically a UN agency, the GATT was constructed under UN sponsorship in the 1940s and since then generally had behaved as if it were a UN agency. After seating the PRC, the UN General Assembly recommended that its specialized agencies review their China representation; thereupon GATT withdrew Taiwan's observer status.

Taiwan's trade after 1980 was conducted primarily on the basis of bilateral reciprocal trade agreements with its trading partners.

"Greater China": Problems of Hong Kong and Taiwan 125

Tariffs on imports from those countries with whom Taiwan had such an agreement were more favorable than those in the general customs duty list. In the late 1980s, 98 percent of Taiwan's imports received the reciprocal duty rates.[73] In terms of tariff schedules, therefore, Taiwan's trade regime was similar to that of GATT members who generally levied duties according to two schedules, one containing MFN rates, the other containing generally applicable mandated rates.

As a consequence of the liberalizing efforts undertaken by Taiwan in response to U.S. pressures in the 1980s, Taiwan's trade regime had been brought closer to that which would be required if the island were a full GATT member. In addition, upon embarking on the policy of flexible diplomacy, the government undertook a survey of all of its trade rules and regulations to determine what adjustments would be necessary to bring Taiwan into full compliance with GATT.[74]

In mid-1988 and continuing through the first half of 1989, a remarkable series of articles entitled "Lifting the Veil of the GATT" (Jiekai GATT de Miansha) began to appear weekly in the Taiwan press. The articles examined in great detail the nature of GATT rules and their applicability to Taiwan. The series written by Yen Ching-Chang, Executive Secretary of the Taxation and Tariff Commission, Ministry of Finance, appeared in the *China Times* (Zhongguo Shibao), one of the island's most widely read newspapers. It clearly was an attempt to educate Taiwan on the intricacies of GATT and its importance to the island. The approach of the articles, however, was not propagandistic, but rather scholarly and objective in its probing and evaluations. The series suggested that while Taiwan would have to make many detailed adjustments in its practices and procedures, some of which would require potentially painful changes on the part of Taiwanese industry in order to comply fully with GATT, the adjustments were all quite feasible.

The most difficult would be the elimination of quantitative restrictions, especially those based on the country of a product's origin which were blatantly discriminatory in nature. (GATT Article XIII specifies that when in extremis quantitative restrictions are employed by a member, they must be non-discrimatory.) In responding to U.S. pressures for import liberalization Taiwan had loosened restrictions on American goods while retaining tighter limits on import from other sources. In 1989 imports of small sedans

126   *China, Hong Kong, Taiwan and World Trade*

from Japan were banned, for example, and small car imports from Korea subject to quota, while no quantitative limits were levied on automobile imports from the U.S. and Europe. (All automobile imports were subject to the same tariff regardless of the source country.) If Taiwan were to give free access to Japanese and Korean cars in its market, the competitive impact on its own automobile producers could force a substantial contraction of production. Nevertheless the opening of the market to all foreign producers on equal terms could be phased in over a period of time in order to minimize the impact and allow the domestic industry time to adjust.

Except for the case of quantitative restrictions, the adjustments required for GATT compliance were not likely to have a major impact on Taiwan. The list of countries with whom Taiwan did not have reciprocal trade agreements contained GATT members exclusively. MFN rates would have to be applied to imports from these countries, were Taiwan to join the GATT. The list, however, was made up mostly of small countries with whom trade would probably not be large – countries in central Africa and Eastern Europe. Israel, the most important trading country in the group, was oriented toward Europe and the U.S. rather than Asia.

Similarly Taiwan's rules of customs procedures and practices would require revisions, but as Mr Yen concluded, Taiwan's regulations were illogical and antiquated and required modernization in any event. "National treatment" rules of the GATT – regulations that forbade giving more favorable treatment to domestic than to foreign products, especially in taxes – also would require assorted and detailed adjustments. The entertainment tax rate on foreign language films was higher than that on Chinese-speaking films, for example, and thus discriminated against all imported films except those produced in Hong Kong. On the other hand Taiwan's anti-dumping and countervailing duty laws were in accord with GATT regulations. Taiwan did not use export subsidies. In short Taiwan had made so many changes in its trade regime by the late 1980s that adjusting to GATT requirements would not be unduly burdensome to the economy.

In addition to doing its homework in hopeful preparation for GATT membership, Taiwan informally let it be known abroad that it was interested in rejoining the GATT and other international economic organizations. Its campaign started with a news conference in November 1987 in Taipei at which a spokesman for the Foreign Ministry announced that the government was studying a

"Greater China": Problems of Hong Kong and Taiwan 127

proposal to rejoin the GATT.[75] Its efforts were supported by scattered editorial comment and news items abroad,[76] but the reaction of foreign diplomats was primarily a resigned negative. While admitting that Taiwan was too important an economic power to be excluded, most foreign governments were unwilling to support Taiwan's membership unless Beijing assented.

Beijing meanwhile had become more and more agitated over the early successes of the island's forward diplomacy. During a state visit by Taiwan's leader to the Bahamas in early 1989, for example, the massive shift in diplomatic recognition away from Taiwan to the PRC that had been underway since the early 1970s was finally reversed. The Bahamas became the 23rd nation to recognize the Republic of China. Singapore had agreed to give Taiwan investors legal protection.[77] Further Taiwan had opened new trade or representative offices in Canada, Egypt, Liberia, Mexico, Sri Lanka, and Turkey. Australia, Britain, Ireland, France and Norway had begun to issue visas in Taipei (rather than through their embassies in neighboring countries) and other countries eased visa restrictions on Taiwan's citizens. The opening of a European Chamber of Commerce in Taiwan and the willingness of the European Community to send representatives to conferences with Taiwan in neutral countries like Singapore were reactions to booming Taiwan-European trade as well as to the diplomatic initiatives of the island.[78]

Such developments created enough concern in Beijing to cause it to circulate a letter at the UN Security Council asking members to reject Taipei's foreign policy overtures. It asserted that Taiwan's new diplomacy was an attempt to create two Chinas.[79] The official *Beijing Review*[80] termed Taiwan's flexible diplomacy "a futile attempt to gain 'dual recognition'." It asserted that "the Chinese government will never tolerate the materialization of the attempts of creating 'two Chinas' or 'one China, one Taiwan'." Beijing worked quietly but with determination to thwart Taiwan's overtures to the GATT and the Organization for Economic Cooperation and Development (OECD).

It had not escaped Taiwan's notice that Japan's emergence from isolation in the post-war period into full membership in the international economic organizations started with its membership in the OECD and that such a course might be feasible for Taiwan. When the OECD took the initiative in early 1989 to hold a seminar with the newly industrializing countries of Asia, only Taiwan was delighted. The purposes of the seminar were to discuss "Sustaining the Development of the Global Economy" and to "get acquainted."

128 *China, Hong Kong, Taiwan and World Trade*

The notion of such a seminar tread upon many highly sensitive areas for hosts and guests alike. The host countries, essentially the industrial democracies, were concerned about the rising competitive power of the "Four Dragons" – Hong Kong, Taiwan, Singapore, and Korea – who were themselves concerned that the seminar would be for the purpose of "NIC-bashing", to chastize the Newly Industrializing Countries for their aggressive export tactics. The hosts felt compelled to avoid offending China by referring to Hong Kong and Taiwan as "countries" and therefore coined the phrase "Newly Industrializing Economies" (NIEs). With the exception of Taiwan the NICs (or NIEs) had no current desire to join the OECD group which would mean giving up the perquisites of developing country status for the obligations of industrial countries – for example, being aid-donors rather than aid-recipients. OECD officials denied that there was any thought of asking the NICs to join the 24-member OECD group, stating that such thoughts were premature. OECD officials did point out, however, that both Taiwan and Hong Kong could only hope eventually to attain some kind of associate status, since the organization as an intergovernmental group could not accommodate "ecomomic entities." Taiwan was reported in return to have suggested that it might be permitted to sit on committees like the Development Assistance Committee that administers OECD members' aid to developing countries.[81] The conference concluded ambiguously with an agreement to pursue the dialogue in the future with more focus and greater attention to specifics.

Reactions to Tiananmen Square

In early June of 1989 the government of Taiwan vehemently condemned the bloodshed and repression on the mainland, but indicated there would be no change in the island's policy toward the mainland. Visits to relatives could continue in both directions as before and trade would be tolerated. During the first half of that year trade with the mainland through Hong Kong had jumped again by 50 percent to an estimated $3 billion at an annual rate. It probably dropped later in the year after the events in Tiananmen Square; nonetheless Taiwanese businessmen, as reported in surveys, remained largely optimistic.[82] Those who had an investment on the mainland would continue to do business; some Taiwanese, however, admitted they were looking elsewhere.

"Greater China": Problems of Hong Kong and Taiwan 129

In general the mood of the government and the people was one of caution. While refusing to ban indirect trade with the mainland, the government urged the West to toughen its economic sanctions. It was probably true that there was no feasible way to stop Taiwan's trade with the mainland, as Taipei claimed. In the background, however, the PRC's long-standing threat to use force against the island in the event of turmoil there probably loomed larger than ever. Such demonstrations as occurred on the island in support of the students in Beijing were small and short-lived compared with those in Hong Kong. The government confined its reactions to stepping up its campaign to publicize abroad its economic accomplishments and political liberalization. It instructed its diplomats to befriend rather than avoid PRC officials abroad and to expand their contacts in countries recognizing Beijing.

Fear reemerged that Taiwan's independence movement would be boosted by events on the mainland, especially among Taiwanese students. Yet even if discussion of independence became more vociferous, confrontation with the government was not inevitable. As one senior opposition party leader pointed out, Taiwan wants "to become a real country. In China they want to change their way of life." Opinion polls in July[83] had shown President Lee to be increasingly popular.[84] Continued liberalization and tolerance could be sufficient to keep the supporters of independence a small minority.[85]

Whether the widespread revulsion in the West and condemnation of China for the events of June would lead to any greater acceptance of Taiwan in the international community probably would depend on the flow of events in China. By late summer of 1989 there was no evidence of increasing warmth toward Taiwan. The logic of Taiwan's claim for acceptance was strong. The West's desire to avoid offending Beijing that had limited the West's contacts with Taiwan was now stripped of optimism about the totality of China's commitment to free enterprise and Western ways on which it had been based. Yet even if the West's reactions to China had been influenced to some degree by rose-colored glasses, it remained in the West's national interest to avoid forcing China back into the isolation, poverty and repression of the Mao era (see Chapter 5). Taiwan was caught in this Western dilemma. If, however, Beijing were to undertake a new round of ruthless repression, intensified Western revulsion might induce the West to ignore any objections the PRC might make to Taiwan's membership in one or several of the international organizations.

130   *China, Hong Kong, Taiwan and World Trade*

After Tiananmen Square, nevertheless, the times were more propitious than they had been for two decades for Taiwan's at least partial emergence from isolation. Among the international organizations it might join, membership in the General Agreement was the most likely of all potentials. With cautious and prudent initiatives Taiwan might gain acceptance by the GATT.

As the world's trade organization the GATT was most relevant to Taiwan's strength and its coverage suffered the largest omission as a consequence of Taiwan's exclusion. In addition Beijing's response to Taipei's overtures toward the GATT had been far less hostile and dogmatic than its reaction to other aspects of Taiwan's elastic diplomacy. Indeed the PRC had made it clear that it was not opposed to Taiwan in the GATT and had said for publication "Beijing welcomes Taiwan to sit down and have consultations on the GATT issue."[86] Beijing did assert, however, that Taiwan's application should be handled by Beijing after the PRC had become a member. Mainland officials also admitted that it would be possible for a separate customs territory of a country to become a GATT member, if supported by two-thirds of the member countries (Article XXXIII). The largest obstacle to Taiwan's entry always had been the issue of its name, but Taiwan had recently become much more flexible on this issue. Taipei appeared to recognize that the psychic satisfaction of being addressed as the "Republic of China" was less important than moving out of the league of pariah countries into which it had fallen. A name mutually acceptable to both China and Taiwan appeared feasible.[87]

After Tiananmen Square Beijing's own negotiations with the GATT for its accession were put on hold with the agreement of all concerned. Even without a reversion to centralized control that Beijing had undertaken in late 1988 there was much in the PRC trade regime and internal economy that was not in compliance with the GATT. Taiwan in contrast was already much closer to GATT consistency. Since it was not at all clear when negotiations between the PRC and the GATT would resume or how quickly they could be concluded, Beijing's continued insistence that Taiwan's membership follow its own would place an indefinite delay on making the GATT more representative of world trade and might receive a more frosty reception as time passed.

In addition, if Taiwan were to accept a name that Beijing had proposed, such as Taiwan Customs District or Taiwan Province of China (and the Kuomintang had always agreed that Taiwan was

"Greater China": Problems of Hong Kong and Taiwan 131

only one of China's provinces), the conservatives in Beijing could trumpet the acceptance as the necessary first step in the reunification process. Since reunification was a goal of such high priority to Beijing, the influential octagenarians there would probably be willing to pay a significant price to see the process started in their lifetime. Taiwan had always worried that if it were to succumb on the name issue, the demand of the opposition for independence would be strengthened. A retreat on the name issue for the purpose of acceptance into a major international organization could be perceived on the island as the first step towards its becoming "a real country"; it could encourage or divert a demand for independence, and would have to be carefully managed by Taipei.

Finally, Beijing was obviously chastened by the withdrawal of Western businessmen and the cessation of Western credits following the repression. With a population made restive by inflation, corruption and a compelling desire for an improved standard of living, the regime had a strong motive for sustained economic growth and modernization. In addition its accumulated foreign debt of over $40 billion on which service charges were mounting also argued for continued trade with the West and access to Western capital. The urgency of Beijing's overtures to the West in the late summer of 1989 (many of which were awkward in the extreme) suggested that the PRC would go out of its way to avoid giving further offense to the world trading community. The GATT represented that community. The rejection of an offer by Taiwan to accept a name that the PRC had suggested would make Beijing appear unreasonable and vindictive in the West and further weaken its standing.

If the times were becoming propitious for Taiwan's return to the community of nations and for its partial entry into the league of industrial democracies, Taiwan's drive for acceptance would be successful only if it persevered in its liberalizing course at home. It was important that the opening of its economy be sustained, together with the restructuring that this implied, that privatisation of the extensive business holdings of the government and the KMT proceed and that political liberalization continue at a steady pace. In the eyes of most of Taiwan's people the government of President Lee was moving in the right direction and making few, if any, mistakes. An air of excitement pervaded the island, a sense of pride and of a bright future. Émigrés were returning home. Horizons were broadening. The challenges of the future were many and difficult – relations with the mainland were unpredictable, environmental degradation at home was generating strident demands for attention, world markets were increasingly competitive, and the obligations of belonging to international institutions meant a total break with the successful policies of the past – but after forty years the island had achieved self-confidence. The horrors of the Beijing massacre for Taiwan could have a silver lining.

5 The Outlook and Implications for U.S. and Western Policy

OUTLOOK FOR CHINA

Everyone's crystal ball is considerably more cloudy today than it was two or three decades ago. A greatly accelerated pace of change and much deeper economic interdependencies throughout the world have made the future increasingly opaque. Perhaps the only remaining certainty about the future is that of change itself.

With that caveat, and with due humility, one can speculate about the nature and direction of future change in China and in China's relations with Hong Kong, Taiwan, and the rest of the world. In the early 1990s the most important questions appear to concern the future of China's economic modernization program, the future of the Chinese Communist Party and the impact of changes in China on China's external relationships.[1]

That China must resume its rightful place in the world is accepted as gospel in China: China should be a world power. Party members and people have been united in their support of that goal. They have also agreed that for China to return once again to a position of power in the world, China must strengthen its economy. It must modernize and extend its production in order to be able to produce the quantity, quality, and variety of goods and services that provide the muscle of economic power.

Differences arose in China over how best to modernize, how much opening to the West was required, how much income inequality, how much centralization of control. Whether the differences were primarily among party members or fairly widespread through the party and general population is uncertain. Such evidence as exists suggests that the dispute over how best to modernize was primarily intra-party; that non-party Chinese (the great majority of the population – party members numbered less than 50 million in a total population of over 1 billion), favored the "open door" and decentralization policies. Their support for economic reform was

134   *China, Hong Kong, Taiwan and World Trade*

probably based primarily on the fact that most of them were better off as a result of the modernization program. There was nonetheless a body of committed communists convinced of the evils of capitalism and unequal incomes, and the corruption, crime, prostitution and, pollution that they believed were the inevitable accompaniments.

In the aftermath of Tiananmen Square a degree of economic austerity not previously experienced during the economic reform is likely, as well as political repression. How a sharp drop in the standard of living might affect support for the program and how it might affect the party are crucial.

By the second half of 1988 the third and by far the most severe crisis of the economic reform period was well under way. Excessive investment and consumer demand fuelled by an uncontrolled money supply and wage increases had raised inflation in the cities to nearly 31 percent, the highest level in the history of the People's Republic. Once again the government had resorted to administrative measures and central controls in an attempt to rein in the economy, but this time the controls were considerably broader and more stringent. They were so severe that in the first half of 1989 several observers began to worry about the dangers of stagflation and even about contracting production in China. The worries were based on the failure of inflation to drop much despite a considerable slowdown in the growth of industrial production. It was not at all clear how far growth would have to dip before inflation once again fell into the single digits. The worries were based on the apparent inability of Beijing to control activity in the coastal provinces. Thus, even before the political turmoil of late spring, the economic problems confronting China were formidable. The degree of their aggravation resulting from the political repression put the future of the Chinese economy as well as of the reform program into question.

The reasons were many. The budget deficit, the main source of inflationary pressure on the demand side, was almost certain to be larger because of higher expenditures and little likelihood of increased revenues. Workers had been given bonuses during the turmoil to keep them at their jobs. Subsidies to consumers to compensate them somewhat for rises in the cost of living were likely to rise in an attempt to contain urban unrest. The massive movement of troops in May had entailed unforeseen expenses; promises of more resources for the military may have been necessary to ensure military support for Deng and the conservatives. The import-

Outlook and Implications for U.S. and Western Policy 135

ance of food supplies meant that payments to farmers could no longer be postponed; the size of the grain harvest itself was crucial.

The chief hope for higher revenues was through the forced sale of government bonds to workers and improved enforcement of tax regulations. Higher taxes in the face of rising unemployment would only exacerbate social tensions and hence, except for the tiny private enterprise sector, were unlikely in the near term. An environment of fear might improve tax collections, but the austerity program itself would lower the tax base. Since making money was no longer favored by Beijing, the growth of private and collective enterprise, the vibrant sectors of the economy, would slow or cease and bankruptcies would rise. And how successful Beijing would be in controlling provincial and local enterprise was problematic – in collecting taxes as well as in slowing growth. Retrenchment probably would fall most heavily on state enterprise. There it could be enforced and taxes could be collected, but its tax base would shrink.

In addition to a larger budget deficit, aggregate supply was in danger of dropping. Productivity would be reduced by the time required to be spent on indoctrination and correct thinking, a reversion to Maoism instituted during the summer of 1989. An atmosphere of fear itself could reduce productivity as could lingering resentment against the political repression, especially in urban areas. On the other hand, productivity in state enterprise, already low, probably would not be much affected by lingering apathy. To the extent that the coastal provinces succeeded in retaining their autonomy, productivity would be less affected. Bottlenecks in raw material supply, power, and transport, however, had been so severe they would open only slowly, if at all, as the pace of growth dropped. During the first four months of 1989 production of iron, coal, petroleum, and other important raw materials contracted as credit and raw material scarcities diverted remaining flows to the more profitable processing industries.[2] Meanwhile, hoarding of scarce materials was more likely as enterprises scrambled to maintain production. The contraction of imports necessitated by balance of payments stringencies would add to supply difficulties.

Reduced foreign aid, official foreign lending, and World Bank investment would not affect supply immediately because of what was already in the pipeline, but unless foreign governmental restrictions were lifted soon, they would have a serious effect in 1990 and beyond. The return of private sector foreign managers to their joint ventures or existing investments in China and the return of foreign

136   *China, Hong Kong, Taiwan and World Trade*

buyers, if delayed, would further depress the supply of foreign exchange. The danger of economic contraction in China was real.

Even if foreign business were to return in large numbers soon, however, and even if foreign credits again became available, the outlook, while improved, would still be perilous. Doing business with China had now been proved to be more risky than many of China's trading partners had believed. China's political and social stability was no longer assured; the possibility of civil war could even be contemplated. The consequence meant that China's interest costs would rise and its terms of trade would fall. China's exports would have to be cheaper and the return available to foreign investors higher for China to attract the same amount of business.

Hanging over China were rising debt service requirements on its outstanding foreign debt. Principal repayments and interest due were scheduled to rise to a peak in 1992. To meet them China would have to husband its foreign exchange, push exports even more aggressively, and slash imports. A larger share of GNP would have to be diverted to the export sector. Exchange depreciation, debt rescheduling and new borrowing would help, but would probably be resisted by the leadership's pride. Going hat-in-hand to foreigners would not be easy unless it was clear that their requests would be accepted without an embarrassing jump in interest rates. The alternative was belt-tightening at home. Thus, while some additional credits probably would be sought, austerity in China for at least two or three years was likely.

Whether prolonged austerity in China would be accepted with the same resignation that it had been in the past probably would depend on its degree and its stability. Even a sizeable drop in living standards (e.g., 5 percent to 7 percent) but in only one year followed by stability at that lower level would probably be accepted with resignation for several years as a lesser evil than inflation. Expectations were higher, however, and appetites had been whetted. The decade of liberalization and contact with the West had acquainted directly or indirectly most Chinese with the comforts of basic consumer durables and a more varied diet. Discontent would be likely to mount with the duration of austerity. If austerity were to produce significantly declining real incomes and production for a period of years, unrest would probably rise and more political repression would be necessary. The chances of a coup d'état would grow.

The decade of reform may well have introduced another historical discontinuity into China's reaction patterns. A group of activist

Outlook and Implications for U.S. and Western Policy 137

Chinese expatriates working to overthrow the existing regime was once again in late 1989 active outside of China, raising reminiscences of the support obtained from overseas Chinese by Sun Yat-sen in the 1911 revolution against the Manchu dynasty. A number of the student leaders of the Beijing demonstrations and several of their advisers in June 1989 were able to escape to the West. There they set about informing the world of what actually had happened in Tiananmen Square, organizing Chinese students and intellectuals around the world into an umbrella opposition group, the "China Democratic Front," and seeking financial support. Their goals were broad and the way to achieve them was not defined – to end dictatorship in China and to establish human rights and a republic there. The leader and immediate source of support for the group was the innovative and wealthy Chinese industrialist, Wan Runnan, who had founded China's Stone Group, a highly successful private computer company. The group was reportedly receiving funds from the government of Taiwan as well as from the Hong Kong Alliance in Support of the Patriotic Movement in China.[3] If the group were to succeed in maintaining its unity and momentum, its existence could be expected to contribute to social and political instability on the mainland.

When Deng returned to Beijing with the support of military conservatives, he announced almost immediately that the economic reform program would continue. In fact the new leadership was trapped into support for the reform and open door policies by the necessity of servicing China's existing foreign debt. They would be able to do so with greater ease if foreigners continued to believe in China's future as an important trading partner. Deng's support for continued reform, however, was probably less cynical and rather a continuation of his long-standing conviction that China's future in the world depended on economic reform. Many of his new colleagues appeared not to share his conviction. It was notable that in the third period of retrenchment, unlike earlier periods, no innovative reform measures were announced. New measures, like obligatory bond purchases, were designed to curtail inflation, not further to change the system. It appeared highly unlikely that the conservative Deng regime would take any additional steps toward economic reform. At the most the status quo would be maintained.

What measures could China take to control inflation and also support continued reform? An immediately relevant precedent was close at hand. One of the most successful and little known cases of

138 *China, Hong Kong, Taiwan and World Trade*

bringing rampant inflation quickly under control occurred when the communists under Mao took control of mainland China in 1949. Then the degree of inflation in China was vastly more severe than it was forty years later, yet it was essentially eliminated within a year.

Upon assuming control Mao immediately tackled the budget deficit, primarily by raising taxes but at the same time by reorganizing and rationalizing China's entire administration for revenue collection and expenditure. The reorganization gave the central government control over taxes that formerly had been levied and collected at the local level. In the process it was able to make collection more efficient by eliminating illegal diversions, a form of corruption that had been rampant under the Nationalists. Forty years later the fact that taxes were once again collected at the local level and then passed up through layers of administrative divisions to the central government again provided rich opportunities for corruption, this time often in the form of tax-bargaining and avoidance. A return to collection by the central government with revenues then being shared with local governments could enhance enforcement and tax receipts. It would also aid in making Beijing's rules effective in the provinces.

In 1949 Mao had exercised strict control over the money supply through control of the budget deficit and through a tight, deflationary bank credit policy. In addition the regime had indexed wages to prices. Interest rates on savings deposits and government bonds were also indexed, thus making savings in both forms more attractive. When prices started to fall, moreover, China introduced a "double guarantee" of savings deposits: these deposits increased in money value as prices rose, but would retain their original cash value if prices fell. It was a "no-lose" very attractive offer. Consumption was reduced and the budget deficit was successfully financed through higher savings.[4]

The astonishing speed with which hyperinflation was brought under control by the new Mao regime probably was traceable as much to political factors as to soundly-based economic measures. The Nationalists had been widely discredited throughout much of the country for the economic and political turmoil that had grown under their control. The new regime was welcomed at least as a return to stability by some, enthusiastically by many. Ideological zeal gave it a degree of credibility as an effective governing force that its predecessor had lacked. In addition the people were willing to cooperate in and support any measures necessary to eliminate

Outlook and Implications for U.S. and Western Policy   139

inflation and bring a return to stability. Then, too, because the new regime was prepared to be ruthless in enforcing its regulations, fear played a role in its success. Also the challenge of controlling inflation in the China of 1949 was administratively more simple than it would be in 1989. Inflation was then an urban phenomenon, not nationwide; the rural areas were largely non-monetized, consisting of self-sufficient peasant households. But recognizing the favorable environment for inflation control that existed in 1949–50, still eliminating inflation within a year was a remarkable accomplishment due in large part to the fact that it was based on sound economic principles and market forces.[5]

Many of the measures that worked in 1949 could be made to work four decades later, albeit more slowly. Inflation control in 1990 in China, however, was a problem not because of lack of knowledge of what should be done, but rather because of a lack of the political will to do it. The Communist Party of the early years was corruption-averse. Fired by the ideology of equality of sacrifice in building a new, corruption-free China where everyone would work for the good of China and share an iron rice-bowl, the party won respect for its selflessness. It *did* share the sacrifice. Building a new China for the highly nationalistic Chinese easily replaced individual or family betterment as the prime incentive.

The categorical assertion that "power corrupts," however, once again was exemplified historically in the case of China; the powerful Chinese Communist Party was corruptible and corrupted. The Deng regime recognized the political dangers of widespread party corruption, but took no more than token measures to correct it. In failing to take meaningful steps to contain and eliminate corruption even after the emphasis given the issue in the student demonstrations and the wide support they won in the country, the party lost a prime opportunity to reestablish its moral authority and thus its popular support.

The longer the party delays in reforming itself, the more discredited it will become in the eyes of the Chinese people. A failure of the party to reform itself is likely to entail a de facto failure of the economic reform program; economic reform and party reform have become interconnected. Correction of the imbalances in the economy appears feasible only if the party itself is reformed. Crippling limitations of infrastructure and raw material supply, for example, worsened during the first decade of reform as the demand for fuel, power, transportation grew nearly three times more rapidly than

140   *China, Hong Kong, Taiwan and World Trade*

their supply. The bottlenecks became worse and lasted longer; cycles increased in intensity.

The structural imbalances can be corrected administratively by increasing allocations of labor and capital to the bottleneck sectors. If prices remain below market-clearing levels, however, opportunities for and the temptations toward corruption will contine to multiply. Sending armies of tax examiners around the country to reduce corruption and enforce tax collections or reforming the tax collection system will not be effective unless the examiners or collectors are corruption-free. Meanwhile, state subsidies will mushroom, waste and inefficiencies will be aggravated and control of inflation will be more difficult.

Success in eliminating corruption requires that the opportunities for corruption be minimized. Retention of the dual price system without steady progress in reducing the scope of low state-fixed prices not only maintains the opportunities and rewards for corruption, but it retains the crippling limitations of raw material and infrastructure supply. If the capacity of the bottleneck industries does not increase more rapidly than industrial production, these bottlenecks will continue to choke off growth after each period of retrenchment making yet another dose of retrenchment necessary after a shorter and shorter interval of growth. Thus real growth in each successive five or ten-year period will be less than that before and the economic reform indefinitely prolonged. Meanwhile China will fall farther and farther behind the West.

Success in eliminating corruption requires more than minimizing opportunities. Ministries that successfully oppose price reform because it will raise their costs must be bridled. Penalties large enough to be a deterrent to corruption and their enforcement regardless of status or privileged position also are necessary.

The Deng regime did an obeisance in the direction of clean government in late July by banning the children and spouses of senior officials in the party and government from engaging in business activity. It also announced that special supplies of food would no longer be available to top leaders, nor such luxuries as imported cars or lavish entertainment funds. It promised to punish criminals involved in corruption, bribes and profiteering and to treat as equal everyone before the law.[6] It said nothing, however, about how these promises and directives would be enforced.

A rule of law is probably the only feasible replacement for the idealistic order based on shared poverty that kept China corruption-

Outlook and Implications for U.S. and Western Policy   141

free in the Mao era. During the decade of economic reform, prodded by the West, China had made considerable progress in shifting from the rule of man to the rule of law. Laywers had been trained, laws and regulations had been drafted to protect individuals against arbitrary official acts. New courts, arbitration panels, codes of laws, and procedures as well as constitutional reform and new commercial laws had been established by the National Peoples' Congress. Except in the case of legally defined criminal acts, however, enforcement lagged; especially in the economic realm the rule of man continued. The order to spill blood in Tiananmen Square was an expression from the highest level of contempt for a rule of law. That attitude of scorn was also reflected by China's judicial system.[7]

There is still time for the party to reform itself, but a new leadership is probably necessary for its renewal as well as for a renewal of the economic reform program. A new leadership, pledging a rule of law as the basis for its own actions and for a renewal of the economic reform program, would be likely to draw much popular support in China. The goal of building a new China on the foundation of a clearly defined and enforced legal order could provide the visionary direction and focus necessary to energize the Chinese people once again. Such a vision, articulated by a new leader, could make the sacrifices and turmoil that would accompany a major price reform endurable. The devotion to their homeland, the diligence and self-discipline that can be invoked in the Chinese in the name of "China" are traits that will not disappear. They can be marshalled by the right leader at the right time. To an outsider it appears that that time is at hand.

A major price reform, perhaps accompanied by a currency conversion to a "New Renminbi" with a major exchange rate depreciation and perhaps with a temporary period of wage and interest rate indexing, will become more necessary to a renewal of the economic reform program the longer the present hiatus lasts. The turmoil and instability that would be part of such drastic changes could be contemplated only by a leadership enjoying widespread popular support. But the longer the repressive conservative regime lasts, the more readily welcomed a credible new leader would be. That new leader will become credible only to the degree that he can promise a credible reform of the Communist Party; a shift to the rule of law is probably the only feasible course for such party reform. Thus party reform and the rule of law appear to be

142 *China, Hong Kong, Taiwan and World Trade*

the necessary prerequisites for a successful economic reform program.

Sooner or later the Chinese Communist Party will ask itself whether it is worth putting party doctrine above the interests of China. Meanwhile, the hiatus in the economic reform program seems likely to endure as long as China is ruled by Party conservatives. Such an interregnum could see important shifts in the internal cohesion of China. Decentralization in the economic reform decade gave provincial and local party and government officials much more authority and independence from Beijing, an independence that Beijing seemed reluctant to counteract.

The reluctance was partly ideologically based. The coastal provinces, the SEZs and the maverick province of Sichuan were to provide the engine of growth that would spread to the internal provinces. To enforce retrenchment in the coastal areas would have involved discouraging foreign investment and exports, something foreign-exchange-short Beijing was loathe to do. In addition local party members and officials, even if loyal to Beijing, had the economic interests of their localities as well as their own economic interests as top priority.

As the coastal areas grew, they and their party and government officials amassed wealth that they invested outside of China, mostly in Hong Kong often under the cover of a Hong Kong corporation. Such wealth made the localities increasingly independent of Beijing and helped to finance their continued development. If Beijing were to attempt to replace the leaders of these areas, growth there would inevitably slow and might cease. Thus failure to control the provinces was a product both of Beijing's ambivalence and its decreasing ability to exert control. It may also have stemmed from Beijing's awareness of how widespread throughout the party corruption was and a fear of alienating a large segment of the leadership's support through a concerted attack on corruption.

The increasing independence of China's provinces aroused speculation among observers about the strength of centripetal forces in China.[8] China is a vast country whose people throughout history have been both submissive and rebellious. The historic tendency of China to fragment territorially is well documented. Provincial separation hastened the decline of the Tang dynasty in the ninth century and figured in each of the dynastic successions after that. For a brief period during the 10th century, China dissolved into smaller kingdoms, only to be reunited by the Sung in 960 A.D.

Outlook and Implications for U.S. and Western Policy   143

Although subsequent periods of dynastic decline and transition were accompanied by similar episodes of dissolution, the notion of unity of the Chinese realm as a single polity governed by the imperial court endured.

Still the geographic, political, economic and linguistic distinctness among provinces persisted through the centuries. It was the basis for the warlordism that prevailed after the fall of the Manchu dynasty in 1911, the last period of extreme decentralization that led to the establishment of a republic in China. The persistence of centrifugal tendencies in China's provinces was less an attempt on their part to rid themselves of central control than to protect their right to independent action. China's size and deficiencies in communications and transportation had always implied that the power of the center was limited. Further, the imperial bureaucracy remained at approximately the same size as it had been in the sixteenth century even as the population doubled and doubled again. Imperial interference in local affairs was impractical; decentralization of power in fact was extensive and the provinces' scope for independent action large.

Imperial supervision of the provinces hinged to a great extent on the ability of the regime to enlist the services of local gentry and family groups. Civil law and commercial matters generally were under the jurisdiction of family lineages, a system consistent with Confucian ideals of self-regulation. The provinces, however, recognized the need for a central power to maintain peace and order and to protect them from incursions by their neighbors. In a country continuously threatened by disintegrating forces, the emperor's legitimacy rested in the final analysis on his ability to suppress local anarchy, civil strife, and banditry.

Despite the ongoing forces of disintegration and lawlessness, China is ethnically and culturally homogeneous, historically a single nation. In fact China as a nation has evinced unusual cohesiveness. Chinese unity is based in a strong sense of cultural identity and historical consciousness. Nonetheless, the prolonged disorder, corruption, and declining public welfare traditionally associated with periods of dynastic change suggest that although the unity of the Chinese nation may be everlasting, the leadership of the Communist Party is not. Historically the interregnum periods have been intervals of strong provincial autonomy or civil war.

The next section discusses four scenarios of internal Chinese developments in the context of appropriate U.S. and Western policies toward China, Hong Kong, and Taiwan. The four scenarios

144   *China, Hong Kong, Taiwan and World Trade*

are: (1) a continuation of an aged, conservative, wobbly regime; (2) a return to a program of progressive economic reform and participation in the international division of labor; (3) political decentralization or systemic collapse; (4) a return to tight central controls, reduced international trade, and political repression.

IMPLICATIONS FOR WESTERN POLICY: CHINA

The Status Quo

Western policy toward China during the interregnum of the conservative Deng regime faces a dilemma. Deng and his cohorts are at the end of their life span. Confronted by severe economic problems as well as social and political discontent, their regime is unstable. Its support lies in the military, which imparts considerable strength to the group, but the unity of the army itself is questionable. Its willingness to follow the orders of officers was found wanting in Beijing in May 1989. When Deng dies, as he must sooner rather than later, turmoil in China is likely. Western policy in the interim should avoid condoning repression and the blatant disregard of human rights exhibited in China after June 3–4. At the same time Western policy should do what it can to insure that China remains open to the world and embarked on a course that will improve the economic and political well-being of the Chinese people. These are the basic principles that should guide policy both during the interregnum and in the course of the new regime(s) that will follow. At the same time the West must be constantly aware that the futures of Hong Kong and Taiwan are hostages to events in China and that policies fashioned to influence the mainland can have significant repercussions on the other two areas.

Dissillusionment in the West

With the advantage of hindsight it is clear that Deng and the new conservative leadership grossly underestimated Western reactions to their ruthless spilling of blood in Tiananmen Square in early June 1989. Consciously or unconsciously, that decision involved a cold-blooded calculus of benefits and costs. Whatever the disapproval with which the West would greet the use of tanks and guns against the students, China's leaders reasoned or intuited, it would be overcome by China's sheer weight in the West's geopolitical consid-

Outlook and Implications for U.S. and Western Policy   145

erations. Gorbachev's visit to Beijing had only just confirmed the thaw in Sino-Soviet relations under way for half a decade; NATO and Japan could not afford to alienate China at such a time. Western business, moreover, was interested in money, not politics; maintaining the "open door" policy would continue to make China's cheap labor available and thus would sustain foreign investment in and trade with China.

Hong Kong would be hard-hit. More business, professional and skilled labor would leave, but a large corps of mainlanders had been active in Hong Kong's finance and business for years and more would gain additional experience over the next eight years. The newcomers would be able to carry on after 1997 and sustain Hong Kong's prosperity with the aid of the people remaining in the colony. Taiwan's monumental bluff of forty years' duration – its claim that it would reconquer the mainland – would be called and shown to be footless. There was no possible danger from a population less than 2 percent that of the mainland. Further, Taiwanese business, too, was more interested in money than politics. From the Beijing vantage point the risks of violent repression were small; the advantages – unequivocally restoring order and reestablishing CCP control – were immense.

The misjudgment of the Chinese leadership was in part ascribable to the West itself. Especially the Americans and Europeans, but to some degree the Japanese too, tended to exaggerate the implications of China's economic reform program and "open door" policy. Statements by Deng that China was fashioning its own road to socialism, borrowing mechanisms from capitalism in order to reach socialism more expeditiously, were either discounted as propaganda for domestic consumption or disbelieved. Their rejection hinged on a Western faith that the advantages of capitalism would prove themselves to the Chinese and be accepted by China as superior to socialism. Viewing China as the birthplace of civilization and seeking to return to civilized ways, many foreigners – but by no means all – found it inconceivable that China could return to savagery.

Many Americans and Europeans had constructed an image of China modelled on their image of themselves. The disillusionment that followed Tiananmen Square worked to intensify their reactions to the occasion.

Then, too, since China's opening to the world in the early 1970s China had sought and had been granted by the West preferential

146   *China, Hong Kong, Taiwan and World Trade*

treatment. Chinese representatives around the world were always quick to demand special exceptions for their country from Western laws, regulations or customs; in many cases the West acquiesced in such exceptions. When the West did not acquiesce, it disagreed gently. Even in the case of such offenses (in Western eyes) as the Chinese invasion of Vietnam to teach its southern neighbor "a lesson," the episodes of violent and bloody repression in Tibet or the sale of missiles to the Middle East, the West had, at the most, protested. It had never given China a "black eye," had never severely chastised the Chinese or penalized them for infractions of acceptable behavior.

The West has not done China a service in the past by its consistent pattern of granting exceptional treatment. In treating China differently, it confirmed China's belief that it *is* different and thus can expect exceptional treatment. It is true that China is big. It is true that China is important. If China is to become an integral part of the world community of nations, however, China must learn to adjust to the world, to give as well as to take, to participate in international forums and abide by their decisions even when in discussion it had argued against them. Although China is big, in the world community it plays the role of a minority; both minorities and majorities must make adjustments for the successful functioning of a community. In the 1980s, China consistently demanded that the rest of the world adjust to it.

In brief, Deng's China had always gotten away with what it wanted to do. The Chinese had no reason to think June 1989 would be any different. Both China and the West had misjudged each other. Disillusionment heightened the reaction of each side to the other and aggravated the ensuing bitterness.

It would be a mistake to think that the bitterness felt in American and European circles was not shared to some degree by China. The moderation of Chinese stridency at Western reactions after the first month or two, the increased subtlety of their propaganda were evidence of the importance to them of Western capital and technology, not a manifestation of diminished hostility on the part of the leadership toward the West. The fact that their representatives in Chinese embassies abroad avoided all but officially sanctioned contact with foreigners suggested either orders from above or the representatives' own fear of the consequences of unsanctioned contacts. In either case it suggested a deep mistrust in China's leaders of all foreigners, a mistrust at least partly founded in their own misjudgment.

Outlook and Implications for U.S. and Western Policy 147

China's own lack of knowledge about the West, a product both of ethnocentrism and isolation, undoubtedly intensifies the effect of misjudgment and creates opportunities for surprise in China and the West. Two months after Tiananmen Square, attempting to stimulate Western private investment in China, a Chinese state agency wrote to Volvo, a large Swedish automobile manufacturer, offering a factory and cheap convict labor if it would set up operations in China. After an original reaction of disbelief, Volvo declined, but the Chinese official who had written the letter continued to stress what a good bargain this would be; that the state would feed the prisoners who would be guarded in the factory by prison officers.[9] That such an offer could be made speaks volumes for the gulf between China and the West. It is illustrative of the enormity of opportunities for misunderstanding and misjudgments of policy on both sides.

Potential Policy Pitfalls
In most practical ways of immediate concern the West is more important to China than China is to the West. To resume its rightful place in the world, China needs the West. When China has achieved the sinews of economic strength, the direction of vulnerability may shift, but for now China's national interests are more dependent on the West than the West's are on China.

So long as *perestroika* is the rule in USSR, the West has little to fear from any common cause that the Soviet Union and China may make together. The amount of practical aid that China can get from the USSR will be decidedly limited by the Soviet's own acute scarcity of resources; similarly China's resource scarcity limits what China can do for the USSR. Those resource scarcities will not be quickly overcome in either country. Even if the leadership changes in either or both countries, the constraints of resource scarcities will limit their scope for foreign adventures.[10]

This is not to say that the dangers of a shift to vitriolic anti-Westernism in China (or the USSR) should be ignored. Dictators clinging to power in the face of rising domestic resentment and hostility can act in irrational ways; contingency planning is always wise and prudent. For example, a Chinese leadership, feeling trapped, could seek to divert domestic discontent by an attempt to bring Taiwan back to the fold through the use of force. "Turmoil" on Taiwan or the use of Taiwan as a counter-revolutionary base would be adequate justification for China. The Chinese, moreover,

148 *China, Hong Kong, Taiwan and World Trade*

would not view an attempt to seize control of Taiwan as a foreign operation; even Taipei agrees that Taiwan is part of China. Nonetheless, a Chinese leadership, considering resort to military action under conditions of domestic and social instability, would be given pause by the risk of unreliable soldiers or officers, or of encouraging a military coup.

The more likely course of events is Chinese preoccupation with its own purely domestic affairs. The Chinese are aware of the strength of Taiwan's armed forces and of American attitudes toward Taiwan; such an operation would at best be very expensive for the mainland. The decade of the Open Door Policy has made Chinese leaders more acutely aware of how weak and backward China is in the world. It has also made them more aware of the importance of the West to China's national goals. A significant foreign adventure on China's part would be likely to occur only in extremis as an act of desperation.

Progressive Economic Reform

The importance of China to the West lies in the long-run opportunity that economic modernization and reform in China can offer, an opportunity that would benefit the West as well as China. It is not in Western national interests that China remain poor and backward. If China does remain so, because of a return to isolation or because of the mismanagement of its leaders, an opportunity would be lost. Western well-being would not be injured, but it would not be as high as it could be if China were to grow, prosper, and remain peaceful. A prospering China, growing largely on the basis of its own efforts – as must be the case – but aided by Western technology, capital and trade that reflects an evolving pattern of comparative advantage could raise productivity, production, and consumption among its neighbors and throughout the world. Successful economic development would commit China more tightly to further growth, to staying the course. China's vested interest in peace and international economic intercourse would rise. Deepening economic interdependence would make the West more vulnerable to China, as it would also make China more dependent on the West. Enhanced vulnerabilities enlarge risks, it is true, but these are the risks that the West has been accepting in greater volume ever since the industrial revolution. They have occasionally led to war, but for the most part they have nurtured peace.

Outlook and Implications for U.S. and Western Policy 149

A turning inward on the part of China, a return to the isolation of the pre-Deng era, would be a commitment of China to a policy of slow growth or stagnation. It could be an abandonment of the goal of catching up with the West and of returning China to its rightful place. It would represent a second-best alternative for the Deng regime, but one which might be chosen under certain conditions at home or abroad. A deterioration of domestic political stability could lead to the rigid controls and repressive tactics of a full police state as well as to an attempt on the part of the regime to protect its own tenure by cutting off all contact with foreigners. As such it would be an act of desperation by a vulnerable regime.

A return to isolation by China could also be the consequence of a move in the West to limit severely the commercial activities of the Western private sector with or in China. A boycott of China by the major industrial powers, for example, would make it difficult or impossible for China to acquire modern technology. Under such conditions China's leaders might well conclude that the only way they could pursue the goal of making China strong is through a policy of forced draft growth at home. If the West were to refuse its technology and capital to China, the second-best alternative would be the only remaining choice for China.

Thus the policy adopted by the West in the immediate aftermath of Tiananmen Square was well-founded. In limiting official contacts, halting military sales, freezing loans to China from international institutions and bilateral aid projects, reducing cultural, scientific and technical cooperation, the West expressed its horror and revulsion. It gave post-Mao China its first-ever "shiner." Except for military sales, the West did not attempt to curtail commercial activities on the part of its businessmen in China. The private sector was left to its own devices in deciding whether and at what level to continue to do business with China. A continuation of the reform and modernization program was still a choice for China. Pressures in the U.S. Congress and European parliaments for more severe sanctions were correctly resisted by Western leaders as being excessive for that time. Rather, the West chose to use the carrot of a potential lessening of existing sanctions in response to lessened repression in China in the hope of alleviating the arbitrary punishment for the Tiananmen demonstrators being meted out by Beijing.

Technology and capital represent the most potent levers in the West's box of foreign policy tools for influencing China. Control over trade, aid, and private foreign investment in China should be

150   *China, Hong Kong, Taiwan and World Trade*

used with care, discretion, and prudence. Reactions by China to Western initiatives are always difficult to estimate and are subject to a larger margin of error than are those of other countries. The dangers of going too far or not far enough are great. Also Americans and some European have come to take Hong Kong and Taiwan for granted and thus tend to forget about them. In the context of relations with the People's Republic such callousness about the two small polities is an abrogation of many of the principles that the West professes to hold dear. In the scheme of geopolitics Hong Kong and Taiwan are not important enough to matter. But principles are not limited in their application to the large and powerful; by definition they are comprehensive and fundamental. In punishing China for infractions of human rights in the PRC the West should take care not to abridge existing human rights in Hong Kong and Taiwan. A Western embargo of trade with China would devastate Hong Kong's economy, demolish Hong Kong's prosperity at least temporarily, and cause China to lose interest in maintaining Hong Kong as a capitalist enclave.

Sooner or later China will return to an active program of economic growth based on participation in the international division of labor because of the force of the evidence favoring such a program as a means toward economic strength. As China achieves success in its development policy, it may become more assertive in its foreign policy. It would be likely to become a less passive member of international organizations, pursuing more actively its national interests in such forums and bilaterally. Such enhanced activity and assertiveness would be expected to some degree in any event as China gained experience operating in the West, regardless of the success of its economic policy. If its economic policy is successful, however, the benefits that China derives from following the rules of accepted procedure would be greater and China would be more willing to play according to the rules. If China remains weak, if its growth lags behind that of the West, its assertiveness is less likely to be benign. Every country can be expected to push its national interests as far as they can be pushed without significant cost to itself. The less China has to lose, the more likely is its international behavior to be disruptive.

China's comportment as a member of the GATT will reflect its commitment to economic growth and its perception of what it has to lose by ignoring GATT strictures. The dangers to China's trading partners, to the world trade mechanism, and to China itself are the

Outlook and Implications for U.S. and Western Policy   151

greater the more inexperienced, poor and slow-growing China is. Thus the earlier years of China's GATT membership are likely to be the most hazardous.

The West has been correct in insisting as it has on special provisions to govern China's return to the GATT while China is still experimenting with its economic system. Selective safeguards like those endorsed by the GATT in the Hungarian Protocol of Accession would protect China as well as the West. They would protect China from the effects of Western reactions to unintentional Chinese excesses, reactions that could come not only from China's immediate trade partners, but from third countries that might otherwise also be injured by Chinese actions. While China's international trade regime lacks internal coherence and consistency and while the transparency of China's trade activities is less than complete in China itself, inadvertent Chinese excesses are likely. As China gains experience in managing its own economy and with the world trading mechanisms, such inadvertencies can be expected to drop as would recourse to selective safeguards by the West.

Intentional flouting of GATT rules by developing countries cannot easily be distinguished from the unintentional because of the many preferences and privileges the GATT confers on such members. If the Uruguay Round succeeds in making the GATT a more effective mechanism, if a GATT surveillance process shames members into better behavior, if GATT and the IMF collaborate to treat the balance of payments exception to import controls as an exception rather than the rule, flouting of GATT rules will be more difficult. In the end, however, it is the decision of the member's leadership that is decisive in determining the members' comportment.

It is in the best interest of both China and the GATT that China's application for reinstatement remain inactive until the struggle over the structure of China's economy is resolved. In any event China is unlikely to push for reactivation of its membership application if there is doubt about its successful completion. When China is once again clearly embarked on a program of economic reform consistent with GATT principles, China should be welcomed into the world trading organization. Then the opportunity for the mutual benefit that can be derived by China, the GATT and GATT's members will be too great to be denied.

In the meantime China could revert to isolationism and lose interest in the GATT; its external trade could shrink. For the West

152 *China, Hong Kong, Taiwan and World Trade*

this would imply a foregone opportunity about which it would have no choice. Or China could tend toward political decentralization with each province pursuing its own open- or closed-door policy. The major implications of these scenarios for Western policy toward Hong Kong and Taiwan are discussed below.

These are of course not the only possible courses for future developments in China; many variations and combinations are in the realm of the possible. A variation of the firmly entrenched conservative regime might be a military dictatorship that wins substantial popular support through widespread patronage, nepotism, bribery and corruption. Such a regime is as possible in China as it has been in Latin America. The interest of a military regime in economic development is likely to be a poor second to its interest in politics and security. A Chinese version would imply a no-growth, crisis-prone economy. Such a regime could perceive membership in the GATT as an opportunity to further its political interests in the world. As a member it could be disruptive. If the Uruguay Round should not be successful in strengthening the GATT, a disruptive member of China's size could politicize and further weaken the GATT. The consequence could be de facto GATT impotency.

Meanwhile events in the People's Republic have telescoped opportunities for Hong Kong and opened new vistas for Taiwan. In each case the interregnum era in China has exacerbated risks but created new opportunities.

IMPLICATIONS FOR WESTERN POLICY: HONG KONG

China's disregard for human rights galvanized Hong Kong and introduced a slow awakening in the West to the special problem of the legal status of Hong Kong people. In the first instance this is a British problem, but it is also a problem for the European Community of which Britain is a member. In the border-free EC, citizens of any member country are citizens of, and therefore have rights of residence and work in, the whole Community. The legal status of the Hong Kong people, moreover, is a proper moral concern for the entire world that claims to be "free." At the least the British should undertake to lead an OECD-wide effort to offer rights of citizenship to those Hong Kong people who seek the protection of a non-Chinese passport. With the assurance of such protection far fewer Hong Kong people probably would actually

Outlook and Implications for U.S. and Western Policy 153

choose to emigrate, knowing that after 1997 international law would guarantee their right to move. The developing world also should be encouraged to offer citizenship to Hong Kong residents. An organized international effort would easily be able to cope with the 3 million people actually involved.

At the same time it should be possible for Western governments to adjust their own rules or regulations in such a way as to avoid undue encouragement to immediate emigration from Hong Kong. In the case of the United State the five-year residency requirement for citizenship would encourage an immediate increase in the outflow of Hong Kong people as soon as the U.S. immigration quota for Hong Kong is raised. A special exception should be made for the unique circumstances of Hong Kong. The issue of "green cards" immediately upon the increase in the U.S. quota, but with the provision that Hong Kong people could use these certificates of legal immigration at any time in the future (i.e., with no time-limit on their validity) would offer individual Hong Kong residents a choice of when to leave. Then those who preferred to remain in Hong Kong in the hope of a continuation of the status quo there could do so without fear.

A more liberal policy on the part of the Western World toward Hong Kong emigrants is endangered, however, by Hong Kong's threat to repatriate forcibly large numbers of "boat people" who are refugees from Vietnam. Such action, if implemented, risks alienating much of the West. The same Western countries to which Hong Kong people would like to migrate in 1997 are those which have accepted Vietnamese refugees for resettlement.

Potential Benefits of GATT Membership

Hong Kong's status as a full member of the GATT affords it a unique although limited strength. The GATT is a technical organization concerned with trade not politics. China has, however, guaranteed that after 1997 Hong Kong can continue as an independent GATT member. This guarantee implies a Chinese promise to avoid any actions or policies on its part that would make Hong Kong's adherence to GATT rules impossible. Implicit in the guarantee is the maintenance of a clear and defined customs border between Hong Kong and the mainland in order that goods produced on the mainland be kept distinct from goods originating in Hong Kong. Such a border will also be essential if the PRC tariff structure

154   *China, Hong Kong, Taiwan and World Trade*

differs from that of Hong Kong. Since Hong Kong will remain a duty-free area while China can be expected to maintain relatively high tariffs, a customs border is necessary to differentiate between imports through Hong Kong destined for the PRC and those whose final destination is Hong Kong.

The customs border need not have a geographic location; it may be solely administrative. Any attempt by corrupt officials on either side of the border to circumvent customs controls must be subject to severe penalties. If by 1997 China is a GATT member such penalties might include not only those levied by China or Hong Kong itself, but also those which a strengthened post-Uruguay Round GATT might bring to bear through its system of surveillance and enhanced enforcement. A strengthened GATT would be likely to support Hong Kong, and recommend compensation against China in the event of Chinese trade infractions against or involving Hong Kong. Hong Kong officials might not even have to participate in the case against China before the GATT, should GATT surveillance of rules of origin be strengthened.

If the regime in Beijing after 1997 is committed to growth and economic reform, any circumvention of customs control would be likely to be inadvertent. Then Beijing itself would cooperate with the GATT in correcting the situation. If the circumvention were by design, however, this would imply that Beijing had lost interest in economic reform and the "open door" policy; then the future of Hong Kong would be bleak.

If after 1997 China is not yet a member of the GATT but still an applicant, Hong Kong's GATT membership could be an advantage. Pending China membership in the GATT could encourage the PRC to keep its promise to Hong Kong of "one country, two systems."

The additional strength imparted to Hong Kong from its GATT membership should not be overstated. If a future regime in China perceives support for the GATT to be in its own national interest, if China sees a prosperous Hong Kong as furthering its national interests, China's infractions of GATT rules will be minor and China will attempt to honor its promises to Hong Kong. But if GATT and Hong Kong come to have a relatively low priority for the Chinese leadership, China would not hesitate to flout GATT rules. China is no different from other member countries in this regard. Still, in marginal cases at least, China would seek to avoid GATT condemnation. If GATT becomes a more potent actor in the world trade scene, China would be more likely to adjust its

Outlook and Implications for U.S. and Western Policy 155

comportment to GATT requirements. Then the cost to China of doing otherwise would be higher.

In one sense Hong Kong's membership in the GATT could be a disadvantage. If Hong Kong were to be stripped of GATT membership – perhaps because other members could no longer distinguish between products of Hong Kong and the mainland – the loss to the Hong Kong business community could be devastating in its psychological impact. Such an eventuality could arise if the Chinese leadership lost interest in the contribution Hong Kong could make to its national goals. If that were the case, it would be likely to imply that the prosperity of the Hong Kong economy had been waning for some time. This would further imply that the size and strength of the Hong Kong business community had dropped sizably. Chinese loss of interest in Hong Kong could also stem from mismanagement or lack of control by Beijing – for example, from inadvertence, or from unsanctioned meddling by Communist Party representatives in Hong Kong. But here, too, the decline of Hong Kong would be unlikely to be precipitous; the Hong Kong business community would have shrunk.

Although the number of non-PRC businessmen remaining in Hong Kong's probably would not be large in the event of Hong Kong's being stripped of GATT membership, the psychological blow would not be confined to Hong Kong. Hong Kong émigrés and foreign business would no longer have any basis for viewing Hong Kong as offering more opportunities than those in the PRC itself. In this sense the horizon for world business would have shrunk.

It is in the best interest of Hong Kong as well as of the United States and its allies that China continue with its economic reform and "open door" policies. A China committed to growth would honor its promises to Hong Kong because it would be in its own interest to do so. In any event until 1992 while China is pressed by rising debt service requirements, Hong Kong will be useful to it in earning foreign exchange. A China whose GATT membership was still pending would have an even more compelling reason to make a "one country, two systems" work.

Depending on the flow of events in the early 1990s, China could perceive that its national interest might lie in a phasing of its membership in the GATT, not a step-by-step membership for the entire mainland, but by a province-by-province membership. That province whose economy most nearly approached GATT requirements – Guangdong in all probability – would, as a customs

156　　*China, Hong Kong, Taiwan and World Trade*

territory, be the first part of China to accede. Additional coastal provinces would accede as their economies and price systems more nearly approached the conditions prevailing in world markets. In time, with appropriate management from Beijing – and it need not take too long – all provinces of China would be members. Since all would be practicing the same trade regime, the customs territories would be unified into a single China membership.

Hong Kong could be of enormous aid to China in such a process and such a process could facilitate China's economic reform and modernization program. The major obstacle that China has confronted in its economic modernization program lies in the difficulty of reforming its price system. Its unreformed price system also is the basis for GATT concerns over offering unconditional Chinese membership in the organization. The shift to market-based pricing is most complete in Guangdong province where extensive contacts with Hong Kong and the activities of Hong Kong businessmen have transformed the province's economy. There the Hong Kong dollar circulates widely; many prices are stated in Hong Kong dollars and are the same as Hong Kong prices. Guangdong is in fact much more a part of the Hong Kong economy that it is part of China's. Because of the influence of Hong Kong, Guangdong is more nearly ready for GATT membership than is any other part of China.

In December 1988 China announced that ten areas of Hong Kong law concerning economic and commercial matters would be introduced systematically into Shenzhen, the SEZ in Guangdong, and then into other economically advanced cities and areas.[11] The idea was sound and could be expanded. If China were to put the Guangdong economy under the administration of Hong Kong, to be operated on the basis of Hong Kong law, it would establish a de facto province-wide training program for regional managers and officials, enhance efficiency, and solve the problem of confidence in Hong Kong. It could curtail corruption in Guangdong by establishing and enforcing a rule of law and offering alternative employment opportunities to party members. Foreign investors and traders would be reassured and trade between the rest of China and Guangdong-Hong Kong would thrive. Bankruptcy would be enforceable because the new business springing up would absorb workers released by bankruptcy. Hong Kong's financiers would provide training in operating a more efficient financial system and in regulating the money supply. In due course experienced Guangdong officials and enterprise managers would provide, through investment

Outlook and Implications for U.S. and Western Policy 157

and joint ventures, the stimulus and training to neighboring provinces that Hong Kong had supplied to Guangdong. As members of the GATT, Guangdong personnel would obtain valuable experience for the rest of China while being able to participate in the benefits that GATT membership is perceived by China to offer. The philosophy of "one country, two systems" could be applied with benefit within the PRC itself.

Such a course would be contemplated only by a Chinese regime committed to an economic reform program. It would require skillful management and support from Beijing and a determination that China's legal system advance at least as rapidly as its economy. In addition, political decentralization in China tending toward a systemic collapse could also further tighten the integration of Guangdong and Hong Kong economies. Such a scenario offers the possibility of an extension of Hong Kong's economic system into Guangdong and the province's early application for membership in the GATT. Meanwhile, while the conservative Deng regime is in control there is little Hong Kong can do beyond an attempt to maintain and strengthen its economy and its legal system.

Apart from its economic and legal systems, Hong Kong's strength in the past has stemmed from its infrastructure and its human resources. The government already is working to expand and improve its physical infrastructure. In view of the more intense competition from cheaper unskilled labor elsewhere in the world, it would serve Hong Kong well if its government were to expand its educational system to encompass more technical training in order to raise the skills and productivity of its labor force.

Except for the United Kingdom, there is little that the West can do for Hong Kong. The United States and its allies can and should aid in offering citizenship to Hong Kong residents; they can and should keep their markets open to Hong Kong products and allow their private sectors free reign in decisions about trade with and investment in Hong Kong. They should support the British in their efforts to induce the PRC to aid in restoring confidence in Hong Kong, and urge the British to be more stalwart in those efforts. The United States, however, has neither a tradition of nor any sound legal basis for intervention in the affairs of Hong Kong. Any direct U.S. initiative in the fluid environment of the conservative Deng regime could do more harm than good.[12]

158   *China, Hong Kong, Taiwan and World Trade*

IMPLICATIONS FOR WESTERN POLICY: TAIWAN

A Window of Opportunity

Despite the anger, frustration and fear invoked in Taiwan by Tiananmen Square, Deng's great error could not have been more propitiously timed for Taiwan's advantage. The island's previously repressive political regime had moderated notably; its economy continued to be one of the most rapidly growing, while at the same time undergoing an adjustment in the structure of its industrial composition and a rapid opening of sectors previously closed to the rest of the world. Perhaps the most potent recent change had been the shift in Taiwan's foreign policy stance from one of withdrawal and isolation from the world to an active pursuit of international contacts and diplomatic respectability.

Taiwan's previous foreign policies had been self-defeating. Scorning all contact with representatives from the mainland and remaining adamantly uncompromising on the issue of name, Taiwan had frustrated the efforts of its few remaining friends to help it remain part of the world. The anachronism of one of the world's most successful economies and trading entities being totally unrecognized and unrepresented in world forums, even statistically, deepened. The international respect which Taiwan's economic accomplishments should have won for it was confined to the press. Diplomatically, respect for Taiwan had diminished and its power to influence the world had disappeared. Its foreign policy had been a failure.

Especially under President Lee Teng-lui, Taiwan's policy toward the mainland became more subtle and less self-defeating. Personal contacts and trade between Taiwan and the mainland were partially legalized. The flat refusal of Taiwan to participate in any forums at which the mainland was represented was moderated and Taiwan even became more flexible about the name to which it would respond.

By mid-1989 the success of Taiwan's new foreign policy had been at best modest. Most of the rest of the world, much more impressed by PRC's size and potential power than by Taiwan's actual accomplishments, was dissuaded from responding favorably and openly to Taiwan's overtures by PRC opposition. Member countries made it clear that Taiwan's return to the GATT or entrance into the OECD hinged on China's acquiescence.

The shock and revulsion with which most of the world viewed Tiananmen Square changed the attitude of the world toward China.

Outlook and Implications for U.S. and Western Policy   159

Where formerly China had been treated as a fair-haired child, now it became a pariah. The shift in world favor away from China, however, was not accompanied by an opposite shift toward Taiwan. It was not at all clear for how long the PRC would remain in disfavor or how deep that disfavor was. But much of the world had been disillusioned by China at the same time that it had observed Taiwan taking many commendable steps. Clearly a window of opportunity had opened which Taiwan should be able to exploit to its own diplomatic advantage.

To do so, it is imperative that Taiwan continue to liberalize its economic and political systems. Any turn backward toward repression or even any long pause in moving steadily step-by-step toward representative government and an open economy could mean the loss of the opportunity. If the Lee government is successful in containing the politically rambunctious Taiwanese who have been infused with enthusiasm by their new political freedoms, if Lee continues to be successful in inducing mainlanders elected to the legislature 40 years earlier to retire and in replacing them by Taiwanese, if the opening of the economy to imports, and to foreign investment and foreign services continues, the world will become increasingly responsive to Taiwan's overtures.

Conditions for GATT Membership

Taiwan's search for diplomatic status and recognition is probably most likely to be successful in its overtures for GATT membership. Here its case is strong. It is the world's eleventh largest exporter. It has grown from being a backward, poverty-stricken former colony into an industrialized economy in little more than a quarter of a century. In applying for membership as an industrial country (Taiwan's return to the GATT as a developing country is out of the question), it would win plaudits as the first of the NICs voluntarily to graduate out of LDC status. Its representatives could aid in counseling GATT LDC members in how to manage the vicissitudes of world trade and their own sustained economic development. As a small resource-poor economy totally dependent on trade its vital national interests lie in supporting the GATT and helping to make the organization work. There could be no question of Taiwan's becoming a disruptive GATT member.

Taiwan will have no trouble in convincing the world of the strength of its case. Most of the major trading nations have already

160 *China, Hong Kong, Taiwan and World Trade*

admitted unofficially that Taiwan should be in the GATT, but they demurred to the PRC's insistence that it should be the first to rejoin. Taiwan's task after Tiananmen Square is to ascertain how many GATT members can be convinced that it is no longer in their or GATT's interest to delay Taiwan's membership, and how long this would take.

Again the arguments that Taiwan can present are strong. Taiwan's trade regime, in contrast to that of Beijing, requires relatively few corrections to be brought into full compliance with the GATT. Taiwan has been making and continues to make these adjustments as well as exchange rate and financial sector changes required for full adherence to the GATT. In 1989 it published in English a description of the structure of Taiwan's tax system including customs duties and other areas of concern to GATT members.[13] It would be enthusiastically willing to work with GATT experts in facilitating the introduction of further necessary changes. With Taiwan in the GATT its trading partners would have a multilateral as well as a bilateral forum for discussing trade disputes. Bilateral relations between Taiwan and its trading partners would be smoothed because in each case GATT would share the blame with the domestic administration for any industries injured by adherence to GATT rules. All parties would benefit. The only cost to the U.S. or to the West would lie in the potential deterioration of Sino-West relations that might be the consequence of admitting Taiwan to the GATT before the PRC.

Taiwan's January 1, 1990 application for GATT membership created a dilemma for the world trading community. Taiwan's choice of name was astute. It applied as the separate customs territory of Taiwan, Penghu, Kinmen, and Matsu, underlining by its inclusion of the tiny islands off the coast of the mainland the fact that Taiwan is part of China. The article under which it applied (XXXIII) permits the government of a separate customs territory that has full autonomy over it external commercial relations to accede to the GATT on approval of a two-thirds majority of the existing members.

Most of the important trading countries would nevertheless be reluctant to commit themselves to support Taiwan's application for membership until the future of the PRC is clarified. As long as a conservative regime in Beijing is beset with intractable economic problems and social and political restiveness, there is the danger that a ready acceptance of Taiwan into a major international

Outlook and Implications for U.S. and Western Policy   161

organization would be perceived in Beijing as an additional sanction, a further turning of the world's collective back on China and one foreshadowing the world's refusal to aid in China's efforts to catch up with the world by denying its technology and capital to China. A ready acceptance of Taiwan back into the community of nations could cause a conservative and proud regime in Beijing to withdraw from the world. The ready acceptance of Taiwan into the GATT could also be perceived in Beijing as acceptance by the West of "two Chinas" and thus as foreshadowing de facto independence for Taiwan. Such an acceptance would run the risk of an invasion of Taiwan by the mainland and a bloody and bitter battle there.

GATT members may need much more evidence that a conservative regime in Beijing is (1) likely to be of long duration and (2) more likely to retreat from rather than undertake any further steps toward a market-controlled economy. Even if and when these conditions come to prevail, the important trading countries may still be reluctant to admit Taiwan without China's agreement.

Thus it seems likely that Taiwan has an interval of time, two or so years, during which it can continue to lay the groundwork for eventual accession to the GATT. It could use this interval to good advantage in strengthening the political acceptability in Taiwan of such a move. Conservative mainlanders have been rugged in their opposition to most of Taiwan's new foreign policy, objecting to increasing contacts with the mainland and to Taiwan's abandonment of the name "Republic of China." Time by itself could reduce the size of this opposition group but the ground at home for Taiwan's return to the world could meanwhile be usefully strengthened. Taipei's new flexibility on name has been opposed by conservatives for implying a retreat from the Nationalist position of representing all of China. It has also been opposed by that part of the opposition who supported independence for Taiwan as implying subjugation to Peking. Taipei needs to do more at home in explaining the advantages, political and economic, that would flow to Taiwan as a consequence of being in the GATT, in order to preempt support for the opposition. Although the independence movement in Taiwan has been small, it has been active and vociferous abroad. The issue has been too sensitive and emotionally wrought to warrant complacency on the part of Taipei.

Taiwan could also use this interval to good advantage in practising the art of diplomacy. Taiwan has never had much opportunity to develop the skills required to influence other countries. Restricted

162   *China, Hong Kong, Taiwan and World Trade*

as it has been in official contacts with foreigners, such negotiating skills as it may have developed would be those associated with commercial bargaining. Its foreign service in the narrow sense of the term is tiny, there having been so few foreign postings open to it.

Finally, Taiwan can use the interval to pursue the process leading to accession. After receiving a formal application for accession, the GATT must form working groups to process the application through the various stages of established GATT procedures. These procedures take time and must be completed before an applicant can become a member.

If during this interval the regime in China should change to one based on the rule of law and favoring economic reform, an extension of the market mechanism and China's participation in the international division of labor, Taiwan would have two potential options. The new regime might be more forthcoming about Taiwan's joining the GATT before the PRC becomes a member, also the new regime on the mainland might be willing to agree to Taiwan's early entry as evidence of its own intent to cooperate with the GATT in making it an effective and widely representative organization. Much would depend on whether relations between China and the West had deteriorated badly during the interregnum.

Should Beijing continue to insist that Taiwan's return to the GATT must follow that of the PRC, and should be West delay action on Taiwan's application, Taiwan could bargain. Beijing's new regime undoubtedly would still be facing severe economic problems at home, whose solution would require more capital and rising productivity. Taiwan could play the role in China's eastern provinces that Hong Kong had played for the south; indeed Taiwanese businessmen trading with and investing in Fujian province already have had a large and stimulating impact on economic growth there. If Taiwan were to legalize direct trade and investment with the mainland, commerce would grow rapidly. Much of the Taiwanese shoe industry already has moved across the straits; other labor-intensive industries would follow. Taiwanese businessmen have been eager for legalized direct trade for some years and the mainland had been actively encouraging it. It would benefit economies on both sides of the straits. A Beijing oriented toward reform would find it hard to resist the offer of legalized trade and investment in return for the PRC's acquiescence in Taiwan's early membership in the GATT.

A liberal, outward-facing regime in Beijing might look with favor on a provincially-based development program and phased GATT

Outlook and Implications for U.S. and Western Policy 163

membership by provinces. Taiwan could be as helpful as could Hong Kong in support of growth in China's eastern seaboard.

Political Decentralization in China

Differential provincially-based development programs would arise as an integral part of another scenario for China's future – that of political as well as economic decentralization in China, the evolution of a federal system or even systemic collapse. With weakness at the center and strong, independent provinces, Beijing would have little strength or inclination to threaten Taiwan or the West. No single province would have the military strength for a successful invasion of the island and collusion among them would be unlikely. Such a development of China, undesirable from the viewpoint of the long-term interests of the West, would imply regional protectionism and a contraction of the division of labor within China. It would be likely to mean a much closer integration of some provinces with the West, but increasing isolation and poverty of others. Political decentralization of the PRC would be the scenario most favorable to an early return of Taiwan to the international organizations. The danger in this case to both Taiwan and the West would be a repetition sometime in the future of the events starting in 1971 that eventually led to Taiwan's isolation.

Return to Central Control in China

If developments on the mainland in the next two or so years take the opposite course, if a conservative regime in Beijing appears to be more firmly entrenched, if China extends its central controls over prices and production, and if China's trade with the West drops sharply, Taiwan's chances for GATT membership might improve. Especially if Deng has died and been replaced by a repressive dictatorship would this be so. Under such a scenario the West would be more responsive to Taiwan's overtures.

Then the U.S. should consider taking the initiative to support Taiwan's application. If it decided to do so, it should assure Beijing that U.S. support for Taiwan's GATT membership reflects U.S. support for the "one country, two systems" policy and thus its acknowledgement that Taiwan is part of China. The United States should also assure Beijing that such a U.S. initiative in no way implies any lack of support for future GATT membership by PRC,

164   *China, Hong Kong, Taiwan and World Trade*

but rather that the U.S. will stand ready to aid Beijing in this effort when the Chinese economy is once again moving toward compliance with GATT principles. The U.S. should also convey to Taipei and Beijing that its support for Taiwan's membership is based upon Taiwan's use a name that implies nothing about its claim to represent all of China.

Such a move would not be risk-free. It could force the PRC back into total isolation, but (by hypothesis) it had been moving in that direction with no evidence of any likelihood of a reversal. It could trigger a military invasion of Taiwan and an attempt to regain control of the island by force. If the Beijing regime were well-entrenched, however, the political cost to it in lives and materiel would probably be weighed more rationally than by an insecure leadership. The risk, however, would exist and would have to be carefully estimated at the time.

The PRC would probably threaten to reduce its imports of U.S. goods and those of any other GATT member supporting Taiwan's application. Since trade with China already had dropped in importance, U.S. diplomats should be able to counter the effectiveness of such attempted blackmail.

The West should not be faced with an either-or choice in the matter of membership in a technical trade organization. A government that is qualified for membership and already accounts for a large segment of world trade should be admitted if it applies – after its own careful evaluation of the risks to itself in so doing. The GATT accepts a "government" as a member; since Taiwan's GATT name carries no country-status implication, China has no reason to object. The West has done itself and China a disservice in according preferential treatment to China in the past. Since Taiwan is willing to bow on the name issue and is qualified in other ways, it should be admitted to the world's trade organization.

A populist military dictatorship in China would probably be no less adamant than its predecessors about Taiwan's reintegration with the mainland. Whether a military dictatorship would honor the PRC's promise of "one country, two systems" is problematic. Whether its perception of the cost of retaking Taiwan by force would be more cavalier than that of a politically insecure regime or whether it would put more weight on the loss of life involved is also impossible to determine a priori. Both Taiwan and the West would have to weigh carefully the risks to Taiwan of its membership in the GATT under such conditions.

Outlook and Implications for U.S. and Western Policy   165

The countries of the West will confront an evolving complex mix of policy considerations as the People's Republic of China struggles to define its own nature and destiny in the near and perhaps long-term future. There is little that the West can do to influence the outcome. The West's influence is at the margin in providing or withholding a last straw or a push for events that probably would happen anyway. In the case of China's application for membership in the GATT, however, the West does have one small lever of influence. So long as the application is still pending, China is likely to be at least somewhat constrained in its policies toward Hong Kong and Taiwan in order to avoid giving further offense to its major trading partners. But in general China is too big, too patient and too volatile, too submissive and too rebellious, too corrupt, and too idealistic to be manipulatable from abroad. Essentially the West can only hope that sooner rather than later the Chinese people will have a leadership that their qualities of diligence, self-discipline, and devotion merit.

Notes

CHAPTER 1: INTRODUCTION

1. *Far Eastern Economic Review* (July 28, 1988, p. 88).
2. Dean Carver, "China's Experiment with Fiscal and Monetary Policy," in Joint Economic Committee *China's Economy Looks Toward the Year 2000, Vol. 1, The Four Modernizations,* Washington, DC, 1986, p. 111.

CHAPTER 2: CHINA'S ECONOMIC REFORMS

1. Chen Tiwei, Why is China Opening to the Outside?" *Beijing Review,* no. 15 (April 1, 1985): 18–22.
2. Robert F. Dernberger, "China's Economic Reforms," *Asia Pacific Report, 1989, Focus: China in the Reform Era,* C. E. Morrison and R. F. Dernberger, eds. (Honolulu: East-West Center, 1989), 55.
3. Robert Michael Field, "China: The Changing Structure of Industry," *China's Economy Looks Toward the Year 2000, The Four Modernizations,* Vol. 1, Joint Economic Committee (Washington, D.C.: GPO, 1986), 530; Shahid Javed Burki, "Reform and Growth in China," *Finance and Development* (Washington, D.C.: International Monetary Fund, December 1988), 46.
4. *Renmin Ribao,* March 30, 1981, p. 6.
5. Field, "China: The Changing Structure of Industry," 506.
6. A. Doak Barnett, *China's Economy in Global Perspective* (Washington, D.C.: The Brookings Institution, 1981), 299.
7. Harry Harding, *China's Second Revolution* (Washington, D.C.: The Brookings Institution, 1987), 31.
8. Barnett, *China's Economy in Global Perspective,* 28.
9. Harding, *China's Second Revolution,* 30, citing official sources.
10. This section draws heavily on the detailed discussion of the early years of China's economic reform in Part 1, Barnett, *China's Economy in Global Perspective,* 12–121.
11. Ibid., 310.
12. *Financial Times,* August 20, 1979.
13. Ibid.
14. Ibid., section 5 (*Economy*).
15. Central Intelligence Agency, Directorate of Intelligence, *China: Economic Performance in 1987 and Outlook for 1988,* EA88–10018, Washington, D.C., May 1988, p. 5; Harding, *China's Second Revolution,* 106; *Financial Times,* March 8, 1989, p. 4.
16. *Financial Times,* March 8, 1989, p. 6.

166

Notes to pp. 33–38 167

17. *Journal of Commerce* (July 24, 1989).
18. *China: Finance and Investment,* World Bank Country Study (Washington, D.C.: World Bank, 1988), 353–54.
19. Ibid., 300.
20. *Far Eastern Economic Review* (August 10, 1989); 47.
21. International Monetary Fund, *International Financial Statistics,* various issues.
22. *New York Times,* October 28, 1988.
23. Ford S. Worthy, "Why There's Still Promise in China," *Fortune,* February 27, 1989.
24. *Beijing Review* (January 30–February 5, 1989): 20; *Far Eastern Economic Review* (March 2, 1989): 49.
25. *World Bank Development Report 1988* (Washington, D.C.: World Bank, 1988), 228; *Beijing Review* (January 30–February 5, 1989): 24.
26. Chinese economists at the end of the decade were studying Chinese economic cycles, examining the reasons for their greater intensity after 1978 than before. *Far Eastern Economic Review* (March 2, 1989): 48.
27. James A. Yunker, "A New Perspective on Market Socialism," *Comparative Economic Studies* 30, no. 2 (Summer 1988): 69–116, summarizes the history of the argument.
28. Christine P. W. Wong, "Between Plan and Market: The Role of the Local Sector in Post-Mao China," *Journal of Comparative Economics* 11, no. 3 (September 1987): 387.
29. Ibid., 389.
30. *Far Eastern Economic Review* (September 8, 1988).
31. Li Yunqi, "Can China Make use of Inflation?" *Intertrade* (July 1988): 22.
32. *Journal of Commerce* (February 22, 1989): 15.
33. Central Intelligence Agency, *China: Economic Performance in 1985,* Report to the Joint Economic Committee, March 17, 1986, Photocopy.
34. William A. Byrd, "The Impact of the Two Tier Plan/Market System in Chinese Industry," *Journal of Comparative Economics* 2, no. 3 (September 1987): 299.
35. World Bank, *China: Finance and Investment* (Washington, D.C.: World Bank, 1988), 53, 77.
36. *MOR [Market Opinion Research] China Letter* (January/February 1989): 4.
37. *Beijing Review* (October 3, 1988): 7; *Far Eastern Economic Review* (January 28, 1988): 72.
38. Harding, *China's Second Revolution,* 104.
39. Dwight H. Perkins, "Reforming China's Economic System," *Journal of Economic Literature* 26, no. 2 (June 1988): 612–27; Nicholas R. Lardy, "Prospects and Some Policy Problems of Agricultural Development in China," *American Journal of Agricultural Economies* 68, no. 2 (May 1986): 451.

168   *Notes to pp. 33–38*

40. Lardy, "Prospects and Some Policy Problems of Agricultural Development in China," 451–57; Nicholas R. Lardy, "Agricultural Reform," *Journal of International Affairs* 39, no. 2 (Winter 1986): 91–104.
41. Gregory C. Chow, "Development of a More Market-Oriented Economy in China," *Science,* January 16, 1987, p. 296.
42. Wu Jinglian and Zhao Renwei, *Journal of Comparative Economies* 11, no. 3 (September 1987): 309–18.
43. Harding, *China's Second Revolution,* 112.
44. *Asian Wall Street Journal Weekly,* February 13, 1989; *Wall Street Journal,* March 2, 1989; Harding, *China's Second Revolution,* 129.
45. *Far Eastern Economic Review* (September 8, 1988).
46. *The Economist,* August 27, 1988, p. 22.
47. *Journal of Commerce* (July 28, 1988); *Economist,* November 9, 1988; *Wall Street Journal,* March 2, 1989. The CIA stated that, in 1987, 12 percent of state enterprises lost money. See Joint Economic Committee, 100th Congress, 2nd Session, April 13 and 21, 1988, "Allocation of Resources in Soviet Union and China – 1987," Part 13, p. 127.
48. *New York Times,* September 26, 1988.
49. *Asian Wall Street Journal Weekly,* February 13, 1989 and February 27, 1989.
50. *Far Eastern Economic Review* (September 8, 1988).
51. Wong, "Between Plan and Market," 292–95; D.H. Perkins, *Journal of Economic Literature* 26, no. 2 (June 1988): 616; Zhang Shaojie, Cui Heming, Xu Gong, and Ji Xiaoming, "Investment: Initial Changes in the Mechanism and Preliminary Ideas about Reform," *Reform in China: Challenges and Choices,* Bruce L. Reynolds, ed. (Armonk, N.Y.: M.E. Sharpe, Inc./China Economic System Reform Research Institute [CESRRI], 1987), 109; Steven Butler, "Realm Between Two Tracks," *Financial Times,* December 14, 1988.
52. *Journal of Commerce* (December 22, 1988).
53. *Beijing Review* (January 30–February 5, 1989): 21–23; *Far Eastern Economic Review* (March 2, 1989): 50; Joint Economic Committee, *China's Economy Looks Toward the Year 2000,* Vol. 2 (Washington, D.C.: GPO, 1986), 1–132; "Road Works Ahead: Traffic Congestion Is Choking China's Cities," *Far Eastern Economic Review* (July 7, 1988): 79.
54. Shaojie *et al., Reform in China,* 54–55.
55. *China Daily,* September 13, 1988.
56. *New York Times,* April 11, 1989, p. D21; *Beijing Review* (April 10–16, 1989): 11; *Far Eastern Economic Review* (March 9, 1989): 81.
57. Ellen Salem, "Things Fall Apart, The Centre Cannot Hold," *Far Eastern Economic Review* (October 27, 1988): 38; Wang Zhigang, "Local Power and Central Planning," (in Chinese) *Outlook Weekly* (September 26, 1988): 4–7.
58. *Asian Wall Street Journal Weekly,* October 17, 1988; "Profiteers Did It," *The Economist,* October 22, 1988; *Journal of Commerce* (November 4, 1988); *Washington Post,* October 21, 1988.

Notest to pp. 38–47 169

59. *Journal of Commerce* (October 28, 1988).
60. *Asian Wall Street Journal Weekly,* January 30, 1989.
61. *Far Eastern Economic Review* (January 19, 1989): 63.
62. Michel Korzes, "Contract Labor, the 'Right to Work' and New Labor Laws in the People's Republic of China," *Comparative Economic Studies* 30, no. 2 (Summer 1988): 117–32.
63. Harding, *China's Second Revolution,* 119; *Far Eastern Economic Review* (January 19, 1989): 63; *Wall Street Journal,* January 27, 1989; *Journal of Commerce* (December 7, 1988); *Journal of Commerce* (November 1, 1988).
64. *Beijing Review* (August 22, 1988): 23.
65. See, for example, *Far Eastern Economic Review* (January 12, 1989): 45; *The Economist,* December 10, 1988, p. 31; Daniel Southerland, "Some Chinese Fear 'Economic Warlordism,'" *Washington Post,* December 12, 1988; Edward A. Gargan, "Along the Chinese Coastline Economic Dragon Awakens," *New York Times,* August 13, 1988; *The Economist,* August 13, 1988, p. 62.
66. *Beijing Review* (August 22–28, 1988): 18.
67. *New York Times,* December 16, 1988.
68. *New York Times,* November 1, 1988; *Journal of Commerce* (November 1, 1988); *Journal of Commerce* (December 7, 1988).
69. *Far Eastern Economic Review* (December 11, 1986): 82; *Asian Wall Street Journal Weekly,* December 22, 1986, p. 6; *Journal of Commerce* (April 11, 1988).
70. *New York Times,* December 16, 1988.
71. *Asian Wall Street Journal Weekly,* January 30, 1989; William A. Byrd, "Rural Industrialization and Ownership in China," Paper presented at a joint meeting of the Chinese Economic Association in North America and the American Economic Association, New York, December 28–30, 1988. This paper discusses the equivocal empirical evidence of private enterprise efficiency in China.
72. *Journal of Commerce* (July 13, 1988); *New York Times,* August 5, 1988; Salem, "Things Fall Apart," 36.
73. *Asian Wall Street Journal Weekly,* August 15, 1988.
74. *Asian Wall Street Journal Weekly,* March 27, 1989, p. 1.
75. Salem, "Things Fall Apart," 36.
76. Michael Ellman, "China's OTC Markets," *Comparative Economic Studies* 30, no. 1 (Spring 1988): 61; *Asian Wall Street Journal Weekly,* August 15, 1988.
77. *Journal of Commerce* (February 3, 1988); *Journal of Commerce* (April 27, 1988).
78. *Journal of Commerce* (July 15, 1988); 7A; *Far Eastern Economic Review* (March 9, 1989): 73.
79. *Asian Wall Street Journal Weekly,* November 7, 1988.
80. *Asian Wall Street Journal Weekly,* August 22, 1988.
81. *Journal of Commerce* (August 9, 1988).
82. *Wall Street Journal,* April 3, 1989, p. 21; *Wall Street Journal,* March 29, 1989, p. 10; *Far Eastern Economic Review* (January 5, 1989): 54–55.

170   *Notes to pp. 47–56*

83. *New York Times,* April 15, 1989, p. 3.
84. *Journal of Commerce* (April 17, 1989): 9A; *Journal of Commerce* (April 5, 1989): 5A; *Financial Times,* February 15, 1989.
85. *Far Eastern Economic Review* (March 30, 1989): 11.
86. *Beijing Review* (April 17–23, 1989): 9.
87. *Far Eastern Economic Review* (March 2, 1989): 48.
88. Alvin and Heidi Toffler, "Socialism in Crisis: China's Answer," *World Monitor* (January 1989): 41.
89. *Asian Wall Street Journal Weekly,* March 27, 1989, p. 1.
90. *Asian Wall Street Journal Weekly,* July 3, 1989, p. 14.
91. *Wall Street Journal,* March 22, 1989, p. 11.
92. *The Economist,* April 8, 1989, p. 40.
93. *Beijing Review* (April 17–23, 1989): 26.
94. Salem, "Things Fall Apart," 36, 40.
95. Like all Chinese statistical data, those on foreign trade are criticized and frequently adjusted by Western analysts. See, for example, *Intertrade* (July 1988): 54; Alan Whiting, "China's Economy in a Global and Regional Context," *U.S.–China Trade: Problems and Prospects,* Eugene K. Lawson, ed. (New York: Praeger, 1988), 32; Doak Barnett, *China's Economy in Global Perspective* (Washington, D.C.: The Brookings Institution, 1981), xviii–xxi; Harry Harding, *China's Second Revolution* (Washington, D.C.: The Brookings Institution, 1987), 140, 142, footnotes. Some Western observers explain China's exclusion of re-exports from its trade data as an attempt by China to minimize the potential size of its trade, about which the West was apprehensive.
96. *New York Times,* November 10, 1975.
97. *Journal of Commerce* (January 19, 1979).
98. General Agreement on Tariffs and Trade (GATT), *International Trade 1987–1988,* Vol. 2 (Geneva: GATT, 1988), Table AA5.
99. *New York Times,* March 9, 1979, p. 63; GATT, *International Trade,* Vol. 2, Table AA3; *The Economist,* March 3, 1979, p. 63; *Beijing Review* (March 6, 1989): 20.
100. *New York Times,* September 16, 1975.
101. Barnett, *China's Economy in Global Perspective,* 132.
102. Department of State, Bureau of Public Affairs, *Gist* (January 1979): 1.
103. Penelope Hartland-Thunberg, "Limits of Trade with China," *Executive* (June 1979): 33–35.
104. *Financial Times,* July 12, 1989, p. 1; *Economist,* August 27, 1988, p. 21; IMF, *International Financial Statistics,* August 1989; Harding, *China's Second Revolution,* 139.
105. Computed from Chinese data. *Beijing Review* (March 6–12, 1989): 23.
106. GATT, *International Trade 88–89,* Vol. 2, p. 3.
107. Ibid., 28.
108. *Forbes,* October 3, 1988, p. 49; *Far Eastern Economic Review* (June 2, 1988): 26.

Notest to pp. 56–60 171

109. *Beijing Review* (March 6, 1989): 20; Eugene K. Lawson estimates 9–10 percent of GNP in "Conclusion," *U.S.–China Trade: Problems and Prospects,* Eugene K. Lawson, ed. (New York: Praeger, 1988), 298.
110. *Far Eastern Economic Review* (August 11, 1988): 48.
111. *Journal of Commerce* (May 23, 1989): 8.
112. Harding, *China's Second Revolution,* 144; International Monetary Fund, *International Financial Statistics,* April 1989; *Beijing Review* (March 6, 1989): 22.
113. *Petroleum Intelligence Weekly,* May 1, 1989, pp. 4, 5; *Statistical Yearbook of China* [English edition] (Hong Kong: Economic Information Agency, various years).
114. Harding, *China's Second Revolution,* 143; *Beijing Review* (March 6, 1989): 21; *Journal of Commerce* (August 5, 1988).
115. Xu Xianquan, "The Commodity Composition of Exports," *China's Foreign Trade,* Zhang Peiji and Ralph W. Huenemann, eds, (Halifax, Nova Scotia: Institute for Research on Public Policy, 1987): 36–42.
116. James T.H. Tsao, *China's Development Strategies and Foreign Trade* (Lexington, Mass.: Lexington Books, 1987), 81; John Frankenstein, "Understanding Chinese Trade," *Current History* (September 1986): 257–75.
117. *Washington Post,* January 31, 1989; *Wall Street Journal,* August 26, 1988; *Statistical Yearbook of China, 1988.*
118. *The Economist,* October 3, 1987; *Wall Street Journal,* April 22, 1987; *Journal of Commerce* (August 26, 1988); *New York Times,* August 26, 1988; Penelope Francks, "Learning from Japan: Plant Imports and Technology Transfer in the Chinese Iron and Steel Industry," *Journal of Japanese and International Economics* (Tokyo Center for Economic Research) 2, no. 1 (March 1988): 42–62.
119. *Statistical Yearbook of China,* various years.
120. Ai Wei, "Technology Trade Between the United States and Mainland China in Recent Years," *Issues and Studies* 24, no. 8 (August 1988): 82–119.
121. Li Shude, "Sino-U.S. Trade: A Chinese Perspective," *U.S.-China Trade: Problems and Prospects,* Chapter 2; Nicholas R. Lardy, *China's Entry into the World Economy: Implications for Northeast Asia and the U.S.* (New York: Asia Society, 1987), 21–26.
122. Jerome Turtola, "Textile Trade Tensions," *China Business Review* 13 (September–October 1986): 26–31.
123. Phillip D. Fletcher, "Imports from China at Issue," *China Business Review* 13 (September–October 1986): 22–25.
124. Committee for Fair Trade with China, "History of the Committee for Fair Trade with China," Medina, Washington, January 1, 1988, p. 3, Photocopy.
125. *Inside U.S. Trade* 5, no. 23 (June 5, 1987): 3–5.
126. Lardy, *China's Entry into the World Economy,* 24.
127. *Washington Post,* August 15, 1978.
128. *Business Week,* November 6, 1978, p. 164; *The Economist,* December 9, 1978.
129. *Wall Street Journal,* March 6, 1979.

172 *Notest to pp. 78–93*

130. *World Business Weekly,* December 31, 1979, p. 50.
131. *The Economist,* December 8, 1979; Barnett, *China's Economy in Global Perspective,* 145–146.
132. *Washington Post,* June 21, 1979; *New York Times,* July 12, 1979.
133. *Asian Wall Street Journal Weekly,* April 21, 1988 and April 17, 1981.
134. Lawrence J. Brainard, "Soviet International Financial Policy: Traditional Formulas on New Innovations?" *Gorbachev's Economic Plans,* U.S. Congress Joint Economic Committee, Vol. 1, November 23, 1987, pp. 108–109; Shahid Javed Burki, "Reform and Growth in China," 46–59; *Financial Times,* November 12, 1986, p. 5; IMF and World Bank officials.
135. *Beijing Review* (March 6–12, 1989): 26–29.
136. *China Reconstructs,* April 1989, p. 26; *Journal of Commerce* (February 16, 1989); *Financial Times,* June 29, 1989, p. VII.
137. *The Economist Survey,* June 3, 1989; *Asian Wall Street Journal Weekly,* April 10, 1989.
138. *Asian Wall Street Journal Weekly,* June 13, 1988.
139. *The Economist,* May 6, 1989, p. 77.
140. *Beijing Review* (March 6–12, 1989): 42.
141. *Far Eastern Economic Review* (January 19, 1989): 48–49.
142. *Financial Times,* April 28, 1988.
143. *Wall Street Journal,* June 7, 1989, p. C1; *Journal of Commerce* (June 9, 1989): A5.
144. Barnett, *China's Economy in Global Perspective,* 223.
145. *Asian Wall Street Journal Weekly,* July 17, 1989, p. 4; *Far Eastern Economic Review* (July 27, 1989): 57; *New York Times,* August 14, 1989, p. D1.
146. Most of the material in the following paragraphs on doing business in China was derived from conversations with foreign business executives in China and Hong Kong during a visit to the area in September 1988. See also the annual *National Trade Estimates Report on Foreign Trade Barriers* by the Office of the U.S. Trade Representative, the Department of Agriculture, and the Department of Commerce and *Importing from China* (Hong Kong: Trade Media Ltd., 1988).
147. Nicholas R. Lardy, "Economic Developments in the People's Republic of China," Paper presented at the Eighteenth Sino-American Conference, Stanford, June 8–11, 1989, pp. 22–30.

CHAPTER 3: CHINA AND THE WORLD TRADING SYSTEM

1. John Yochelson, ed., *Keeping Pace: U.S. Policies and Global Economic Change,* Ballinger, Cambridge, Mass. for CSIS, 1988.
2. *Financial Times,* September 14, 1989, p. 1.

Notest to pp. 78–93 173

3. The details of China's preparations for membership in the Bank, Fund and the GATT are discussed in Harold K. Jacobson and Michel Oksenberg *China and the Keystone International Economic Organizations,* University of Michigan, 18 September 1987, Chapter 2 (draft).
4. *Journal of Commerce* (February 9, 1981; October 14, 1981).
5. *Financial Times,* January 14, 1986.
6. *Financial Times,* January 14, 1986.
7. *Financial Times,* January 13, 1986.
8. This and the following section draw on my chapter "China and the GATT: Time for Modernization" in John Yochelson, ed., *Keeping Pace: U.S. Policies and Global Economic Change,* Ballinger, Cambridge, Mass., 1988, pp. 175–202.
9. *Financial Times,* February 3, 1983.
10. *Financial Times,* September 15, 1981.
11. William J. Davey, *GATT: Its Present Operation and Prospects for the Future,* a paper presented at the Southwest Legal Foundation Symposium on Private Investment Abroad: International Business in 1986 – Problems and Solutions, June 17–19, 1986 pp. 39–40 (xeroxed).
12. Eliza R. Patterson, "Improving GATT Rules for Non-Market Economies," *Journal of World Trade Law,* Vol. 20, Number 2, March–April 1986, p. 187.
13. Kapur, Harish, *China and the European Economic Community: The New Convention,* Nijhoff, 1986, p. 41.
14. Phillip J. Bryson, Joseph M. Van Brabant, "Non-Market Pricing in the Socialist World Market" *Kyklos,* Vol. 28–2, 1975.
15. William J. Davey, *GATT: Its Present Operations and Prospects for Its Future,* p. 12.
16. Federal Reserve Bank of N.Y., *Quarterly Review,* Winter 1982–83, p. 41.
17. World Bank, *World Development Report 1988,* p. 242; Federal Reserve Bank of N.Y., op. cit., p. 50.
18. J. M. Richards, "Protectionism and the ITC," *China Business Review,* Sept.–Oct., 1982, pp. 28–31.
19. Computed from the files of USITC.
20. USITC, *Operation of the Trade Agreements Program, 40th Report 1988,* USITC Publication 2208, July 1989, pp. 193, 195.
21. Shu Ziquing and Wa Siahuang, "Policy Stances of Economies That Are Not in the GATT Toward That Organization," United Nations Department of International Economic and Social Affairs in cooperation with World Institute for Development Economic Research Symposium: Economic Reforms and the Role of Asian Centrally Planned Economic Relations, Paper No. 8 for Session II, Helsinki, 12–16 June 1989, p. 32 (xerox).
22. The Chinese position is forcefully argued in Li, Chung-chou "Resumption of China's GATT Membership," *Journal of World Trade Law,* Vol. 21, No. 4, August 1987, pp. 25–48.
23. John H. Jackson, *The World Trading System,* MIT, 1989, p. 270 (from page proof).
24. J. S. Jackson, op. cit., p. 268.

174 *Notes to pp. 94–105*

25. The Fair Trade Subcommittee of the American Chamber of Commerce in Hong Kong, "Import Controls in China: Protectionism with Chinese Characteristics," *China Business Review,* January–February 1987, pp. 42–45.
26. Jacobson and Oksenberg, op. cit., p. 82.
27. *Journal of Commerce* (June 14, 1989).

CHAPTER 4: "GREATER CHINA": THE SPECIAL PROBLEMS OF HONG KONG AND TAIWAN

1. *Journal of Commerce* (Dec. 29, 1988, p. 3A); *Business Weekly* (October 10, 1988); *Journal of Commerce* (September 13, 1988).
2. Y. C. Jao "Hong Kong's Economic Prospects after the Sino-British Agreement: A Preliminary Assessment" in Hungdah Chin, Y. C. Jao and Yuann-li Wu, eds., *The Future of Hong Kong,* Quorum Books, NY 1987, p. 58.
3. Piers Jacobs, "Hong Kong and the Modernization of China," *Journal of International Affairs,* Vol. 39, No. 2, Winter 1986, pp. 63–75.
4. U.S. Consulate in Hong Kong, *Economic Briefing,* Aug. 17, 1988, p. 6, xerox; *The Economist,* June 3, 1989, Survey, p. 20.
5. *Wall Street Journal,* November 8, 1982.
6. *The Economist,* June 3, 1989, Survey, p. 8; *Financial Times,* June 29, 1989, Survey, p. VI.
7. *Business America,* July 7, 1986, p. 13.
8. Kayser Sung, "Trading on from 1997 with Special Reference to Hong Kong's Textile Agreements," in Jao, Y. C. *et al.,* eds., *Hong Kong and 1997: Strategies for the Future,* Hong Kong, Centre of Asian Studies, University of Hong Kong, 1985, p. 306.
9. *Financial Times,* April 25, 1986.
10. *Financial Times,* Oct. 9, 1986.
11. *Far Eastern Economic Review,* Oct. 6, 1988, p. 62.
12. *Financial Times,* January 6, 1989.
13. *The Economist,* August 27, 1988, p. 64; *Financial Times,* June 12, 1989, p. 4; *Wall Street Journal,* March 29, 1989; *Business Weekly,* June 19, 1989.
14. *Asian Wall Street Journal Weekly,* January 21, 1980; *Far Eastern Economic Review* (January 26, 1989).
15. *Wall Street Journal,* March 29, 1984; *Washington Post,* March 31, 1984.
16. Hsin-Chi Kuan and Siu-Kai Lau, "Hong Kong's Search for a Consensus: Barriers and Prospects" in Chiu, Jao and Wu, eds., *Future of Hong Kong,* pp. 95–114.
17. *The Economist,* February 25, 1989, p. 13; April 22, 1989, p. 38; *Financial Times,* February 23, 1989.
18. *Financial Times,* February 22, 1989.

Notes to pp. 105–107 175

19. *Far Eastern Economic Review,* February 23, 1989, p. 42; *Financial Times,* August 12, 1988; December 8, 1988.
20. *New York Times,* May 23, 1989; *Financial Times,* May 26, 1989; *The Economist,* May 27, 1989; *Journal of Commerce* (June 2, 1989).
21. *Financial Times,* June 6, 1989.
22. *The Economist,* April 22, 1989, p. 38; *New York Times,* March 13, 1989, p. D4; unpublished study of the Hong Kong government.
23. *Financial Times,* June 29, 1989.
24. *Washington Post,* July 22, 1989, p. 18.
25. *Financial Times,* June 1, 1989.
26. *Journal of Commerce* (July 7, 1989, p. 5A).
27. *Washington Post,* July 14, 1989.
28. *Wall Street Journal,* July 10, 1989.
29. *Financial Times,* June 29, 1989.
30. *Wall Street Journal,* June 15, 1989.
31. *Wall Street Journal,* June 16, 1989.
32. *Journal of Commerce* (June 8, 1989); *Financial Times,* June 29, 1989.
33. *Financial Times,* June 29, 1989, p. VII.
34. *Wall Street Journal,* July 14, 1989.
35. *Far Eastern Economic Review* (July 27, 1989): 56–7.
36. Alvin Rabushka, *The New China: Comparative Economic Development in Mainland China, Taiwan and Hong Kong,* Westview Press, Boulder, for Pacific Research Institute for Public Policy, 1987, pp. 103–39.
37. *The Economist,* January 3, 1981, p. 30; *World Business Weekly,* May 19, 1980, p. 5; Leonard Ungar, "Derecognition Worked," *Foreign Policy,* Fall, 1979, No. 36, pp. 105–21; Frank Ching, "A Most Unenvied Province," *Foreign Policy,* Fall, 1979, No. 36, pp. 122–46; Roy Rowan "Taiwan Gears Up To Go It Alone," *Fortune,* February 12, 1979, p. 75.
38. Bela Balassa and John Williamson, "Adjusting to Success: Balance of Payments Policy in the East Asian NIC's," Institute for International Economics, Washington, 1987, pp. 58–9; *The Business Guide To Taiwan,* Research Institute of America in collaboration with the Center for Strategic and International Studies, New York and Washington, 1980, pp. 7–8.
39. Schive Chi, "An Economy in Transition," *Free China Review,* April 1989, p. 4; *Taiwan Statistical Data Book,* various years.
40. *Foreign Trade and Development of the Republic of China,* Ministry of Economic Affairs, Taipei, 1988.
41. Shive Chi, op. cit.
42. Balassa and Williamson, op. cit.; *Far Eastern Economic Review* (December 29, 1988): 42; (March 16, 1989): 86.
43. *Journal of Commerce* (October 7, 1988); *New York Times,* Dec. 13, 1988.
44. *Fortune,* December 5, 1988, p. 177.
45. *Asian Wall Street Journal Weekly,* April 10, 1989, p. 4; April 24, 1989, p. 2B; April 17, 1989, p. 1.
46. Osman Tseng, "Upgrading the Banks," *Free China Review,* January 1989, pp. 12–17.

176 *Notest to pp. 118–25*

47. *Journal of Commerce* (October 7, 1988).
48. Osman Tseng, op. cit.
49. *Journal of Commerce* (July 26, 1989, p. 3A; July 18, 1989, p. 3A).
50. *Far Eastern Economic Review,* July 20, 1989, p. 65; *Financial Times,* July 18, 1989, p. 1.
51. *New York Times,* July 16, 1988.
52. *Financial Times,* November 1, 1988.
53. *Wall Street Journal,* November 9, 1989, p. A18.
54. *Journal of Commerce* (January 3, 1989).
55. *Journal of Commerce* (July 13, 1989, p. 4A).
56. *Far Eastern Economic Review* (January 26, 1989, p. 54; January 19, 1989, p. 70).
57. Edward Chow, "Foreign Workers – Local Problems," *Free China Review,* April 1989, p. 36.
58. *Journal of Commerce* (October 7, 1988, p. 6A).
59. *Financial Times,* July 12, 1989, p. 5; Richard Sorich, "Taiwan Unfreezes Its Mainland China Policy," *The World and I,* November 1988, p. 140.
60. *Wall Street Journal,* July 13, 1988.
61. *Journal of Commerce* (July 15, 1988); *New York Times,* July 13, 1988.
62. *Journal of Commerce* (November 25, 1988).
63. *Financial Times,* July 7, 1988.
64. *Financial Times,* August 15, 1988.
65. *Financial Times,* October 19, 1985, p. 33.
66. *Financial Times,* May 21, 1986, p. 4.
67. *Journal of Commerce* (January 4, 1989); *New York Times,* January 19, 1989.
68. *Asian Wall Street Journal Weekly,* April 24, 1989, p. 3B.
69. *New York Times,* May 2, 1989.
70. *New York Times,* April 22, 1980; Richard E. Feinberg, *The Soviet Union and the Bretton Woods Institutions: Risks and Rewards of Membership,* Institute for East-West Security Studies, Public Policy Papers, 1989; William R. Feeney, "Chinese Policy Toward Multi-lateral Economic Institutions," Samuel S. Kim, ed., *China and the World: New Directions in Chinese Foreign Relations,* Westview Press, Boulder, 1989, pp. 237–64.
71. William Adams Brown, Jr., *The United States and the Restoration of World Trade,* Washington D.C., The Brookings Institution, 1950, pp. 75, 116–17, 126, 156–7; John H. Jackson, *World Trade and the Law of the GATT,* Indianapolis, Bobs-Merrill, 1969, p. 650; Clair Wilcox, *A Charter for World Trade,* NY, Arno Press, 1972, p. 42.
72. *China Times* (Zhongguo Shibao, Taipei), "Taiwan's Participation in the GATT – An Analysis," June 20, 1988.
73. *China Times* (Zhongguo Shibao, Taipei), July 25, 1988.
74. Arthur K. Yeh, "Taiwan's Membership with General Agreement on Tariffs & Trade," a paper presented at the Conference on Taiwan's Role in International Economic Organizations, co-sponsored by the Brookings Institution and the Institute for National Policy Research, Washington, D.C., September 11, 1989, xerox, contains a full discus-

Notes to pp. 127–38 177

sion of the advantages to Taiwan and the GATT of Taiwan's membership.
75. *New York Times,* November 30, 1987; *Journal of Commerce* (December 1, 1987).
76. *Wall Street Journal,* April 22, 1988; *Journal of Commerce* (November 22, 1988).
77. *Wall Street Journal,* August 16, 1989, p. A8.
78. *Asian Wall Street Journal Weekly,* April 24, 1989, p. 4B.
79. *New York Times,* January 19, 1989; *Far Eastern Economic Review* (February 2, 1989); *Free China Review,* March 1989, p. 4.
80. April 3–9, 1989, p. 7.
81. *Financial Times,* January 26, 1989; *Far Eastern Economic Review* (February 9, 1989, p. 59); *Journal of Commerce* (February 16, 1989).
82. *Far Eastern Economic Review* (July 19, 1989, p. 56); *Journal of Commerce* (July 7, 1989, p. 5A).
83. *Asian Wall Street Journal Weekly,* August 7, 1989, p. 14.
84. *Asian Wall Street Journal Weekly,* May 29, 1989, p. 1.
85. *Washington Post,* April 15, 1989; *Asian Wall Street Journal Weekly,* June 12, 1989, p. 6; *Wall Street Journal,* June 13, 1989, p. 17; *Financial Times,* June 30, 1989, p. 5; Martin L. Lassiter, *Policy in Evolution: U.S. Role in China's Reunification,* Westview Press, Boulder, 1989, pp. 179–187.
86. *Journal of Commerce* (May 8, 1989, p. 3A).
87. Byron S. J. Weng, "Divided China and the Question of Membership in International Economic Organizations," a paper presented at the Conference on Taiwan and International Organizations for Economic Cooperation, co-sponsored by the Institute for National Policy Research (Taipei) and the Brookings Institution (Washington, D.C.), September 10–12, 1989, Washington, D.C., xerox, contains a full analysis of the role of names in Taiwan's relations with international organizations.

CHAPTER 5: THE OUTLOOK AND IMPLICATIONS FOR U.S. AND WESTERN POLICY

1. The article by Roger W. Sullivan, "A Government in Transition" in *The China Business Review,* July/August 1989, p. 8, is thoughtful and thought-provoking.
2. *Far Eastern Economic Review* (June 22, 1989, p. 45).
3. *Wall Street Journal,* August 22, 1989, p. 10; *Far Eastern Economic Review,* August 24, 1989, p. 16.
4. John King Fairbank, *The United States and China,* Fourth Edition, Harvard University Press, Cambridge, Mass., 1983, pp. 371–372; S. C. Tiang, "Money and Banking in Communist China," Joint Economic Committee, *An Economic Profile of Mainland China,* Vol. 1: General Economic Setting, Washington, February 1967, pp. 325–330.

178   *Notes to pp. 139–60*

5. Alexander Eckstein, "Conditions and Prospects for Economic Growth in Communist China (Part I)" *World Politics,* Vol. VII, no. 1, October 1954, pp. 23–26; T. J. Hughes and D. E. T. Luard, *The Economic Development of Communist China 1949–1960,* second edition, Oxford University Press, London, 1961, pp. 23–31; Alexander Eckstein, *Communist China's Economic Growth and Foreign Trade: Implications for U.S. Policy,* McGraw-Hill, N.Y., 1966, pp. 25–28; Jan S. Prybyla, *The Political Economy of Communist China,* International Textbook Company, Scranton, Pa., 1970, pp. 79–85.
6. *Washington Post,* July 29, 1989, p. 1.
7. *Far Eastern Economic Review* (July 13, 1989, pp. 23–4), Jerome Alan Cohen, "Law and Leadership in China"; *New York Times,* August 4, 1989, p. B9, David Margolich, "At the Bar".
8. The following summary of the history of regional autonomy in China is based on a research paper by my intern, Charles Matt. Among the sources he consulted are: Wang Zhigang, "Flexibility and Weighing the Losses," *Outlook Weekly,* (Zhongguo Jingji Fazhan Zoushi Tanfanglu) October 3, 1988, pp. 6–8; Bianco, Lucien, *Origins of the Chinese Revolution,* 1915–1949, Stanford University Press, Stanford, California, 1971, translated from the French by Muriel Bell; *The New Encyclopedia Britannica,* Vol. 16, Knowledge in Depth Series, 15th edition, 1985, pp. 32–254; John K. Fairbank, ed., *Cambridge History of China,* Vol. 10, "Late Ching, 1910–1911"; vol. 14, "The Peoples' Republic, Part I: The Emergence of Revolutionary China, 1949–1965, Cambridge University Press, 1978; James E. Sheridan, *China in Disintegration: The Republican Era in Chinese History 1912–1949,* N.Y.: Free Press, 1975; Wakeman, Frederick Jr., *The Fall of Imperial China,* The Free Press, N.Y., 1975.
9. *Financial Times,* August 10, 1989, p. 3.
10. See the sensitive article by Winston Lord, "China and America: Beyond the Big Chill," *Foreign Affairs,* Fall, 1989.
11. *Far Eastern Economic Review* (March 2, 1989, p. 66).
12. Hungdah Chiu, "The Hong Kong Agreement and American Foreign Policy," *Issues and Studies*, Vol. 22, No. 6, June 1986, pp. 76–91.
13. *Taxation in the Republic of China,* Ministry of Finance, Taxation and Tariff Commission, 1989, Taipei, Taiwan.

Bibliography

Ai Wei. "Technology Trade Between the United States and Mainland China in Recent Years." *Issues and Studies* 24, no. 8 (August 1988): 82–119.

Balassa, Bela and John Williamson. *Adjusting to Success: Balance of Payments Policy in the East Asian NIC's.* Washington, D.C.: Institute for International Economics, 1987.

Baldwin, Robert E., J. David Richardson, eds. *Issues in the Uruguay Round,* NBER Conference Report. Cambridge, Mass.: National Bureau of Economic Research, 1988.

Barnett, A. Doak. *China's Economy in Global Perspective.* Washington, D.C.: The Brookings Institution, 1981.

———. "Ten Years After Mao." *Foreign Affairs* (Fall 1986): 54.

Bianco, Lucien. *Origins of the Chinese Revolution, 1915–1949.* Translated by Muriel Bell. Stanford, Calif.: Stanford University Press, 1971.

Brainard, Lawrence J. "Soviet International Financial Policy: Traditional Formulas or New Innovations?" *Gorbachev's Economic Plans, Volume 1.* Joint Economic Committee, 100th Cong., 1st sess., 1987, pp. 100–15.

Brick, Andrew B. *The Case for Taipei's Membership in International Economic Organizations.* Washington, D.C.: The Heritage Foundation, no. 82, October 27, 1988.

Brick, Andrew B. *Hong Kong: Now a Matter of U.S. Interest.* Washington, D.C.: The Heritage Foundation, no. 95, October 18, 1989.

Brown, Jr., William Adams. *The United States and the Restoration of World Trade.* Washington, D.C.: The Brookings Institution, 1950.

Bryson, Phillip J. and Joseph M. Van Brabant. "Non-Market Pricing in the Socialist World Market." *Kyklos* 28, no. 2 (1975).

Burki, Shahid Javed. "Reform and Growth in China." *Finance and Development.* Washington, D.C.: International Monetary Fund, December 1988.

The Business Guide to Taiwan. New York and Washington, D.C.: Research Institute of America in collaboration with the Center for Strategic and International Studies, 1980.

Butler, Steven. "Realm Between Two Tracks." *Financial Times,* December 14, 1988.

Byrd, William A. "The Impact of the Two-Tier Plan Market System in Chinese Industry." *Journal of Comparative Economics* 2, no. 3 (September 1987): 299.

———. "Rural Industrialization and Ownership in China." Paper presented at the joint meeting of the Chinese Economic Association in North America and the American Economic Association, New York, December 23–30, 1988. Photocopy.

Carver, Dean. "China's Experiment with Fiscal and Monetary Policy." *China's Economy Looks Toward the Year 2000, Volume 1, The Four*

180   *Bibliography*

Modernizations. Joint Economic Committee, 99th Cong., 2nd sess., 1986, pp. 110–31.

Chen, Tiwei. "Why is China Opening to the Outside?" *Beijing Review,* April 1, 1985, pp. 18–22.

Chi, Schive. "An Economy in Transition." *Free China Review,* April 1989, p. 4.

China: External Trade and Capital. World Bank Country Study. Washington, D.C.: The World Bank, 1988.

China: Finance and Investment. World Bank Country Study. Washington, D.C.: The World Bank, 1988.

China: Socialist Economic Development, Volume 1: The Economy, Statistical System, and Basic Data. World Bank Country Study. Washington, D.C.: The World Bank, 1983.

Chiu, Hungdah. "Certain Legal Aspects of Recognizing the People's Republic of China." *Case Western Reserve Journal of International Law* 2, no. 2 (Spring 1979): 389–419.

——. "The Hong Kong Agreement and American Foreign Policy." *Issues and Studies* 22, no. 6 (June 1986): 76–91.

——, ed. *China and the Taiwan Issue.* New York: Praeger, 1979.

Chong, Frank. "A Most Unenvied Province." *Foreign Policy* 36 (Fall 1979): 122–46.

Chow, Edward. "Foreign Workers – Local Problems." *Free China Review,* April 1986, p. 36.

Chow, Gregory C. "Development of a More Market-Oriented Economy in China." *Science,* January 16, 1987, p. 296.

Central Intelligence Agency. *China: Economic Performance in 1985.* Report prepared for the Joint Economic Committee, March 17, 1986. Photocopy.

——, Directorate of Intelligence. *China: Economic Performance in 1987 and Outlook for 1988.* EA88–10018, May 1988.

Cohen, Jerome Alan. "Law and Leadership in China." *Far Eastern Economic Review,* July 13, 1989, pp. 23–24.

Committee for Fair Trade With China. *History of the Committee for Fair Trade With China: Creation of a Lobby to Normalize U.S.-China Economic Relations.* Medina, Washington D.C.: CFTC, January 1988. Photocopy.

Conn, David. "Economic Theory and Comparative Economic Systems: A Partial Literature Survey." *Journal of Comparative Economics* 2 (1978): 355.

Davey, William J. "GATT: Its Present Operation and Prospects for the Future." Paper presented at the Southwest Legal Foundation Symposium on Private Investment Abroad: International Business in 1986 – Problems and Solutions, June 17–19, 1986, Dallas. Photocopy.

Dernberger, Robert F. "China's Economic Reforms." *Asia Pacific Report, 1989, Focus: China in the Reform Era,* C. E. Morrison and R. F. Dernberger, eds. Honolulu: East-West Center, 1989: pp. 53–64.

Dumbaugh, Kerry. *The 13th Party Congress: Implications for China's Future.* Washington, D.C.: The Center for Strategic and International Studies, November 1987.

Bibliography

Durham, Harry C. Jr. "Comparative Economies and International Trade." *Bulletin* (Association for Comparative Economic Studies) 18, no. 2–3 (Winter 1975): 47.

Eckstein, Alexander. *Communist China's Economic Growth and Foreign Trade: Implications for U.S. Policy.* New York: McGraw-Hill, 1966.

——. "Conditions and Prospects for Economic Growth in Communist China." *World Politics* 7, no. 1 (October 1959): 23–26.

Ellis, James L. "Eastern Europe: Changing Trade Patterns and Perspectives." *East European Economies: Slow Growth in the 1980s: Selected Papers,* Vol. 2. Washington, D.C.: Joint Economic Committee, 1986, pp. 6–30.

Ellman, Michael. "China's OTC Markets." *Comparative Economic Studies* 30, no. 1 (Spring 1988): 61.

The Fair Trade Subcommittee of the American Chamber of Commerce in Hong Kong. "Import Controls in China: Protectionism with Chinese Characteristics." *China Business Review* (January–February 1987): 42–45.

Fairbank, John K., ed. *Cambridge History of China,* Vol. 10. Cambridge: Cambridge University Press, 1978.

——, ed. *Cambridge History of China,* Vol. 14. Cambridge: Cambridge University Press, 1978.

——. *The United States and China,* 4th ed., Cambridge: Harvard University Press, 1983.

Federal Reserve Bank of New York. *Quarterly Review* (Winter 1982–83): 41–51.

Feeney, William R. "Chinese Policy Toward Multilateral Economic Institutions." *China and the World: New Directions in Chinese Foreign Relations,* Samuel Kim, ed. Boulder, Colo.: Westview Press, 1989, pp. 237–264.

Feinberg, Richard E. *The Soviet Union and the Bretton Woods Institutions: Risks and Rewards of Membership.* Public Policy Papers. Institute for East-West Security Studies, 1989.

Field, Robert M. "China: The Changing Structure of Industry." *China's Economy Looks Toward the Year 2000, Vol. 1, The Four Modernizations.* Joint Economic Committee, 99th Cong., 2nd sess., 1986, pp. 505–47.

Fischer, William A. "Chinese Industrial Management: Outlook for the Eighties." *China's Economy Looks Toward the Year 2000, Vol. 1, The Fourt Modernizations.* Joint Economic Committee, 99th Cong., 2nd sess., 1986, pp. 548–70.

Fletcher, Philip D. "Imports from China at Issue." *China Business Review* no. 13 (September–October 1986): 22–25.

Foreign Trade and Development of the Republic of China. Taipei: Ministry of Economic Affairs, 1988.

Francks, Penelope. "Learning from Japan: Plant Imports and Technology Transfer in the Chinese Iron and Steel Industry." *Journal of Japanese and International Economics.* (Tokyo Center for Economic Research) March 1988, pp. 42–62.

Frank, Isaiah. *The "Graduation" Issue in Trade Policy Toward LDCs.* World Bank Staff Working Paper No. 334. Washington, D.C.: The World Bank, 1979.

Bibliography

Frankenstein, John. "Understanding Chinese Trade." *Current History* (September 1986): 257–275.

Gadbow, R. M. "Reciprocity and its Implications for U.S. Trade Policy." *Law and Policy in International Business* 14, no. 3 (1982).

Gargan, Edward A. "Along the Chinese Coastline Economic Dragon Awakens." *Economist*, August 13, 1988, p. 62.

General Agreement on Tariffs and Trade. *International Trade 88–89*, Vol. 2 Geneva: GATT, 1989.

Generalized System of Preferences: Review of the First Decade. Report by the Secretary-General. Paris: Organization of Economic Cooperation and Development, 1983.

Goldman, Marshall I. "Soviet Perceptions of Chinese Economic Reforms" *Journal of International Affairs* 39, no. 2 (Winter 1986): 41–55.

—— and Merle Goldman. "Soviet and Chinese Economic Reform." *Foreign Affairs* 66, no. 3 (1987–88): 551–73.

Harding, Harry. *China's Second Revolution.* Washington, D.C.: The Brookings Institution, 1987.

——, ed. *China's Foreign Relations in the 1980's.* New Haven, Conn.: Yale University Press, 1984.

Harrison, Selig S. "Taiwan After Chiang Ching-kuo," *Foreign Affairs* 66, no. 4 (Spring 1988): 790–808.

Hartland-Thunberg, Penelope. "China and the GATT: Time for Modernization." *Keeping Pace: U.S. Policies and Global Economic Change,* John Yochelson, ed. Cambridge: Ballinger, 1988, p. 175–202.

——. "Limits of Trade with China." *Executive*, June 1979, pp. 33–35.

Hudec, Norbet. "Adjudication of International Trade Disputes." London: The Trade Policy Research Center, no. 16, 1978.

Hughes, J. J. and D. E. T. Luard. *The Economic Development of Communist China 1499–1960,* 2nd ed. London: Oxford University Press, 1961.

International Monetary Fund. *Exchange Arrangements and Exchange Restrictions, Annual Report.* Washington, D.C.: IMF, 1986, p. 168.

Jackson, John H. *World Trade and the Law of the GATT.* Indianapolis: Bobbs-Merill, 1969.

——. *The World Trading System.* Cambridge, Mass.: Massachusetts Institute of Technology, 1989.

Jacobs, Piers. "Hong Kong and the Modernization of China." *Journal of International Affairs* 39, no. 2 (Winter 1986): 63–75.

Jacobson, Harold K. and Michael Oksenberg. *China and the Keystone International Economic Organizations.* University of Michigan, 1987. Photocopy of draft.

Jao, Y. C. "Hong Kong's Economic Prospects After the Sino-British Agreement: A Preliminary Assessment." *The Future of Hong Kong,* Y. C. Jao and Yuann-li Wu, eds. New York: Quorum Books, 1987.

Joint Economic Committee. *Allocation of Resources in the Soviet Union and China, Part 6.* 96th Cong., 2nd sess. Washington, D.C.: GPO, 1980.

——. *China: A Reassessment of the Economy.* 94th Cong., 1st sess. Washington, D.C.: GPO, 1975.

——. *China's Economy Looks Toward the Year 2000: Volume 1, The Four Modernizations.* 99th Cong., 2nd sess. Washington, D.C.: GPO, 1986.

Bibliography 183

Joint Economic Committee. *China's Economy Looks Toward the Year 2000: Volume 2, Economic Openness in Modernizing China*. 99th Cong., 2nd sess. Washington, D.C.: GPO, 1986.

——. *Chinese Economy Post-Mao: Volume 1, Policy and Performance*. 95th Cong., 2nd sess. Washington, D.C.: GPO, 1978.

——. *An Economic Profile of Mainland China: Volume 1, General Economic Setting*. 90th Cong., 1st sess. Washington, D.C.: GPO, 1967.

——. *Foreign Trade and International Finance, East European Economies: Slow Growth in the 1980s*. 99th Cong., 2nd sess. Washington, D.C.: GPO, 1986.

——. *Gorbachev's Economic Plans, Volume 1*. 100th Cong., 1st sess. Washington, D.C.: GPO, 1987.

Kapur, Harish. *China and the European Economic Community: The New Convention*. Boston: Nijhoff, 1986.

Keidel, Albert. "Chinese Coal Industry" *China's Economy Looks Toward the Year 2000, Volume 2 Economic Openness in Modernizing China*. Joint Economic Committee, 99th Cong., 2nd sess. Washington, D.C.: GPO, 1986, pp. 60–86.

Kim, Samuel S., ed. *China and the World: Chinese Foreign Policy in the Post-Mao Era*. Boulder, Colo.: Westview Press, 1984.

——, ed. *China and the World: New Directions in Chinese Foreign Relations*. Boulder, Colo.: Westview Press, 1989.

Kock, Karin. *International Trade Policy and the GATT 1947–1967*. Stockholm: Almquist & Miksell, 1969.

Komiya, Ryutaro, "Japanese Firms, Chinese Firms: Problems for Economic Reform in China" Part I: *Journal of Japanese and International Economies* 1, no. 1 (March 1987): 31–61; Part II: 1, no. 2 (June 1987): 229–47.

Korzes, Michael. "Contract Labor, the 'Right to Work' and New Labor Laws in the People's Republic of China." *Comparative Economic Studies* 30, no. 2 (Summer 1988): 117–32.

Kostecki, M.M. *East-West Trade and the GATT System*. New York: St. Martin's Press, 1978.

Kuan, Hsin-Chi and Lau Siu-Kai. "Hong Kong's Search for a Consensus: Barriers and Prospects." *Future of Hong Kong*, Y. C. Jao and Yuann-li Wu, eds. New York: Quorum Books, 1987.

Lardy, Nicholas R. "Agricultural Reform." *Journal of International Affairs* 39, no. 2 (Winter 1988): 91–104.

——. *China's Entry into the World Economy: Implications for Northeast Asia and the U.S.* New York and London: The Asia Society, 1987.

——. "Economic Developments in the People's Republic of China." Paper presented at the 18th Sino-American Conference, Stanford, June 8–11, 1989. Photocopy.

——. *Economic Policy Toward China in the Post-Reagan Era*. China Policy Series, no. 1. New York: National Committee on United States-China Relations, Inc., January 1989.

——. "Prospects and Some Policy Problems of Agricultural Development in China." *American Journal of Agricultural Economies* 68, no. 2 (May 1986).

Lassiter, Martin L. *Policy in Evolution: U.S. Role in China's Reunification*. Boulder, Colo.: Westview Press, 1989.

184 Bibliography

Lawson, Eugene K., ed. *U.S.-China Trade: Problems and Prospects.* New York: Praeger, 1988.

Li Chung-chou. "Resumption of China's GATT Membership." *Journal of World Trade Law* 21, no. 4 (August 1987): 25–48.

Li Shude. "Sino-U.S. Trade: A Chinese Perspective." *U.S.-China Trade: Problems and Prospects,* Eugene K. Lawson, ed. New York: Praeger, 1988.

Li Yunqi. "Can China Make Use of Inflation?" *Intertrade* (July 1988): 22.

Lippit, Victor D. *The Economic Development of China.* M. E. Sharpe, Inc., 1987.

Lord, Winston. "China and America: Beyond the Big Chill." *Foreign Affairs* 68, no. 4 (Fall 1989): 1–26.

Mah, Feng-Hwa. *The Foreign Trade of Mainland China.* Chicago: Aldine-Atherton for the Social Science Research Council, 1971.

Margolich, David. "At the Bar." *New York Times,* August 4, 1989, B9.

Maresse, Michael. "Unconventional Gains from Trade." *Journal of Comparative Economics* 7 (1983): 382.

Market Opinion Research. *MOR China Letter.* Detroit: MOR, January/February 1989.

Martin, Edward W. *Southeast Asia and China: The End of Containment.* Boulder, Colo.: Westview Press, 1977.

Mitchell, Laurance W. *U.S.-China Aerospace Cooperation.* U.S. Department of State, Foreign Service Institute, May 22, 1988. Photocopy.

Nakajima, Seiichi. "The Chinese Economy in 1988." *China Newsletter* no. 79 (March-April 1989).

The New Encyclopedia Britannica, 15th ed., Vol. 16, pp. 2–254.

Oksenberg, Michel. "China's Confident Nationalism." *Foreign Affairs* (Fall 1987) 501–23.

———. "Economic Policy Making in China: Summer 1981." *China Quarterly* 90 (June 1982): 165–194.

Patterson, Eliza R. "Improving GATT Rules for Non-Market Economies." *Journal of World Trade Law* 20, no. 2 (March–April 1986): 187.

Perkins, Dwight M. "Reforming China's Economic System." *Journal of Economic Literature* 26, no. 2 (June 1988): 612–27.

Prybyla, Jan S. *The Political Economy of Communist China.* Scranton, Pa.: International Textbook Company, 1970.

Rabushka, Alvin. *The New China's Comparative Economic Development on Mainland China, Taiwan and Hong Kong.* Boulder, Colo.: Westview Press, 1987.

Richards, J. M. "Protectionism and the ITC." *China Business Review* (September–October 1982): 28–31.

Roessler, Frieder. "The GATT Declaration on Trade Measures Taken For Balance of Payments Purposes: A Commentary." *Case Western Reserve Journal of International Law* 12, no. 1 (Winter 1980): 383–403.

Rowan, Roy. "Taiwan Gears Up To Go It Alone." *Fortune,* February 12, 1979, p. 75.

Salem, Ellen. "Things Fall Apart, the Center Cannot Hold." *Far Eastern Economic Review,* October 27, 1988, p. 38.

Sheridan, James E. *China In Disintegration: The Republican Era in Chinese History 1912–1949.* New York: Free Press, 1975.

Bibliography

Shu Ziqing and Wa Siahuang. "Policy Stances of Economies that are not in the GATT Toward that Organization." U.N. Department of International Economic and Social Affairs. Paper presented at the Second Session of the World Institute for Development Economic Research Symposium, June 12–16, 1989. Photocopy.

Sorich, Richard. "Taiwan Unfreezes its Mainland China Policy." *The World and I,* November 1988, p. 140.

Southerland, Daniel. "Some Chinese Fear 'Economic Warlordism'." *New York Times,* August 13, 1988.

Sullivan, Roger W. "A Government in Transition." *China Business Review,* July/August 1989, p. 8.

Sung, Kayser. "Trading on From 1997 with Special Reference to Hong Kong's Textile Agreements." *Hong Kong and 1997: Strategies for the Future.* Y. C. Jao, *et al.,* ed. Hong Kong: Center of Asian Studies, University of Hong Kong, 1985.

Sutter, Robert. *Chinese Foreign Policy: Developments After Mao.* New York: Praeger, 1986.

——. "Hong Kong's Future and Its Implications for the United States." *China's Economy Looks Toward the Year 2000: Volume 2, Economic Openness in Modernizing China.* Joint Economic Committee, 99th Cong., 2nd sess., 1986, pp. 371–83.

Szuprowicz, Bohdan and Maria R. Szuprowicz. *Doing Business With the People's Republic of China: Industries and Markets.* New York: John Wiley and Sons, 1978.

Taxation in the Republic of China. Taipei, Taiwan: Ministry of Finance, 1989.

Teng Weizao and N.T. Wang, eds. *Transnational Corporations and China's Open Door Policy.* Lexington, Mass.: Lexington Books, 1988.

Tiang, S. C. "Money and Banking in Communist China." *An Economic Profile of Mainland China: Volume 1.* Joint Economic Committee, 90th Cong., 1st sess., 1967, pp. 323–39.

Toffler, Alvin and Heidi Toffler. "Socialism in Crisis: China's Answer." *World Monitor,* January 1989, p. 41.

Tsao, James T. M. *China's Development Strategies and Foreign Trade.* Lexington, Mass.: Lexington Books, 1987.

Tseng, Osman. "Upgrading the Banks." *Free China Review,* January 1989, pp. 12–17.

Turtola, Jerome. "Textile Trade Tensions." *China Business Review* 13 (September–October 1986): 26–31.

Ungar, Leonard. "Derecognition Worked." *Foreign Policy* 36 (Fall 1979): 105–21.

United States Department of State, Bureau of Public Affairs. *Gist,* January 1979.

U.S. International Trade Commission. *Operation of the Trade Agreements Program, 40th Report 1988.* USITC Publication 2208, July 1989.

Wakeman, Frederick Jr. *The Fall of Imperial China.* New York: The Free Press, 1975.

Walder, Andrew G. "The Informal Dimension of Enterprise Financial Reforms." *China's Economy Looks Toward the Year 2000: Volume 1, The Four Modernizations.* Joint Economic Committee, 99th Cong., 2nd sess. Washington, D.C.: GPO, 1986, pp. 630–645.

186 *Bibliography*

Wang Zhigang. "Flexibility and Weighing the Losses." *Outlook Weekly* [Zhongguo Jingji Fazhan Zoushi Tanfanglu] October 3, 1988, pp. 6–8.

Weng, Byron S. J. "Divided China and the Question of Membership in International Economic Organizations." Paper presented at the Conference on Taiwan and International Organizations for Economic Cooperation, Washington, D.C., September 10–12, 1989.

Whiting, Alan. "China's Economy in a Global and Regional Context." *U.S.-China Trade: Problems and Prospects,* Eugene K. Lawson, ed. New York: Praeger, 1988.

Wilcox, Clair. *A Charter for World Trade.* New York: Arno Press, 1972.

Winfield, G. F. "The Impact of Urbanization on Agricultural Processes." *Annals* (American Academy of Political and Social Science), January 1973, p. 3.

Wolf, Thomas A. "Optimal Foreign Trade for the Price Insensitive Soviet-Type Economy." *Journal of Comparative Economics* 6 (1982): 27.

Wong, Christine P. W. "Between Plan and Market: The Role of the Local Sector in Post-Mao China." *Journal of Comparative Economics* 11, no. 3 (September 1987): 387.

———. "Ownership and Control in Chinese Industry: The Maoist Legacy and Prospects for the 1980s." *China's Economy Looks Toward the Year 2000: Volume 1. The Four Modernizations.* Joint Economic Committee, 99th Cong., 2nd sess. Washington, D.C.: GPO, 1986, pp. 571–603.

Worthy, Ford, S. "Why There's Still Promise in China." *Fortune,* February 27, 1989.

Wu Jinglian and Zhao Renwei. "The Dual Pricing System in China's Industry." *Journal of Comparative Economics* 11, no. 3 (September 1987): 309–18.

Yeh, Arthur K. "Taiwan's Membership in the General Agreement on Tariffs and Trade." Paper presented at the Conference on Taiwan's Role in International Economic Organizations, Washington, D.C., September 10–12, 1989. Photocopy.

Yochelson, John, ed. *Keeping Pace: U.S. Policies and Global Economic Change.* Cambridge, Mass.: Ballinger, 1988.

Yunker, James A. "A New Perspective on Market Socialism." *Comparative Economic Studies* 30, no. 2 (Summer 1988): 69–116.

Index

NOTE: Figures are in *Italic*, Tables are in **Bold**

Agriculture
China 71; decline in labor
productivity 15; output
growth required by Deng
Xiaoping leadership 16, 21;
reforms successful 32; still
main occupation 9
Taiwan 113–14
Anti-dumping duties 87
Anti-dumping investigations, by
USA 91–92
Asian fears concerning new
regional developments 75

Balance of payment exception
(GATT) 151
Chinese reliance on 89
Balance of payments deficits 68,
90
USA 76
Balance of payments surpluses 76
Balance of trade deficits 68
Banking, a private enterprise in
China 45
Banking controls, created serious
currency shortage in China 47
Banking system
China, to replace the budget
44–45
Taiwan, first steps towards open
financial sectors 118
Bankruptcy 41, 49, 135, 156
Banks
China, specialized 44
in Taiwan 117
Basic Law 104, 111
second draft 105
Beijing (place)
demonstrations and crackdown,
reaction in foreign financial
markets 65
Beijing (administration)
lost control of revenues 44
manipulating financial and fiscal
levers of indirect control 44

restricted autonomy of
provinces and municipalities
47
shift to conservative regime 3
suffering from technical
inefficiencies 94
unable to control provinces 142
worked to thwart Taiwan's
overtures to GATT and
OECD 127
worried by sucesses of
Taiwanese diplomacy 127
see also China
Boat people, effect of repatriation
on West 153
Bond market, lacking in China
45–46
Bonuses 134
Borrowing, by China 60–61 **63**;
provincial 62, 64–65
Bottlenecks 51, 71, 135
affecting foreign trade 54
determining demand growth
48–49
and the dual-price system 36–40
effect of continual lagging 42
imposing constraints on Chinese
economy 17
must be removed 140
reform period, price
differentials widened for basic
industrial inputs 36
willingness to sacrifice
investment in 49
worsening 139–40
Budget deficit *21*, 56, 49, 52–53
figures misleading 18
financing of: in Western
countries 45–46; in China 46
likely to increase 134
under Mao 138
Bureaucracy
interference by 70
problems with 69

187

188 *Index*

Capital
  tool for influencing China 149–50
  trade in 76
Capital flight, from Hong Kong 109
Capitalism, vs. market socialism 25–26
Catching-up process, retarded 73
Central Bank of China *see* People's Bank of China
Central plan 27
Centrally controlled economies and GATT 88–89
Change, Chinese acceptance of 8–9
Chiang Kai-shek 99
China
  as an international investor 62, 64
  apprehensive about foreign borrowing 60
  assumption of rightful place in the world 23–25, 72, 133
  attempted to become more attractive to foreign business 70
  austerity 134; acceptability of 136; 1988 program 49–50
  backwardness of 13
  benefiting from the debt crisis 77
  choice between prosperity and return to isolation 148–49
  dangers of economic contraction 135–36
  debt service burden 131; and exchange rate fluctuations 64; needs economic reform policies 137; rising 136
  did not take advice of economists and advisers 24, 46–47
  economy: grew during Mao leadership 16;
  mismanagement of 52; modernization and stimulation of 1–2; status of changing 79

  encouraged Taiwanese investment 121
  exceptional treatment for 79, 96, 145–46, 154
  foreign currency earnings through Hong Kong 103
  foreign trade and investment 53–70, 71; foreign investment 60–66; obstacles to 66–70
  future of 165; affecting Taiwan's GATT application 160–61
  and GATT 5–6, 130; future accession to 150–52; post-1997 155; pros and cons of accession 78–81; problem areas in 82–96; province-by-province membership 155–56, 162–63; recognized GATT worries over transparency of its system 92; usefulness of Hong Kong's membership 153–57
  GNP, growth of 23
  growing importance as a trading nation 55
  growth: program dependent on participation in world trade 11; would be inhibited by selective safeguard provision 95
  historic tendency to territorial fragmentation 142–43
  and Hong Kong, loss of interest in 155; much foreign trade funneled through Hong Kong 102; in own interests to maintain Hong Kong's system intact 110; potential mismanagement of absorption of Hong Kong 7–8; relations with 99–101
  ignorance of Western business/financial concepts and practices 60–61, 66
  implications of change in world economy during the 1980s 73

Index

impossible to compare internal and export prices 94

insulated from effects of world changes 8

internal market large enough to permit economies of scale 42–43

largest source of Hong Kong imports 99

laws, regulations and bureaucracy a constant problem 69

laws/regulations governing foreign investment, slow evolution of 66–67

membership of international organizations 150–51

modernization ix, 23–25, 68, 81; political aspects 133–34

nature of 165

neighboring markets expanding 75

never a national market 26

no long-term debt strategy 64

objected to EC's quota restrictions 93

objected to USA's failure to extend unconditional MFN treatment 93

opening of to West (1970s), importance of 3–4

outlook for 133–44

part in Taiwan's return to GATT 162

plans to protect domestic market 4

political decentralization 152, 157; effect on Taiwan 163

political and social stability no longer assured 136

possible retreat from world trade 10–11

possible shrinking of external trade 151–52

potential as growth locomotive 11

preferential treatment for 145–46, 164

problem of emigration policy 94

provincial price chaos 10

rebuilding of 141

replaced Taiwan in World Bank and IMF 61

resumption of economic growth 150–51

return to central control, effect on Taiwan 163–65

scenarios of internal development: political decentralization or systematic collapse (Hong Kong) 152–57; progressive economic reform 148–52; return to tight central controls (Taiwan) 158–65; the status quo 144–48

scrupulous in meeting debt obligations 65

seeking to follow path of Japan, Taiwan and S. Korea 4

stagnating prices 8

and Taiwan 158–65; benefiting from affluence of 77; friendly overtures to 1; liberalization of relations 119–21; position on 122; possible attempt to absorb Taiwan as a diversion 147–48

task of shift from stability to dynamic change 8

technology, need for 74

trade: change in composition 56; two-way 53; with E. Europe and USSR 89

trading partners, importance of political relations with 57–59

transparency of trading practices and economic policies important 88

and the United Nations 61

unity of 143

use of IMF resources 61, 64–65, 78

use of World Bank 61–62, 64–65, 78

and the West: mutual importance 147, 148–49; need for apparent post-Tiananmen Square 131

190   *Index*

see also Beijing; One country, two systems
China Democratic Front 137
China Enterprise Management Association 30
China International Trade and Investment Corporation (CITIC) 62, 64
China, Nationalist
founder member of GATT 6
see also Taiwan
China–Hong Kong–Taiwan 97–99, 133
Chinese expatriates, working to overthrow Deng regime 137
Chinese Nationalists
endorsed liberalization of policies toward the mainland 121
retreat to Taiwan 112–13
Chinese products, poor quality of 68
Citizenship quarrel, Hong Kong–Britain 105–6, 152–53, 157
Citizens' rights, Hong Kong 152–53
Coal shortages, reasons for 36–37
Coastal provinces 135
amassed wealth invested outside China 142
attractive to migrants 38
favoured in reform process 38
and foreign trade 94
Collective enterprises 27, 33, 43, 135
and contract system 34–35
Commerce, increased between China, Hong Kong and Taiwan 2
Commodity economy 24
Communications and transport, China's deficiencies limit power of center 143
Communist Party 133
adjustment to lessening degree of control 2
corruption in 3, 48, 51
effect of conservatives 142

and modernization ix
need for a new leader 141
originally corruption averse 139
reform of 141–42; needed 139–40
to control "two systems" 1–2
Comparative advantage 92
evolving patterns of 73
pattern no longer stable 74
Competitiveness 74
Complimentarity, China–Hong Kong–Taiwan 98
Contract system 34–36
Controls 9
Convict labor, offer to Volvo 147
Corruption 3, 18, 43, 48, 71, 139, 142, 154
and dual-price system 31
elimination of 140
in Guangdong 156
harassment of enterprise managers 30–31
kept under control in Hong Kong 107
political 43, 48
quota allocation sales 38
and state enterprises 35
students sought sources of 51–52
Cost of living, China *23*, 134
Costs, largely ignored 28
Countervailing duties 87, 93
Credit creation, excessive 45
Crises 134
of increasing intensity 17–26
show basic weakness of reform program 71
Cultural Revolution 26
economic ramifications 8
increased Chinese isolation 15–16
Currency circulation, China *22*
Customs border, China–Hong Kong 153–54

Debt crisis 76
Debt rescheduling 136
Debt restructuring 66
Decentralization 38, 94, 133–34

Index

of decision making 29
extreme 143
political 152, 157, 163
through economic reform 29
to provide engine of growth 142
Democracy, demand for 51–52
Deng Xiaoping leadership
10-year program of economic
development 16–17
and clean government 140
deep mistrust of foreigners 146
experimentation with economic
reform 24
identified sources of economic
problems 15
misjudged Western reactions to
Tiananmen Square 144–45,
146
"one country, two systems" 1
"open door" policy 38–39
recognized problems of Party
corruption 139
reluctant to commit resources
to alleviate bottlenecks 49
Developing countries
Asian, expanded share in world
trade 74
becoming international
competitors 74
flouting of GATT rules 151
import demand 74
problem of debt servicing 77
reliance on import restraints 89
see advantages in textile
agreements 85
Dispute settlement mechanism,
GATT 81
Dollar exchange rate 77
Dual exchange-rate system,
complaints from IMF 41
Dual-price system 10, 31–43, 52,
57, 70, 71, 94, 140
bottlenecks 36–40
contract system 34–36
and corruption 3
distortions further exaggerated
38
extended into foreign exchange
trading 41

rural reform 31–32
state sector 40–43
to be eliminated 92
urban reform 32–34
Dumping 87–89, 93

Eastern Europe, and GATT
88–89
Economic freedom, and political
freedom 52
Economic growth
rapid, how to achieve 23–24
strong pressures for 30
Economic reform ix
changes in role of banking
44–45
connected with Party reform
139–40
effects of 136–37
experimentation with 24
first decade: ended in tragedy 3;
mixed record of 70–72
goal of 25
intention of 29
invited corruption 3
phased plan might have been
preferable 50–51
political restraints on 52–53
prices must eventually reflect
internal shortages 42
progressive 148–52
to accelerate domestic growth
92
tried to separate ownership of
means of production from
control of production process
24
Economic reform program 1–2
course of the transition 28–43;
autonomy of enterprise
management 28–31;
dual-price system
experimentation 31–43
inheritance of 26–28
legitimized if China acceded to
GATT 80, 81
renewal of 141
"Economic warlordism" 38
Education, in Taiwan 113

Index

E(E)C *see* European (Economic) Community

Efficiency
emphasis on improvement of 15
state-imposed constraints on 34

Electricity generation,
China–Hong Kong 103

Electronic goods, trade in 74

Emigration, from Hong Kong
106, 109, 111, 153

Employment
guaranteed 49
non-agricultural, pressure for
provision of 30

Enterprise management,
autonomy of 28–31

Enterprises
ownership and administration of
27
symbiotic relationship with local
authorities 27
entrepôt trade, Hong Kong 99,
100, 102, 108, 111

Entrepreneurs, Chinese as 29

European (Economic) Community
93
Chinese diplomatic relations
with 54
elimination of all barriers within
Europe by 1992 75
Hong Kong problem 152–53

Excess demand 18–19

Exchange controls 83

Exchange rate depreciation 136,
141
possibility of 66

Exchange rates
artificial 94
more volatile 76, 77
overvalued 28, 69
Taiwan, undervalued 116

Export pricing, by China 91

Export targeting 86–87
form of extra-GATT non-tariff
barriers 87

Exports
China 2, *20*, 56; and unfair
trading charges 10–11
Hong Kong 101, 102; textiles
108
Taiwan 115, 117

Financial regulation, decreased 76

Financial resource distribution,
role of banking system 45

Financial sector
China 44–48
Taiwan, liberalization of 118

Five-Year plans, history of 17

Food availability, importance of
15

Food supplies, importance of 135

Food and water, of concern to
Hong Kong 107–8

Foreign aid and lending to China,
reduction in 135

Foreign business executives
post-Tiananmen Square 135–36
problems of operating in China
66–70

Foreign debt, Chinese definition
of 64

Foreign exchange shortage 92
and offset agreements 68

Foreign investors, affected by
banking controls 47

Foreign trade and investment 17,
53–70, 71
obstacles to 66–70

Four Dragons, rising power of 128

Free enterprise
controlled and directed, Taiwan
117
in Hong Kong 99
rapid growth of in China 33

Free-trade system, Hong Kong 99

Fujian Province 38, 162

GATT 10
and centrally controlled
economies 88–89
China: pros and cons of
accession 78–81; concerns
about export regime 91–96;
concerns about import regime
89–91; future membership
150–52; joining requires
adjustments 95; pricing policy
worries 90–91; problem areas
in 82–96; risks in membership
80–81; transparency of

Index

193

system, worries over 91, 94;
would legitimize economic
reform program 80, 81
establishment of international
trading procedures 4–5
formal withdrawal of Chinese
Nationalists (1950) 124
and Hong Kong 108, 153–54,
155–56; possible loss of
membership 155; relationship
with 101–2
Kennedy Round 84
LDC reliance on exceptions
questioned 89
mission largely accomplished
77–78
and NICs 5
non-discrimination,
transparency and reciprocity
82–84
perceived as being out of date 5
relationship with Hong Kong
and Taiwan 6–7
safeguards, subsidies and
dumping 84–89
selective safeguard action
considered 86
Subsidies Code 87–88
and Taiwan 123–28, 130,
163–65; conditions for
membership 159–63
Tokyo Round 86, 87–88
Uruguay Round 5, 6, 78, 83,
86, 89, 151, 152; surveillance
of members' trading practices
90
withdrawal of Nationalist China
6
GATT-IMF cooperation 83, 89,
90
General Agreement on Tariffs
and Trade *see* GATT
Generalized System of
Preferences (GSP) 81
not applied to Chinese imports
59
Global change, discernable
patterns viii
Good will towards China,

dissipated by mid-1988
repression 7, 95–96
Government, role of in Chinese
economy 90
Government bonds, forced sale of
135
Government control, shift to
provinces 10
Government regulation 24
Governmental control, informal
29
Grain deliveries, incentive prices
for 32
Great Leap Forward, and collapse
of productivity 15
Greater China Common Market
97
"Greater China" economic
alliance 97
Guangdong Province 37, 109,
155–56
attractive to migrants 39–40
integration with Hong Kong,
potential example and
training ground 156–57
leading exporting area 39–40
success of "open door" policy
38
ties with Hong Kong 102–3
trade with Hong Kong 58

Hainan Island 38
insurance against political risk
for foreign investors 28
Heavy industry, China's emphasis
on 8
Hong Kong ix
booming economy 100–101
and China: attitudes affected by
post-1997 experiences 7;
implications for Western
policy 152–57; influence of
becoming more apparent 107;
investment in 103; joint
ventures in China 103;
relations with 97, 99–101,
trade with 98
China's loss of 98
citizenship and emigration
105–6, 152–53

Index

concern over mid-1989 repression 2
confidence in upset 109–10; by Tiananmen Square 7–8
a duty-free area 154
economy: flexibility of 110; vulnerable to Chinese policy changes 108
entrepôt trade 99, 100, 102, 108, 111
expanding world trade aided exports and entrepôt trade 102
export-oriented industrial economy 100
a financial centre 111
as a free port 111
as full member of GATT 6–7, 101–2, 104, 153–54
future of 106–12
growth: government aiming to slow down rate of 111–12; in late 1980s 102–3
Guangdong province: position adjacent to 38, 39; ties with 102–3
importance of in China's future 110
Joint Declaration and Basic Law 103–5
Law (Hong Kong), parts to be introduced to Shenzhen, Guangdong and other areas 156
leading financial centre 100
loss of Chinese interest in 155
must not interfere with mainland China 108–9
only deep water port in S. China 102, 110–11
popular with Chinese investors 62, 64
post-1997, many different fears 107–8
pragmatic and apolitical community 104
speculation by Chinese Communist party members 64
support for Chinese students 105

textile export, importance of 108
and Tiananmen Square 145
to become (post-1997) a Special Administrative region of China 103–4; status quo to continue for limited period 104
under "one country, two systems" 1
Hong Kong Chinese, to be regarded as Chinese nationals 105–6
Hong Kong companies, set up business in China 102
Hong Kong dollar 112, 156 depreciation of 101
Hong Kong people, legal status of 152–53
Hot money 76
Household farming 31–32
Human rights 11, 103, 152
in Hong Kong and Taiwan, care for 150
Taiwan 119
see also repression; Tiananmen Square
Hyperinflation 48
controlled by Mao regime 138

Idealism 51
IMF 4, 60, 124, 151
Chinese involvement 61, 64–65, 78
and GATT 83, 89, 90
new mission in debt management 77
and Taiwan 123
Imperial China, and the provinces 143
Import controls, non-discriminatory 85
Import quotas
non-existent in Hong Kong 101
USA, on Chinese textiles 59
Imports
China 18, 20, 57; contraction of 135
Japan, rising 74

Index

non-tariff barriers against 5
  Taiwan 115, 117; cars 125–26
  textiles, and GATT 85–86
Incentives 13
  ideological 8
  non-existent 28
Income distribution, under market
  socialism 25
Independence, no longer an
  important issue in Taiwan 119
Indigenization, Taiwan 118–19
Indirect control, instruments of 44
Industrial bias, China and USSR
  49
Industrial dispersion 15, 26
Industrial growth, required by
  Deng Xiaoping leadership 16
Industrial inputs 41
  ceiling on rate of
    noninflationary growth 48–49
  competition worked against
    Chinese interests 41–42
  greater efficiency in use of 36
  production lagging 36
Industrial mix, does not maximize
  productivity of China's labor
  and capital 9
Industrial output/production,
  China *19*, 134
  increased 14–15, 36
  variability of 15, 18
Industrial reform,
  experimentation with 33
Industrialization 26
  in Taiwan 114
Industries
  basic, expansion of 16
  small-scale under Mao 26
Inefficient workers, impossible to
  fire 39
Inflation 45, 134
  in China 18–21; control of 1949
    and 1990 137–39; and
    corruption 3, 48–53;
    demand-driven 48; reason for
    difficulty in controlling 50–51;
    resulting from industrial input
    competition 42; urban
    phenomenon 139

Hong Kong 111
  in Taiwan 115
Infrastructure investment, bias
  against 49
Interest rates 44
  more volatitle 77
  Taiwan 117
International finance, changes in
  during 1980s 76–78
International Monetary Fund *see*
  IMF
Investment
  in China 60–66; by Taiwan,
    120–21; direct 60, 62, 66;
    figures misleading 18;
    inefficient 68; in Guandong
    39–40; under Mao leadership
    28
  in Taiwan 114, 116
Investment capital 30
Investment projects, deemed
  indispensible 49
Iron rice bowl 8, 51
Isolation, of China 149, 151–52,
  164

Japan
  and export targeting 86
  imports rising 74
  new source of international
    capital and aid 77
  reasons for productivity growth
    14
  recognition of China 114
  and Taiwanese exports 116
  trade with China 54, 57–58
Jardine Matheson, quit Hong
  Kong 104
Joint Declaration on the Question
  of Hong Kong 103–5
  favourable to Hong Kong
    economy 101–2
  promised self-government 104–5
Joint ventures 103
  in Guangdong 38
  three-way 102
  wages in 67

Labor
  a factor in China's exports 91

Index

migrant 56
Labor Market, progress towards
  flexibility 39
Labor mobility 91
  discouraged in China 39
Labor reforms, resistance to in
  state enterprises 40–41
Labor shortage
  Hong Kong 109
  Taiwan 120
Land reform program, Taiwan
  113
  success of 113–14
Lange, Oskar, *On the Economic
  Theory of Socialism* 25
Large-scale enterprises 43
Law enforcement, lagging 141
LDCs
  almost all basic obligations
    waived in GATT 83
  fear selective safeguard action
    86
  and textile agreements 85–86
Legal regime, shifting and opaque
  94
Lending decisions, perceived as
  risk-free 45
Less Developed Countries *see*
  LDCs
Liberalization
  China, effects of 136
  Taiwan: in political life of
    118–21, 129, 131, 159; of
    imports 117
"Lifting the Veil on GATT,"
  articles in Taiwan Press 125
Light industry, development of
  required 16
Liquid funds, growing volume and
  movement of 76
Liquidity, Taiwanese banking
  system 118
Living standards 53, 98, 136
Loan repayments, by Taiwan 114
Lobbying, importance of learned
  by China 59–60
Local authorities, symbiotic
  relationship with enterprises 27

Local Government
  harassing enterprise managers
    31
  power of 29–30

"Made in Hong Kong," misuse of
  108
Management, efficiency of 25, 35
Managers
  appointment of 30
  harassed by "three pests" 30–31
  more authority through reforms
    34
  under market socialism 25
Manufactured goods, trade in 74
Mao leadership
  and control of inflation 138–39
  emphasis on regional
    self-sufficiency 26
  growth in the economy 16
  moral authority of 51
  relative price structure under
    27–28
Market forces
  determining prices 33
  in pre-reform period 27–28
  under the Mao regime 138–39
Market mechanisms 2, 24, 50
  introduction into China 8–9
Market prices, rising for raw
  materials 37–38
Market socialism 25–26, 43–44
  efficiency of 25
Martial law, lifted in Taiwan 119
Migrant labor 56
Migration, illegal, within China
  39–40
Military expenses, rise in 134
Military regime, possible in China
  152, 164
Modernization ix
  rapid achievement of 23–24
  requires imports 68
  would be aided by Chinese
    return to GATT 81
Money in circulation, pre-reform
  48–48
Money supply
  control of under Mao 138

Index

197

expansion of 45
used as instrument of control 47
Most Favoured Nation (MFN)
status, within GATT 82–83
Most Favoured Nation (MFN)
treatment 58
Multi-fibre Arrangements (MFA)
Hong Kong a member 101
joined by China 78
resented by LDCs 85–86

National sovereignty viii
NICs (Newly Industrializing
Countries)
and export targeting 86
OECD seminar 127–28
relieved from fulfilling GATT
obligations 5
Taiwan seen as first to leave
LDC status 159
Non-tariff barriers 5, 78, 83

OECD (Organization for
Economic Cooperation and
Development) 90
on eventual status of Hong
Kong and Taiwan 128
seminar with Asian NICs
127–28
Officials, deviousness of 69, 70
Offset agreements 68
Oil crisis, affecting Taiwan 114
One country, two systems 1, 98,
112 163
feasibility question after
mid-1989 repression 2
in Hong Kong 99, 154
promise to Hong Kong and
Taiwan 7
Open cities 38
"Open door" policy 1, 38,
133–34, 145
China more aware of own
weakness and backwardness
148
implications of x
Optimism, in China 17
Output planning, role of
provinces and localities 27

Overcapacity 42
Overstaffing 33, 43

Pacific Economic Cooperation
Conference 75
People's Bank of China (PBC)
44–48, 60–61
People's Liberation Army, and
Hong Kong 107
People's Republic of China see
China
Planning process, decentralization
of 26
Pluralism viii
political 11
Political change, in Taiwan 118–21
Political freedom 52
Political necessities 25
Political tensions 3
Politicians, corrupt 43
Population density, Taiwan 120
Population growth, China 2, 16
Price chaos, in provinces 10
Price controls, problems of 9–10
Price distortion 32, 68
Price reform, China 42–43, 92,
141, 156
Price stability 18
Price structure 9
under Mao leadership 27–28;
processing more profitable
than raw material production
30
Prices, China
controlled 31, 32
rising 19–21
Private banks 45
Private enterprises 33, 43, 135
and contract system 34–35
see also free enterprise
Private loans, acceptance of 60
Private property rights 103
Privatization, Taiwan 131
Processing industries 30
Production contracts 28–29
Production practices, Western
13–14
Production quotas/targets,
agriculture 32

198 *Index*

Productivity
  in China 10, 11; low 13, 43;
    reduced post-Tiananmen
    Square 135; stagnant 14;
    sustained rise essential 11
  in Taiwan 116
Profits, Beijing approach to 35
Prosperity in China, ensuing
  results 148
Protectionism 69
  Taiwan 124
Provinces, inland, felt treatment
  of coastal provinces unfair 40
Public utility development,
  China–Hong Kong 103

Quantitative restrictions,
  elimination of difficult for
  Taiwan 125–26
Quotas, China
  mandatory, for farmers,
    eliminated by Beijing 28–29
  of raw materials, profitable sale
    in free market 38
  replaced by targets 32
  see also Imports

Rail network, slow growth partial
  cause of coal shortage 37
Raw materials
  access to 30
  industries largely government
    run 37
  processing within own regions
    30
  quotas sold profitably in free
    market 38
  scarcities aggravated by new
    local processing capacity
    37–38
  shortages 27–28; aggravated 42
  Taiwanese imports 115
Raw materials hoarding 34, 36,
  135
Reciprocity
  aided reduction of trade
    barriers 84
  no criteria for measurement of
    84

principle challenged by LDCs
  84
Reform measures, introduced
  during stop-go policy period
  28–29
Regional competition, Asian 75
Rents, high for foreigners 67–68
Repression
  mid-1989, impact on localities
    uncertain 47–48
  political, effects of
    post-Tiananmen Square 134
  problems induced by 50
Resource allocation
  inefficient 69
  under market socialism 25
Resource misallocation 71, 91
Resource scarcities, USSR and
  China 147
Resources, shift into efficient
  industries/enterprises (China) 11
Retrenchment 28, 137
  and borrowing 62
  in coastal provinces 142
  effect on foreign trade 54
  financial results of 45
  increased problems of selling to
    China 69
  post-Tiananmen Square 135
  resort to quantitative
    restrictions 89
"Right of abode" removed from
  Hong Kong citizens 105–6
Risk management 77
Rule of law 140–41, 156
  and party reform 141–42
Rule of man 141
Rural industry, growth of in
  China 32
Rural reform, and the dual-price
  system 31–32

Safeguards, under GATT 84–85,
  86
Savings
  in China 44; under Mao 138
  high in Taiwan 114
Selective safeguard action 86
Selective safeguard provision, if
  China rejoined GATT 95, 151

Index

Services
  China, trade in 56, 75–76
  Hong Kong 99, 102
Shanghai, decline of 40
Shortages, hidden, in Mao
    economy 28
Sichuan province 142
Singapore 111
Singapore stock exchange 109
Sino-British Agreement 1994 *see*
    Joint Declaration on the
    Question of Hong Kong
Sino-European trade 54
Socialist commodity system 1
Socialist market economy 1–2
Sovereignty demand, effect on
    Hong Kong 100
Special Economic Zones (SEZs)
    38, 142
  and foreign trade 94
stability
  abandonment of a challenge 8–9
  effect of in China 8
Stagflation 42, 47, 134
State enterprises 27, 34, 135
  determination of profits 35;
    government approach to
    35–36
  a drag on the rising economy 43
  inefficiency in 71
  profits and losses 41
  pursuit of efficiency and higher
    profits frustrated 34
  reform of barely started 40
State sector
  declining in China 33–34
  and the dual-price system 40–43
Steel output, limited 37
Stop-go policies 17–18
  did not prevent rise in foreign
    trade 55
  reasons for 22–24
Structural change, dilemmas of in
    China viii–ix
Structural imbalances, correction
    of 140
Students, marching for
    democracry 51–52
Subsidies 32, 87, 93, 94, 107, 134

non-existent in Hong Kong 101
  pervasive in Chinese industry
    91; leading to unfair trading
    charges 10–11
Subsidies Code, GATT 87–88
Surrogate country approach,
    dumping and subsidies 88
Surveillance, by GATT 90

Taiwan ix, 77, 112–32
  an anomalous position 122
  banking problems 118
  bilateral reciprocal trade
    agreements 124–25
  ceded to Japan 98
  and China 158–65, 97;
    liberalization of relations with
    119–21
  concern over mid-1989
    repression 3
  currency appreciation 117
  derecognition by USA 115
  deterioration of competitive
    position in world markets 121
  early success of new diplomacy
    127
  economic aid to developing
    countries 123
  economic growth dependent on
    foreign trde 115
  the eonomic miracle 113–15
  economic progress in the 1980s
    115
  export surpluses 116
  financial sector 117–18
  flexibility over name 130–31;
    astute choice for GATT
    application 160; opposed by
    conservatives 161
  flexible diplomacy 123, 125, 127
  foreign currency reserves 116
  foreign investment in 114, 116
  foreign policy 122–23; new,
    opposition to 161; shift in 158
  and GATT 7, 123–28, 130;
    adjustments needed before
    membership feasible 125;
    would provide forum for
    discussing trade disputes 160;
    sought observer status 124

200 *Index*

informal notification of interest in rejoining international economic organizations 126–27
infrastructure improved 114
looking to the future 131–32
loosened restrictions on USA goods 125–26
name of, a sensitive area 7
need for modernization of customs procedures and practices 126
now sees itself as part of China 148
and "one country, two systems" 1; concept endorsed 123
political change 118–21
population density 120
possibility of military invasion 164
practising the art of diplomacy 161–62
reactions to Tiananmen Square 128–32; supposed 145
replaced by China in World Bank and IMF 61
returned to China 98–99
role in China's Eastern Provinces 162–63
sought to end isolated position 123
sought to influence pace of China's reform 122–23
trade: role of 115–17; two-way (indirect) with the mainland 120–21, 128; with Japan and UK 116
Taiwanese economy, growth of 114
Tariff concessions, reciprocal 83, 84
Tariff reductions, through GATT 5
Tariffs
in China's import regime 90
Taiwan 125
Tax avoidance, China 50
Taxes 41, 44, 71
aimed at private and collective sector 50

enforcement of 135
under Mao
Technological change, acceleration of 73
Technology 149
and "catching up with the West" 13
and contemporary revolution viii
modernization of 11
obsolete/obsolescent 9
tool for influencing China 149–50
Technology imports, a Beijing priority 91
Technology transfer 58, 73, 74
Terms of trade, China 91
Textile agreements 85–86
advantages of 85
Textiles, Chinese exports (and reexports) 56
Tiananmen Square viii
aftermath in China 134
changed world attitude to China 158–59
dissipated good will to China 7–8
effect on Taiwan 158
effect in USA 59
Taiwanese reactions to 112, 128–32, 158; supposed 145
tragedy of 51
Total factor productivity
Chinese agriculture 32
Western 14
Tourism 56, 66
Trade
China 53–60: two-way, projected and achieved 53; use of import and export controls by Beijing 70
Hong Kong, entrepôt trade 99, 100, 102, 108, 111
Taiwan 115–17, 120–21, 128
Trade balances, China 18
Trade deficit, China *20*
Trade disputes, international 10–11
Trade imbalance, Taiwan–USA, caused friction 116–17

Index

Trade sanctions, possibility of 108
Trading practices, opaqueness of 94–95
Transparency 94
  of Chinese trading practices 88
  of trade matters, GATT 82–83
Transport, lack of in China 26
Transportation structure, expansion required 16
Treasury bonds, blackmarket in 46
"Trickle down," working 39–40

UK, and Hong Kong 105–6, 152–53, 157
Under-employment 43
Unemployment compensation 28, 39
Unfair trading practices 91
United Nations, Taiwan voted out 114
Urban reform, and the dual-price system 32–34
USA 93
  anti-dumping investigations 91–92; case against Chinese textile apparel 93
  change in financial role of 76–77
  China: trade with 54; trade relations colored by political relations 58–59; viewed as a Less Developed Country 4
  discrimination against nonmarket economies 59
  immigration requirements 152–53
  increasing share of Taiwanese export market 116
  interest in future of Hong Kong and Taiwan 12
  law prevents MFN treatment of communist countries 93–94
  national interest and China 11–12
  Taiwan: aid to 114; derecognition of 115; GATT membership supported

163–64; pressuring of to liberalize policies 125–26
  use of "constructed cost" in dumping or subsidy cases 93

Voluntary export restraint agreements (VERs) 85, 87

Wage reform, resented in state enterprises 41
Wages
  China: indexed to prices under Mao 138; paid by foreign employers 66–67
  in Taiwan 116, 120
West
  dilemma concerning China post-Tiananmen Square 129, 144
  disillusionment in 144–47
  importance of China to 148–49
  preferential treatment of China a disservice 146, 164
  private sector not influenced by government's post-Tiananmen Square 149
  revulsion at Tiananmen Square 149
Western policy, implications of direction of China's future development 143–65
World Bank 4, 60, 77, 135
  resources used by China 61–62, 64–65, 78
World business community, and China 53
World economy, accelerated changes during the 1980s 73
World recession, hit Hong Kong 100
World trade
  composition and distribution of shifting 74
  growth not depressed by risks 77
  recovery in 1980s 74

Yen-dollar exchange rate 64